Effective Java™

Programming Language Guide

Effective Java™
Programming Language Guide

Joshua Bloch

ADDISON-WESLEY

Boston • San Francisco • New York • Toronto • Montreal
London • Munich • Paris • Madrid
Capetown • Sydney • Tokyo • Singapore • Mexico City

The publisher offers discounts on this book when ordered in quantity for special sales. For more information, please contact:

Pearson Education Corporate Sales Division
One Lake Street
Upper Saddle River, NJ 07458
(800) 382-3419
corpsales@pearsontechgroup.com

Visit AW on the Web: www.awl.com/cseng/

Library of Congress Cataloging-in-Publication Data is available.

ISBN 0-201-31005-8

Text printed on recycled paper.
1 2 3 4 5 6 7 8 9 10–MA–05 04 03 02 01
First printing, June 2001

To my family: Cindy, Tim, and Matt

Contents

Foreword

IF a colleague were to say to you, "Spouse of me this night today manufactures the unusual meal in a home. You will join?" three things would likely cross your mind: third, that you had been invited to dinner; second, that English was not your colleague's first language; and first, a good deal of puzzlement.

If you have ever studied a second language yourself and then tried to use it outside the classroom, you know that there are three things you must master: how the language is structured (grammar), how to name things you want to talk about (vocabulary), and the customary and effective ways to say everyday things (usage). Too often only the first two are covered in the classroom, and you find native speakers constantly suppressing their laughter as you try to make yourself understood.

It is much the same with a programming language. You need to understand the core language: is it algorithmic, functional, object-oriented? You need to know the vocabulary: what data structures, operations, and facilities are provided by the standard libraries? And you need to be familiar with the customary and effective ways to structure your code. Books about programming languages often cover only the first two, or discuss usage only spottily. Maybe that's because the first two are in some ways easier to write about. Grammar and vocabulary are properties of the language alone, but usage is characteristic of a community that uses it.

The Java programming language, for example, is object-oriented with single inheritance and supports an imperative (statement-oriented) coding style within each method. The libraries address graphic display support, networking, distributed computing, and security. But how is the language best put to use in practice?

There is another point. Programs, unlike spoken sentences and unlike most books and magazines, are likely to be changed over time. It's typically not enough to produce code that operates effectively and is readily understood by other persons; one must also organize the code so that it is easy to modify. There may be ten ways to write code for some task T. Of those ten ways, seven will be awkward, inefficient, or puzzling. Of the other three, which is most likely to be similar to the code needed for the task T' in next year's software release?

There are numerous books from which you can learn the grammar of the Java Programming Language, including *The Java Programming Language* by Arnold, Gosling, and Holmes [Arnold00] or *The Java Language Specification* by Gosling, Joy, yours truly, and Bracha [JLS]. Likewise, there are dozens of books on the libraries and APIs associated with the Java programming language.

This book addresses your third need: customary and effective usage. Joshua Bloch has spent years extending, implementing, and using the Java programming language at Sun Microsystems; he has also read a lot of other people's code, including mine. Here he offers good advice, systematically organized, on how to structure your code so that it works well, so that other people can understand it, so that future modifications and improvements are less likely to cause headaches—perhaps, even, so that your programs will be pleasant, elegant, and graceful.

Guy L. Steele Jr.
Burlington, Massachusetts
April 2001

Preface

IN 1996 I pulled up stakes and headed west to work for JavaSoft, as it was then known, because it was clear that that was where the action was. In the intervening five years I've served as Java platform libraries architect. I've designed, implemented, and maintained many of the libraries and served as a consultant for many others. Presiding over these libraries as the Java platform matured was a once-in-a-lifetime opportunity. It is no exaggeration to say that I had the privilege to work with some of the great software engineers of our generation. In the process, I learned a lot about the Java programming language—what works, what doesn't, and how to use the language and its libraries to best effect.

This book is my attempt to share my experience with you so that you can imitate my successes while avoiding my failures. I borrowed the format from Scott Meyers's *Effective C++* [Meyers98], which consists of fifty items, each conveying one specific rule for improving your programs and designs. I found the format to be singularly effective, and I hope you do too.

In many cases, I took the liberty of illustrating the items with real-world examples from the Java platform libraries. When describing something that could have been done better, I tried to pick on code that I wrote myself, but occasionally I pick on something written by a colleague. I sincerely apologize if, despite my best efforts, I've offended anyone. Negative examples are cited not to cast blame but in the spirit of cooperation, so that all of us can benefit from the experience of those who've gone before.

While this book is not targeted solely at developers of reusable components, it is inevitably colored by my experience writing such components over the past two decades. I naturally think in terms of exported APIs (Application Programming Interfaces), and I encourage you to do likewise. Even if you aren't developing reusable components, thinking in these terms tends to improve the quality of the software you write. Furthermore, it's not uncommon to write a reusable component without knowing it: You write something useful, share it with your buddy across the hall, and before long you have half a dozen users. At this point, you no longer have the flexibility to change the API at will and are thankful for all the effort that you put into designing the API when you first wrote the software.

My focus on API design may seem a bit unnatural to devotees of the new lightweight software development methodologies, such as *Extreme Programming* [Beck99]. These methodologies emphasize writing the simplest program that could possibly work. If you're using one of these methodologies, you'll find that a focus on API design serves you well in the *refactoring* process. The fundamental goals of refactoring are the improvement of system structure and the avoidance of code duplication. These goals are impossible to achieve in the absence of well-designed APIs for the components of the system.

No language is perfect, but some are excellent. I have found the Java programming language and its libraries to be immensely conducive to quality and productivity, and a joy to work with. I hope this book captures my enthusiasm and helps make your use of the language more effective and enjoyable.

Joshua Bloch
Cupertino, California
April 2001

Acknowledgments

I thank Patrick Chan for suggesting that I write this book and for pitching the idea to Lisa Friendly, the series managing editor; Tim Lindholm, the series technical editor; and Mike Hendrickson, executive editor of Addison-Wesley Professional. I thank Lisa, Tim, and Mike for encouraging me to pursue the project and for their superhuman patience and unyielding faith that I would someday write this book.

I thank James Gosling and his original team for giving me something great to write about, and I thank the many Java platform engineers who followed in James's footsteps. In particular, I thank my colleagues in Sun's Java Platform Tools and Libraries Group for their insights, their encouragement, and their support. The team consists of Andrew Bennett, Joe Darcy, Neal Gafter, Iris Garcia, Konstantin Kladko, Ian Little, Mike McCloskey, and Mark Reinhold. Former members include Zhenghua Li, Bill Maddox, and Naveen Sanjeeva.

I thank my manager, Andrew Bennett, and my director, Larry Abrahams, for lending their full and enthusiastic support to this project. I thank Rich Green, the VP of Engineering at Java Software, for providing an environment where engineers are free to think creatively and to publish their work.

I have been blessed with the best team of reviewers imaginable, and I give my sincerest thanks to each of them: Andrew Bennett, Cindy Bloch, Dan Bloch, Beth Bottos, Joe Bowbeer, Gilad Bracha, Mary Campione, Joe Darcy, David Eckhardt, Joe Fialli, Lisa Friendly, James Gosling, Peter Haggar, Brian Kernighan, Konstantin Kladko, Doug Lea, Zhenghua Li, Tim Lindholm, Mike McCloskey, Tim Peierls, Mark Reinhold, Ken Russell, Bill Shannon, Peter Stout, Phil Wadler, and two anonymous reviewers. They made numerous suggestions that led to great improvements in this book and saved me from many embarrassments. Any remaining embarrassments are my responsibility.

Numerous colleagues, inside and outside Sun, participated in technical discussions that improved the quality of this book. Among others, Ben Gomes, Steffen Grarup, Peter Kessler, Richard Roda, John Rose, and David Stoutamire contributed useful insights. A special thanks is due Doug Lea, who served as a sounding board for many of the ideas in this book. Doug has been unfailingly generous with his time and his knowledge.

I thank Julie Dinicola, Jacqui Doucette, Mike Hendrickson, Heather Olszyk, Tracy Russ, and the whole team at Addison-Wesley for their support and professionalism. Even under an impossibly tight schedule, they were always friendly and accommodating.

I thank Guy Steele for writing the foreword. I am honored that he chose to participate in this project.

Finally, I thank my wife, Cindy Bloch, for encouraging and occasionally threatening me to write this book, for reading each item in its raw form, for helping me with Framemaker, for writing the index, and for putting up with me while I wrote.

CHAPTER 1

Introduction

THIS book is designed to help you make the most effective use of the Java™ programming language and its fundamental libraries, `java.lang`, `java.util`, and, to a lesser extent, `java.io`. The book discusses other libraries from time to time, but it does not cover graphical user interface programming or enterprise APIs.

This book consists of fifty-seven items, each of which conveys one rule. The rules capture practices generally held to be beneficial by the best and most experienced programmers. The items are loosely grouped into nine chapters, each concerning one broad aspect of software design. The book is not intended to be read from cover to cover: Each item stands on its own, more or less. The items are heavily cross-referenced so you can easily plot your own course through the book.

Most items are illustrated with program examples. A key feature of this book is that it contains code examples illustrating many *design patterns* and idioms. Some are old, like Singleton (Item 2), and others are new, like Finalizer Guardian (Item 6) and Defensive `readResolve` (Item 57). A separate index is provided for easy access to these patterns and idioms (page 239). Where appropriate, they are cross-referenced to the standard reference work in this area [Gamma95].

Many items contain one or more program examples illustrating some practice to be avoided. Such examples, sometimes known as *antipatterns,* are clearly labeled with a comment such as "`// Never do this!`" In each case, the item explains why the example is bad and suggests an alternative approach.

This book is not for beginners: it assumes that you are already comfortable with the Java programming language. If you are not, consider one of the many fine introductory texts [Arnold00, Campione00]. While the book is designed to be accessible to anyone with a working knowledge of the language, it should provide food for thought even for advanced programmers.

Most of the rules in this book derive from a few fundamental principles. Clarity and simplicity are of paramount importance. The user of a module should never be surprised by its behavior. Modules should be as small as possible but no smaller. (As used in this book, the term *module* refers to any reusable software component, from an individual method to a complex system consisting of multiple packages.) Code should be reused rather than copied. The dependencies between modules should be kept to a minimum. Errors should be detected as soon as possible after they are made, ideally at compile time.

While the rules in this book do not apply 100 percent of the time, they do characterize best programming practices in the great majority of cases. You should not slavishly follow these rules, but you should violate them only occasionally and with good reason. Learning the art of programming, like most other disciplines, consists of first learning the rules and then learning when to violate them.

For the most part, this book is not about performance. It is about writing programs that are clear, correct, usable, robust, flexible, and maintainable. If you can do that, it's usually a relatively simple matter to get the performance you need (Item 37). Some items do discuss performance concerns, and a few of these items provide performance numbers. These numbers, which are introduced with the phrase "On my machine," should be regarded as approximate at best.

For what it's worth, my machine is an aging homebuilt 400 MHz Pentium® II with 128 megabytes of RAM, running Sun's 1.3 release of the Java 2 Standard Edition Software Development Kit (SDK) atop Microsoft Windows NT® 4.0. This SDK includes Sun's Java HotSpot™ Client VM, a state-of-the-art JVM implementation designed for client use.

When discussing features of the Java programming language and its libraries, it is sometimes necessary to refer to specific releases. For brevity, this book uses "engineering version numbers" in preference to official release names. Table 1.1 shows the correspondence between release names and engineering version numbers.

Table 1.1:   Java Platform Versions

Official Release Name	Engineering Version Number
JDK 1.1.x / JRE 1.1.x	1.1
Java 2 Platform, Standard Edition, v 1.2	1.2
Java 2 Platform, Standard Edition, v 1.3	1.3
Java 2 Platform, Standard Edition, v 1.4	1.4

While features introduced in the 1.4 release are discussed in some items, program examples, with very few exceptions, refrain from using these features. The examples have been tested on releases 1.3. Most, if not all, of them should run without modification on release 1.2.

The examples are reasonably complete, but they favor readability over completeness. They freely use classes from the packages `java.util` and `java.io`. In order to compile the examples, you may have to add one or both of these import statements:

```
import java.util.*;
import java.io.*;
```

Other boilerplate is similarly omitted. The book's Web site, `http://java.sun.com/docs/books/effective`, contains an expanded version of each example, which you can compile and run.

For the most part, this book uses technical terms as they are defined in *The Java Language Specification, Second Edition* [JLS]. A few terms deserve special mention. The language supports four kinds of types: *interfaces*, *classes*, *arrays*, and *primitives*. The first three are known as *reference types*. Class instances and arrays are *objects*; primitive values are not. A class's *members* consist of its *fields*, *methods*, *member classes*, and *member interfaces*. A method's *signature* consists of its name and the types of its formal parameters; the signature does *not* include the method's return type.

This book uses a few terms differently from the *The Java Language Specification*. Unlike *The Java Language Specification*, this book uses *inheritance* as a synonym for *subclassing*. Instead of using the term inheritance for interfaces, this book simply states that a class *implements* an interface or that one interface *extends* another. To describe the access level that applies when none is specified, this book uses the descriptive term *package-private* instead of the technically correct term *default access* [JLS, 6.6.1].

This book uses a few technical terms that are not defined in *The Java Language Specification*. The term *exported API*, or simply *API*, refers to the classes, interfaces, constructors, members, and serialized forms by which a programmer accesses a class, interface, or package. (The term *API*, which is short for *application programming interface*, is used in preference to the otherwise preferable term *interface* to avoid confusion with the language construct of that name.) A programmer who writes a program that uses an API is referred to as a *user* of the API. A class whose implementation uses an API is a *client* of the API.

Classes, interfaces, constructors, members, and serialized forms are collectively known as *API elements*. An exported API consists of the API elements that are accessible outside of the package that defines the API. These are the API elements that any client can use and the author of the API commits to support. Not coincidentally, they are also the elements for which the Javadoc utility generates documentation in its default mode of operation. Loosely speaking, the exported API of a package consists of the public and protected members and constructors of every public class or interface in the package.

CHAPTER 2

Creating and Destroying Objects

THIS chapter concerns creating and destroying objects: when and how to create objects, when and how to avoid creating them, how to ensure that objects are destroyed in a timely manner, and how to manage any cleanup actions that must precede object destruction.

Item 1: Consider providing static factory methods instead of constructors

The normal way for a class to allow a client to obtain an instance is to provide a public constructor. There is another, less widely known technique that should also be a part of every programmer's toolkit. A class can provide a public *static factory method*, which is simply a static method that returns an instance of the class. Here's a simple example from the class `Boolean` (the wrapper class for the primitive type `boolean`). This static factory method, which was added in the 1.4 release, translates a `boolean` primitive value into a `Boolean` object reference:

```
public static Boolean valueOf(boolean b) {
    return (b ? Boolean.TRUE : Boolean.FALSE);
}
```

A class can provide its clients with static factory methods instead of, or in addition to, constructors. Providing a static factory method instead of a public constructor has both advantages and disadvantages.

One advantage of static factory methods is that, unlike constructors, they have names. If the parameters to a constructor do not, in and of themselves, describe the object being returned, a static factory with a well-chosen name can make a class easier to use and the resulting client code easier to read. For example, the constructor `BigInteger(int, int, Random)`, which returns a `BigInteger` that is probably prime, would have been better expressed as a static factory method named `BigInteger.probablePrime`. (This static factory method was eventually added in the 1.4 release.)

A class can have only a single constructor with a given signature. Programmers have been known to get around this restriction by providing two constructors whose parameter lists differ only in the order of their parameter types. This is a bad idea. The user of such an API will never be able to remember which constructor is which and will end up calling the wrong one by mistake. People reading code that uses these constructors will not know what the code does without referring to the class documentation.

Because static factory methods have names, they do not share with constructors the restriction that a class can have only one with a given signature. In cases where a class seems to require multiple constructors with the same signature, you should consider replacing one or more constructors with static factory methods whose carefully chosen names highlight their differences.

A second advantage of static factory methods is that, unlike constructors, they are not required to create a new object each time they're invoked. This allows immutable classes (Item 13) to use preconstructed instances or to cache instances as they're constructed and to dispense these instances repeatedly so as to avoid creating unnecessary duplicate objects. The `Boolean.valueOf(boolean)` method illustrates this technique: It never creates an object. This technique can greatly improve performance if equivalent objects are requested frequently, especially if these objects are expensive to create.

The ability of static factory methods to return the same object from repeated invocations can also be used to maintain strict control over what instances exist at any given time. There are two reasons to do this. First, it allows a class to guarantee that it is a singleton (Item 2). Second, it allows an immutable class to ensure that no two equal instances exist: `a.equals(b)` if and only if `a==b`. If a class makes this guarantee, then its clients can use the `==` operator instead of the `equals(Object)` method, which may result in a substantial performance improvement. The *typesafe enum* pattern, described in Item 21, implements this optimization, and the `String.intern` method implements it in a limited form.

A third advantage of static factory methods is that, unlike constructors, they can return an object of any subtype of their return type. This gives you great flexibility in choosing the class of the returned object.

One application of this flexibility is that an API can return objects without making their classes public. Hiding implementation classes in this fashion can lead to a very compact API. This technique lends itself to interface-based frameworks, where interfaces provide natural return types for static factory methods.

For example, the Collections Framework has twenty convenience implementations of its collection interfaces, providing unmodifiable collections, synchronized collections, and the like. The great majority of these implementations are exported via static factory methods in a single, noninstantiable class (`java.util.Collections`). The classes of the returned objects are all nonpublic.

The Collections Framework API is much smaller than it would be if it had exported twenty separate public classes for the convenience implementations. It is not just the bulk of the API that is reduced, but the "conceptual weight." The user knows that the returned object has precisely the API specified by the relevant interface, so there is no need to read additional class documentation. Furthermore, using such a static factory method mandates that the client refer to the returned object by its interface rather than by its implementation class, which is generally a good practice (Item 34).

Not only can the class of an object returned by a public static factory method be nonpublic, but the class can vary from invocation to invocation depending on the values of the parameters to the static factory. Any class that is a subtype of the declared return type is permissible. The class of the returned object can also vary from release to release, for enhanced software maintainability.

The class of the object returned by a static factory method need not even exist at the time the class containing the static factory method is written. Such flexible static factory methods form the basis of *service provider frameworks* like the Java Cryptography Extension (JCE). A service provider framework is a system wherein providers make multiple implementations of an API available to users of the framework. A mechanism is provided to *register* these implementations, making them available for use. Clients of the framework use the API without worrying about which implementation they are using.

In the JCE, the system administrator registers an implementation class by editing a well-known `Properties` file, adding an entry that maps a string key to the corresponding class name. Clients use a static factory method that takes the key as a parameter. The static factory method looks up the `Class` object in a map initialized from the `Properties` file and instantiates the class using the

Class.newInstance method. The following implementation sketch illustrates this technique:

```
// Provider framework sketch
public abstract class Foo {
    // Maps String key to corresponding Class object
    private static Map implementations = null;

    // Initializes implementations map the first time it's called
    private static synchronized void initMapIfNecessary() {
        if (implementations == null) {
            implementations = new HashMap();

            // Load implementation class names and keys from
            // Properties file, translate names into Class
            // objects using Class.forName and store mappings.
            ...
        }
    }

    public static Foo getInstance(String key) {
        initMapIfNecessary();
        Class c = (Class) implementations.get(key);
        if (c == null)
            return new DefaultFoo();

        try {
            return (Foo) c.newInstance();
        } catch (Exception e) {
            return new DefaultFoo();
        }
    }
}
```

The main disadvantage of static factory methods is that classes without public or protected constructors cannot be subclassed. The same is true for nonpublic classes returned by public static factories. For example, it is impossible to subclass any of the convenience implementation classes in the Collections Framework. Arguably this can be a blessing in disguise, as it encourages programmers to use composition instead of inheritance (Item 14).

A second disadvantage of static factory methods is that they are not readily distinguishable from other static methods. They do not stand out in API documentation in the way that constructors do. Furthermore, static factory methods represent a deviation from the norm. Thus it can be difficult to figure out from the class documentation how to instantiate a class that provides static factory methods instead of constructors. This disadvantage can be reduced by adhering to standard naming conventions. These conventions are still evolving, but two names for static factory methods are becoming common:

- valueOf—Returns an instance that has, loosely speaking, the same value as its parameters. Static factory methods with this name are effectively type-conversion operators.

- getInstance—Returns an instance that is described by its parameters but cannot be said to have the same value. In the case of singletons, it returns the sole instance. This name is common in provider frameworks.

In summary, static factory methods and public constructors both have their uses, and it pays to understand their relative merits. Avoid the reflex to provide constructors without first considering static factories because static factories are often more appropriate. If you've weighed the two options and nothing pushes you strongly in either direction, it's probably best to provide a constructor simply because it's the norm.

Item 2:   Enforce the singleton property with a private constructor

A *singleton* is simply a class that is instantiated exactly once [Gamma98, p. 127]. Singletons typically represent some system component that is intrinsically unique, such as a video display or file system.

There are two approaches to implementing singletons. Both are based on keeping the constructor private and providing a public static member to allow clients access to the sole instance of the class. In one approach, the public static member is a final field:

```
// Singleton with final field
public class Elvis {
    public static final Elvis INSTANCE = new Elvis();

    private Elvis() {
        ...
    }

    ...  // Remainder omitted
}
```

The private constructor is called only once, to initialize the public static final field Elvis.INSTANCE. The lack of public or protected constructors *guarantees* a "monoelvistic" universe: Exactly one Elvis instance will exist once the Elvis class is initialized—no more, no less. Nothing that a client does can change this.

In a second approach, a public static factory method is provided instead of the public static final field:

```
// Singleton with static factory
public class Elvis {
    private static final Elvis INSTANCE = new Elvis();

    private Elvis() {
        ...
    }

    public static Elvis getInstance() {
        return INSTANCE;
    }

    ...  // Remainder omitted
}
```

All calls to the static method, `Elvis.getInstance`, return the same object reference, and no other `Elvis` instance will ever be created.

The main advantage of the first approach is that the declarations of the members comprising the class make it clear that the class is a singleton: the public static field is final, so the field will always contain the same object reference. There may also be a slight performance advantage to the first approach, but a good JVM implementation should be able to eliminate it by inlining the call to the static factory method in the second approach.

The main advantage of the second approach is that it gives you the flexibility to change your mind about whether the class should be a singleton without changing the API. The static factory method for a singleton returns the sole instance of the class but could easily be modified to return, say, a unique instance for each thread that invokes the method.

On balance, then, it makes sense to use the first approach if you're absolutely sure that the class will forever remain a singleton. Use the second approach if you want to reserve judgment in the matter.

To make a singleton class serializable (Chapter 10), it is not sufficient merely to add `implements Serializable` to its declaration. To maintain the singleton guarantee, you must also provide a `readResolve` method (Item 57). Otherwise, each deserialization of a serialized instance will result in the creation of a new instance, leading, in the case of our example, to spurious `Elvis` sightings. To prevent this, add the following `readResolve` method to the `Elvis` class:

```
// readResolve method to preserve singleton property
private Object readResolve() throws ObjectStreamException {
    /*
     * Return the one true Elvis and let the garbage collector
     * take care of the Elvis impersonator.
     */
    return INSTANCE;
}
```

A unifying theme underlies this Item and Item 21, which describes the *type-safe enum* pattern. In both cases, private constructors are used in conjunction with public static members to ensure that no new instances of the relevant class are created after it is initialized. In the case of this item, only a single instance of the class is created; in Item 21, one instance is created for each member of the enumerated type. In the next item (Item 3), this approach is taken one step further: the absence of a public constructor is used to ensure that no instances of a class are ever created.

Item 3: Enforce noninstantiability with a private constructor

Occasionally you'll want to write a class that is just a grouping of static methods and static fields. Such classes have acquired a bad reputation because some people abuse them to write procedural programs in object-oriented languages, but they do have valid uses. They can be used to group related methods on primitive values or arrays, in the manner of `java.lang.Math` or `java.util.Arrays`, or to group static methods on objects that implement a particular interface, in the manner of `java.util.Collections`. They can also be used to group methods on a final class, in lieu of extending the class.

Such *utility classes* were not designed to be instantiated: An instance would be nonsensical. In the absence of explicit constructors, however, the compiler provides a public, parameterless *default constructor*. To a user, this constructor is indistinguishable from any other. It is not uncommon to see unintentionally instantiable classes in published APIs.

Attempting to enforce noninstantiability by making a class abstract does not work. The class can be subclassed and the subclass instantiated. Furthermore, it misleads the user into thinking the class was designed for inheritance (Item 15). There is, however, a simple idiom to ensure noninstantiability. A default constructor is generated only if a class contains no explicit constructors, so **a class can be made noninstantiable by including a single explicit private constructor**:

```
// Noninstantiable utility class
public class UtilityClass {

    // Suppress default constructor for noninstantiability
    private UtilityClass() {
        // This constructor will never be invoked
    }
    ...  // Remainder omitted
}
```

Because the explicit constructor is private, it is inaccessible outside of the class. It is thus guaranteed that the class will never be instantiated, assuming the constructor is not invoked from within the class itself. This idiom is mildly counterintuitive, as the constructor is provided expressly so that it cannot be invoked. It is therefore wise to include a comment describing the purpose of the constructor.

As a side effect, this idiom also prevents the class from being subclassed. All constructors must invoke an accessible superclass constructor, explicitly or implicitly, and a subclass would have no accessible constructor to invoke.

Item 4:   Avoid creating duplicate objects

It is often appropriate to reuse a single object instead of creating a new functionally equivalent object each time it is needed. Reuse can be both faster and more stylish. An object can always be reused if it is *immutable* (Item 13).

As an extreme example of what not to do, consider this statement:

```
String s = new String("silly");  // DON'T DO THIS!
```

The statement creates a new String instance each time it is executed, and none of those object creations is necessary. The argument to the String constructor ("silly") is itself a String instance, functionally identical to all of the objects created by the constructor. If this usage occurs in a loop or in a frequently invoked method, millions of String instances can be created needlessly.

The improved version is simply the following:

```
String s = "No longer silly";
```

This version uses a single String instance, rather than creating a new one each time it is executed. Furthermore, it is guaranteed that the object will be reused by any other code running in the same virtual machine that happens to contain the same string literal [JLS, 3.10.5].

You can often avoid creating duplicate objects by using *static factory methods* (Item 1) in preference to constructors on immutable classes that provide both. For example, the static factory method Boolean.valueOf(String) is almost always preferable to the constructor Boolean(String). The constructor creates a new object each time it's called while the static factory method is never required to do so.

In addition to reusing immutable objects, you can also reuse mutable objects that you know will not be modified. Here is a slightly more subtle and much more common example of what not to do, involving mutable objects that are never modified once their values have been computed:

```
public class Person {
    private final Date birthDate;
    // Other fields omitted

    public Person(Date birthDate) {
        this.birthDate = birthDate;
    }
```

```
// DON'T DO THIS!
public boolean isBabyBoomer() {
    Calendar gmtCal =
        Calendar.getInstance(TimeZone.getTimeZone("GMT"));
    gmtCal.set(1946, Calendar.JANUARY, 1, 0, 0, 0);
    Date boomStart = gmtCal.getTime();
    gmtCal.set(1965, Calendar.JANUARY, 1, 0, 0, 0);
    Date boomEnd = gmtCal.getTime();
    return birthDate.compareTo(boomStart) >= 0 &&
            birthDate.compareTo(boomEnd)   <  0;
    }
}
```

The isBabyBoomer method unnecessarily creates a new Calendar, TimeZone, and two Date instances each time it is invoked. The version that follows avoids this inefficiency with a static initializer:

```
class Person {
    private final Date birthDate;

    public Person(Date birthDate) {
        this.birthDate = birthDate;
    }


    /**
     * The starting and ending dates of the baby boom.
     */
    private static final Date BOOM_START;
    private static final Date BOOM_END;

    static {
        Calendar gmtCal =
            Calendar.getInstance(TimeZone.getTimeZone("GMT"));
        gmtCal.set(1946, Calendar.JANUARY, 1, 0, 0, 0);
        BOOM_START = gmtCal.getTime();
        gmtCal.set(1965, Calendar.JANUARY, 1, 0, 0, 0);
        BOOM_END = gmtCal.getTime();
    }

    public boolean isBabyBoomer() {
        return birthDate.compareTo(BOOM_START) >= 0 &&
                birthDate.compareTo(BOOM_END)   <  0;
    }
}
```

The improved version of the `Person` class creates `Calendar`, `TimeZone`, and `Date` instances only once, when it is initialized, instead of creating them every time `isBabyBoomer` is invoked. This results in significant performance gains if the method is invoked frequently. On my machine, the original version takes 36,000 ms for one million invocations, while the improved version takes 370 ms, which is one hundred times faster. Not only is performance improved, but so is clarity. Changing `boomStart` and `boomEnd` from local variables to final static fields makes it clear that these dates are treated as constants, making the code more understandable. In the interest of full disclosure, the savings from this sort of optimization will not always be this dramatic, as `Calendar` instances are particularly expensive to create.

If the `isBabyBoomer` method is never invoked, the improved version of the `Person` class will initialize the BOOM_START and BOOM_END fields unnecessarily. It would be possible to eliminate the unnecessary initializations by *lazily initializing* these fields (Item 48) the first time the `isBabyBoomer` method is invoked, but it is not recommended. As is often the case with lazy initialization, it would complicate the implementation and would be unlikely to result in a noticeable performance improvement (Item 37).

In all of the previous examples in this item, it was obvious that the objects in question could be reused because they were immutable. There are other situations where it is less obvious. Consider the case of *adapters* [Gamma98, p. 139], also known as *views*. An adapter is one object that delegates to a backing object, providing an alternative interface to the backing object. Because an adapter has no state beyond that of its backing object, there's no need to create more than one instance of a given adapter to a given object.

For example, the `keySet` method of the `Map` interface returns a `Set` view of the `Map` object, consisting of all the keys in the map. Naively, it would seem that every call to `keySet` would have to create a new `Set` instance, but every call to `keySet` on a given `Map` object may return the same `Set` instance. Although the returned `Set` instance is typically mutable, all of the returned objects are functionally identical: When one returned object changes, so do all the others because they're all backed by the same `Map` instance.

This item should not be misconstrued to imply that object creation is expensive and should be avoided. On the contrary, the creation and reclamation of small objects whose constructors do little explicit work is cheap, especially on modern JVM implementations. Creating additional objects to enhance the clarity, simplicity, or power of a program is generally a good thing.

Conversely, avoiding object creation by maintaining your own *object pool* is a bad idea unless the objects in the pool are extremely heavyweight. A prototypical example of an object that does justify an object pool is a database connection. The cost of establishing the connection is sufficiently high that it makes sense to reuse these objects. Generally speaking, however, maintaining your own object pools clutters up your code, increases memory footprint, and harms performance. Modern JVM implementations have highly optimized garbage collectors that easily outperform such object pools on lightweight objects.

The counterpoint to this item is Item 24 on *defensive copying*. The present item says: "Don't create a new object when you should reuse an existing one," while Item 32 says: "Don't reuse an existing object when you should create a new one." Note that the penalty for reusing an object when defensive copying is called for is far greater than the penalty for needlessly creating a duplicate object. Failing to make defensive copies where required can lead to insidious bugs and security holes; creating objects unnecessarily merely affects style and performance.

Item 5:   Eliminate obsolete object references

When you switch from a language with manual memory management, such as C or C++, to a garbage-collected language, your job as a programmer is made much easier by the fact that your objects are automatically reclaimed when you're through with them. It seems almost like magic when you first experience it. It can easily lead to the impression that you don't have to think about memory management, but this isn't quite true.

Consider the following simple stack implementation:

```java
// Can you spot the "memory leak"?
public class Stack {
    private Object[] elements;
    private int size = 0;

    public Stack(int initialCapacity) {
        this.elements = new Object[initialCapacity];
    }

    public void push(Object e) {
        ensureCapacity();
        elements[size++] = e;
    }

    public Object pop() {
        if (size == 0)
            throw new EmptyStackException();
        return elements[--size];
    }

    /**
     * Ensure space for at least one more element, roughly
     * doubling the capacity each time the array needs to grow.
     */
    private void ensureCapacity() {
        if (elements.length == size) {
            Object[] oldElements = elements;
            elements = new Object[2 * elements.length + 1];
            System.arraycopy(oldElements, 0, elements, 0, size);
        }
    }
}
```

There's nothing obviously wrong with this program. You could test it exhaustively, and it would pass every test with flying colors, but there's a problem lurking. Loosely speaking, the program has a "memory leak," which can silently manifest itself as reduced performance due to increased garbage collector activity or increased memory footprint. In extreme cases, such memory leaks can cause disk paging and even program failure with an OutOfMemoryError, but such failures are relatively rare.

So where is the memory leak? If a stack grows and then shrinks, the objects that were popped off the stack will not be garbage collected, even if the program using the stack has no more references to them. This is because the stack maintains *obsolete references* to these objects. An obsolete reference is simply a reference that will never be dereferenced again. In this case, any references outside of the "active portion" of the element array are obsolete. The active portion consists of the elements whose index is less than size.

Memory leaks in garbage collected languages (more properly known as *unintentional object retentions*) are insidious. If an object reference is unintentionally retained, not only is that object excluded from garbage collection, but so too are any objects referenced by that object, and so on. Even if only a few object references are unintentionally retained, many, many objects may be prevented from being garbage collected, with potentially large effects on performance.

The fix for this sort of problem is simple: Merely null out references once they become obsolete. In the case of our Stack class, the reference to an item becomes obsolete as soon as it's popped off the stack. The corrected version of the pop method looks like this:

```
public Object pop() {
    if (size==0)
        throw new EmptyStackException();
    Object result = elements[--size];
    elements[size] = null; // Eliminate obsolete reference
    return result;
}
```

An added benefit of nulling out obsolete references is that, if they are subsequently dereferenced by mistake, the program will immediately fail with a NullPointerException, rather than quietly doing the wrong thing. It is always beneficial to detect programming errors as quickly as possible.

When programmers are first stung by a problem like this, they tend to overcompensate by nulling out every object reference as soon as the program is finished with it. This is neither necessary nor desirable as it clutters up the program unnecessarily and could conceivably reduce performance. Nulling out object references should be the exception rather than the norm. The best way to eliminate an obsolete reference is to reuse the variable in which it was contained or to let it fall out of scope. This occurs naturally if you define each variable in the narrowest possible scope (Item 29). It should be noted that on present day JVM implementations, it is not sufficient merely to exit the block in which a variable is defined; one must exit the containing method in order for the reference to vanish.

So when should you null out a reference? What aspect of the `Stack` class makes it susceptible to memory leaks? Simply put, the `Stack` class *manages its own memory*. The *storage pool* consists of the elements of the `items` array (the object reference cells, not the objects themselves). The elements in the active portion of the array (as defined earlier) are *allocated*, and those in the remainder of the array are *free*. The garbage collector has no way of knowing this; to the garbage collector, all of the object references in the `items` array are equally valid. Only the programmer knows that the inactive portion of the array is unimportant. The programmer effectively communicates this fact to the garbage collector by manually nulling out array elements as soon as they become part of the inactive portion.

Generally speaking, whenever a class manages its own memory, the programmer should be alert for memory leaks. Whenever an element is freed, any object references contained in the element should be nulled out.

Another common source of memory leaks is caches. Once you put an object reference into a cache, it's easy to forget that it's there and leave it in the cache long after it becomes irrelevant. There are two possible solutions to this problem. If you're lucky enough to be implementing a cache wherein an entry is relevant exactly so long as there are references to its key outside of the cache, represent the cache as a `WeakHashMap`; entries will be removed automatically after they become obsolete. More commonly, the period during which a cache entry is relevant is not well defined, with entries becoming less valuable over time. Under these circumstances, the cache should occasionally be cleansed of entries that have fallen into disuse. This cleaning can be done by a background thread (perhaps via the `java.util.Timer` API) or as a side effect of adding new entries to the cache. The `java.util.LinkedHashMap` class, added in release 1.4, facilitates the latter approach with its `removeEldestEntry` method.

Because memory leaks typically do not manifest themselves as obvious failures, they may remain present in a system for years. They are typically discovered only as a result of careful code inspection or with the aid of a debugging tool known as a *heap profiler*. Therefore it is very desirable to learn to anticipate problems like this before they occur and prevent them from happening.

Item 6:   Avoid finalizers

Finalizers are unpredictable, often dangerous, and generally unnecessary. Their use can cause erratic behavior, poor performance, and portability problems. Finalizers have a few valid uses, which we'll cover later in this item, but as a rule of thumb, finalizers should be avoided.

C++ programmers are cautioned not to think of finalizers as the analog of C++ destructors. In C++, destructors are the normal way to reclaim the resources associated with an object, a necessary counterpart to constructors. In the Java programming language, the garbage collector reclaims the storage associated with an object when it becomes unreachable, requiring no special effort on the part of the programmer. C++ destructors are also used to reclaim other nonmemory resources. In the Java programming language, the `try-finally` block is generally used for this purpose.

There is no guarantee that finalizers will be executed promptly [JLS, 12.6]. It can take arbitrarily long between the time that an object becomes unreachable and the time that its finalizer is executed. This means that **nothing time-critical should ever be done by a finalizer.** For example, it is a grave error to depend on a finalizer to close open files because open file descriptors are a limited resource. If many files are left open because the JVM is tardy in executing finalizers, a program may fail because it can no longer open files.

The promptness with which finalizers are executed is primarily a function of the garbage collection algorithm, which varies widely from JVM implementation to JVM implementation. The behavior of a program that depends on the promptness of finalizer execution may likewise vary. It is entirely possible that such a program will run perfectly on the JVM on which you test it and then fail miserably on the JVM favored by your most important customer.

Tardy finalization is not just a theoretical problem. Providing a finalizer for a class can, under rare conditions, arbitrarily delay reclamation of its instances. A colleague recently debugged a long-running GUI application that was mysteriously dying with an `OutOfMemoryError`. Analysis revealed that at the time of its death, the application had thousands of graphics objects on its finalizer queue just waiting to be finalized and reclaimed. Unfortunately, the finalizer thread was running at a lower priority than another thread in the application, so objects weren't getting finalized at the rate they became eligible for finalization. The JLS makes no guarantees as to which thread will execute finalizers, so there is no portable way to prevent this sort of problem other than to refrain from using finalizers.

Not only does the JLS provide no guarantee that finalizers will get executed promptly, it provides no guarantee that they'll get executed at all. It is entirely possible, even likely, that a program terminates without executing finalizers on some objects that are no longer reachable. As a consequence, **you should never depend on a finalizer to update critical persistent state**. For example, depending on a finalizer to release a persistent lock on a shared resource such as a database is a good way to bring your entire distributed system to a grinding halt.

Don't be seduced by the methods `System.gc` and `System.runFinalization`. They may increase the odds of finalizers getting executed, but they don't guarantee it. The only methods that claim to guarantee finalization are `System.runFinalizersOnExit` and its evil twin, `Runtime.runFinalizersOnExit`. These methods are fatally flawed and have been deprecated.

In case you are not yet convinced that finalizers should be avoided, here's another tidbit worth considering: If an uncaught exception is thrown during finalization, the exception is ignored, and finalization of that object terminates [JLS, 12.6]. Uncaught exceptions can leave objects in a corrupt state. If another thread attempts to use such a corrupted object, arbitrary nondeterministic behavior may result. Normally, an uncaught exception will terminate the thread and print a stack trace, but not if it occurs in a finalizer—it won't even print a warning.

So what should you do instead of writing a finalizer for a class whose objects encapsulate resources that require termination, such as files or threads? Just **provide an *explicit termination method***, and require clients of the class to invoke this method on each instance when it is no longer needed. One detail worth mentioning is that the instance must keep track of whether it has been terminated: The explicit termination method must record in a private field that the object is no longer valid, and other methods must check this field and throw an `Illegal-StateException` if they are called after the object has been terminated.

A typical example of an explicit termination method is the `close` method on `InputStream` and `OutputStream`. Another example is the `cancel` method on `java.util.Timer`, which performs the necessary state change to cause the thread associated with a `Timer` instance to terminate itself gently. Examples from `java.awt` include `Graphics.dispose` and `Window.dispose`. These methods are often overlooked, with predictably dire performance consequences. A related method is `Image.flush`, which deallocates all the resources associated with an `Image` instance but leaves it in a state where it can still be used, reallocating the resources if necessary.

Explicit termination methods are often used in combination with the try-finally construct to ensure prompt termination. Invoking the explicit termination method inside the finally clause ensures that it will get executed even if an exception is thrown while the object is being used:

```
// try-finally block guarantees execution of termination method
Foo foo = new Foo(...);
try {
    // Do what must be done with foo
    ...
} finally {
    foo.terminate();  // Explicit termination method
}
```

So what, if anything, are finalizers good for? There are two legitimate uses. One is to act as a "safety net" in case the owner of an object forgets to call the explicit termination method that you provided per the advice in the previous paragraph. While there's no guarantee that the finalizer will get invoked promptly, it's better to free the critical resource late than never, in those (hopefully rare) cases when the client fails to hold up its end of the bargain by calling the explicit termination method. The three classes mentioned as examples of the explicit termination method pattern (InputStream, OutputStream, and Timer) also have finalizers that serve as safety nets in case their termination methods aren't called.

A second legitimate use of finalizers concerns objects with *native peers*. A native peer is a native object to which a normal object delegates via native methods. Because a native peer is not a normal object, the garbage collector doesn't know about it and can't reclaim it when its normal peer is reclaimed. A finalizer is an appropriate vehicle for performing this task, *assuming the native peer holds no critical resources*. If the native peer holds resources that must be terminated promptly, the class should have an explicit termination method, as described above. The termination method should do whatever is required to free the critical resource. The termination method can be a native method, or it can invoke one.

It is important to note that "finalizer chaining" is not performed automatically. If a class (other than Object) has a finalizer and a subclass overrides it, the subclass finalizer must invoke the superclass finalizer manually. You should finalize the subclass in a try block and invoke the superclass finalizer in the corresponding `finally` block. This ensures that the superclass finalizer gets executed even if the subclass finalization throws an exception and vice versa:

```
// Manual finalizer chaining
protected void finalize() throws Throwable {
    try {
        // Finalize subclass state
        ...
    } finally {
        super.finalize();
    }
}
```

If a subclass implementor overrides a superclass finalizer but forgets to invoke the superclass finalizer manually (or chooses not to out of spite), the superclass finalizer will never be invoked. It is possible to defend against such a careless or malicious subclass at the cost of creating an additional object for every object to be finalized. Instead of putting the finalizer on the class requiring finalization, put the finalizer on an anonymous class (Item 18) whose sole purpose is to finalize its enclosing instance. A single instance of the anonymous class, called a *finalizer guardian*, is created for each instance of the enclosing class. The enclosing instance stores the sole reference to its finalizer guardian in a private instance field so the finalizer guardian becomes eligible for finalization immediately prior to the enclosing instance. When the guardian is finalized, it performs the finalization activity desired for the enclosing instance, just as if its finalizer were a method on the enclosing class:

```
// Finalizer Guardian idiom
public class Foo {
    // Sole purpose of this object is to finalize outer Foo object
    private final Object finalizerGuardian = new Object() {
        protected void finalize() throws Throwable {
            // Finalize outer Foo object
            ...
        }
    };
    ...  // Remainder omitted
}
```

Note that the public class, Foo, has no finalizer (other than the trivial one that it inherits from Object), so it doesn't matter whether a subclass finalizer calls `super.finalize` or not. This technique should be considered for every nonfinal public class that has a finalizer.

In summary, don't use finalizers except as a safety net or to terminate noncritical native resources. In those rare instances where you do use a finalizer, remember to invoke `super.finalize`. Last, if you need to associate a finalizer with a public, nonfinal class, consider using a finalizer guardian to ensure that the finalizer is executed, even if a subclass finalizer fails to invoke `super.finalize`.

CHAPTER 3

Methods Common to All Objects

ALTHOUGH Object is a concrete class, it is designed primarily for extension. All of its nonfinal methods (equals, hashCode, toString, clone, and finalize) have explicit *general contracts* because they are designed to be overridden. It is the responsibility of any class overriding these methods to obey their general contracts; failure to do so will prevent other classes that depend on these contracts from functioning properly in conjunction with the class.

This chapter tells you when and how to override the nonfinal Object methods. The finalize method is omitted from this chapter because it was discussed in Item 6. While not an Object method, Comparable.compareTo is discussed in this chapter because it has a similar character.

Item 7: Obey the general contract when overriding equals

Overriding the equals method seems simple, but there are many ways to get it wrong, and the consequences can be dire. The easiest way to avoid problems is not to override the equals method, in which case each instance is equal only to itself. This is the right thing to do if any of the following conditions apply:

- **Each instance of the class is inherently unique.** This is true for classes that represent active entities rather than values, such as Thread. The equals implementation provided by Object has exactly the right behavior for these classes.

- **You don't care whether the class provides a "logical equality" test.** For example, java.util.Random could have overridden equals to check whether two Random instances would produce the same sequence of random numbers going forward, but the designers didn't think that clients would need or want this functionality. Under these circumstances, the equals implementation inherited from Object is adequate.

- **A superclass has already overridden `equals`, and the behavior inherited from the superclass is appropriate for this class.** For example, most `Set` implementations inherit their `equals` implementation from `AbstractSet`, `List` implementations from `AbstractList`, and `Map` implementations from `AbstractMap`.

- **The class is private or package-private, and you are certain that its `equals` method will never be invoked.** Arguably, the `equals` method *should* be over-ridden under these circumstances, in case it is accidentally invoked someday:

```
public boolean equals(Object o) {
    throw new UnsupportedOperationException();
}
```

So when is it appropriate to override `Object.equals`? When a class has a notion of *logical equality* that differs from mere object identity, and a superclass has not already overridden `equals` to implement the desired behavior. This is generally the case for *value classes*, such as `Integer` or `Date`. A programmer who compares references to value objects using the `equals` method expects to find out whether they are logically equivalent, not whether they refer to the same object. Not only is overriding the `equals` method necessary to satisfy programmer expectations, it enables instances of the class to serve as map keys or set elements with predictable, desirable behavior.

One kind of value class that does *not* require the `equals` method to be overridden is the *typesafe enum* (Item 21). Because typesafe enum classes guarantee that at most one object exists with each value, `Object`'s `equals` method is equivalent to a logical `equals` method for such classes.

When you override the `equals` method, you must adhere to its general contract. Here is the contract, copied from the specification for `java.lang.Object`:

The equals method implements an *equivalence relation*:
- It is *reflexive*: For any reference value x, x.equals(x) must return `true`.

- It is *symmetric*: For any reference values x and y, x.equals(y) must return `true` if and only if y.equals(x) returns `true`.

- It is *transitive*: For any reference values x, y, and z, if x.equals(y) returns `true` and y.equals(z) returns `true`, then x.equals(z) must return `true`.

- It is *consistent*: For any reference values x and y, multiple invocations of x.equals(y) consistently return `true` or consistently return `false`, provided no information used in `equals` comparisons on the object is modified.

- For any non-null reference value x, x.equals(null) must return `false`.

Unless you are mathematically inclined, this might look a bit scary, but do not ignore it! If you violate it, you may well find that your program behaves erratically or crashes, and it can be very difficult to pin down the source of the failure. To paraphrase John Donne, no class is an island. Instances of one class are frequently passed to another. Many classes, including all collections classes, depend on the objects passed to them obeying the `equals` contract.

Now that you are aware of the evils of violating the `equals` contract, let's go over the contract in detail. The good news is that, appearances notwithstanding, the contract really isn't very complicated. Once you understand it, it's not hard to adhere to it. Let's examine the five requirements in turn:

Reflexivity—The first requirement says merely that an object must be equal to itself. It is hard to imagine violating this requirement unintentionally. If you were to violate it and then add an instance of your class to a collection, the collection's `contains` method would almost certainly say that the collection did not contain the instance that you just added.

Symmetry—The second requirement says that any two objects must agree on whether they are equal. Unlike the first requirement, it's not hard to imagine violating this one unintentionally. For example, consider the following class:

```
/**
 * Case-insensitive string. Case of the original string is
 * preserved by toString, but ignored in comparisons.
 */
public final class CaseInsensitiveString {
    private String s;

    public CaseInsensitiveString(String s) {
        if (s == null)
            throw new NullPointerException();
        this.s = s;
    }

    // Broken - violates symmetry!
    public boolean equals(Object o) {
        if (o instanceof CaseInsensitiveString)
            return s.equalsIgnoreCase(
                ((CaseInsensitiveString)o).s);
        if (o instanceof String)  // One-way interoperability!
            return s.equalsIgnoreCase((String)o);
        return false;
    }
    ... // Remainder omitted
}
```

The well-intentioned `equals` method in this class naively attempts to interoperate with ordinary strings. Let's suppose that we have one case-sensitive string and one ordinary one:

```
CaseInsensitiveString cis = new CaseInsensitiveString("Polish");
String s = "polish";
```

As expected, `cis.equals(s)` returns `true`. The problem is that while the `equals` method in `CaseInsensitiveString` knows about ordinary strings, the `equals` method in `String` is oblivious to case-insensitive strings. Therefore `s.equals(cis)` returns `false`, a clear violation of symmetry. Suppose you put a case-insensitive string into a collection:

```
List list = new ArrayList();
list.add(cis);
```

What does `list.contains(s)` return at this point? Who knows? In Sun's current implementation, it happens to return `false`, but that's just an implementation artifact. In another implementation, it could just as easily return `true` or throw a run-time exception. Once you've violated the `equals` contract, you simply don't know how other objects will behave when confronted with your object.

To eliminate the problem, merely remove the ill-conceived attempt to interoperate with `String` from the `equals` method. Once you do this, you can refactor the method to give it a single return:

```
public boolean equals(Object o) {
    return o instanceof CaseInsensitiveString &&
        ((CaseInsensitiveString)o).s.equalsIgnoreCase(s);
}
```

Transitivity—The third requirement of the `equals` contract says that if one object is equal to a second and the second object is equal to a third, then the first object must be equal to the third. Again, it's not hard to imagine violating this requirement unintentionally. Consider the case of a programmer who creates a subclass that adds a new *aspect* to its superclass. In other words, the subclass adds a piece of information that affects `equals` comparisons. Let's start with a simple immutable two-dimensional point class:

```
public class Point {
    private final int x;
    private final int y;
    public Point(int x, int y) {
        this.x = x;
        this.y = y;
    }

    public boolean equals(Object o) {
        if (!(o instanceof Point))
            return false;
        Point p = (Point)o;
        return p.x == x && p.y == y;
    }

    ...   // Remainder omitted
}
```

Suppose you want to extend this class, adding the notion of color to a point:

```
public class ColorPoint extends Point {
    private Color color;

    public ColorPoint(int x, int y, Color color) {
        super(x, y);
        this.color = color;
    }

    ...   // Remainder omitted
}
```

How should the `equals` method look? If you leave it out entirely, the implementation is inherited from `Point`, and color information is ignored in `equals` comparisons. While this does not violate the `equals` contract, it is clearly unacceptable. Suppose you write an `equals` method that returns `true` only if its argument is another color point with the same position and color:

```
// Broken - violates symmetry!
public boolean equals(Object o) {
    if (!(o instanceof ColorPoint))
        return false;
    ColorPoint cp = (ColorPoint)o;
    return super.equals(o) && cp.color == color;
}
```

The problem with this method is that you might get different results when comparing a point to a color point and vice versa. The former comparison ignores color, while the latter comparison always returns `false` because the type of the argument is incorrect. To make this concrete, let's create one point and one color point:

```
Point p = new Point(1, 2);
ColorPoint cp = new ColorPoint(1, 2, Color.RED);
```

Then `p.equals(cp)` returns `true`, while `cp.equals(p)` returns `false`. You might try to fix the problem by having `ColorPoint.equals` ignore color when doing "mixed comparisons":

```
// Broken - violates transitivity.
public boolean equals(Object o) {
    if (!(o instanceof Point))
        return false;

    // If o is a normal Point, do a color-blind comparison
    if (!(o instanceof ColorPoint))
        return o.equals(this);

    // o is a ColorPoint; do a full comparison
    ColorPoint cp = (ColorPoint)o;
    return super.equals(o) && cp.color == color;
}
```

This approach does provide symmetry, but at the expense of transitivity:

```
ColorPoint p1 = new ColorPoint(1, 2, Color.RED);
Point p2 = new Point(1, 2);
ColorPoint p3 = new ColorPoint(1, 2, Color.BLUE);
```

At this point, `p1.equals(p2)` and `p2.equals(p3)` return `true`, while `p1.equals(p3)` returns `false`, a clear violation of transitivity. The first two comparisons are "color-blind," while the third takes color into account.

So what's the solution? It turns out that this is a fundamental problem of equivalence relations in object-oriented languages. **There is simply no way to extend an instantiable class and add an aspect while preserving the `equals` contract.** There is, however, a fine workaround. Follow the advice of Item 14, "Favor composition over inheritance." Instead of having ColorPoint extend

Point, give ColorPoint a private Point field and a public *view* method (Item 4) that returns the point at the same position as this color point:

```
// Adds an aspect without violating the equals contract
public class ColorPoint {
    private Point point;
    private Color color;

    public ColorPoint(int x, int y, Color color) {
        point = new Point(x, y);
        this.color = color;
    }

    /**
     * Returns the point-view of this color point.
     */
    public Point asPoint() {
        return point;
    }

    public boolean equals(Object o) {
        if (!(o instanceof ColorPoint))
            return false;
        ColorPoint cp = (ColorPoint)o;
        return cp.point.equals(point) && cp.color.equals(color);
    }

    ...  // Remainder omitted
}
```

There are some classes in the Java platform libraries that subclass an instantiable class and add an aspect. For example, java.sql.Timestamp subclasses java.util.Date adding a nanoseconds field. The equals implementation for Timestamp does violate symmetry and can cause erratic behavior if Timestamp and Date objects are used in the same collection or are otherwise intermixed. The Timestamp class has a disclaimer cautioning the programmer against mixing dates and timestamps. While you won't get into trouble as long as you don't mix them, there's nothing preventing you from doing so, and the resulting errors could be hard to debug. The TimeStamp class is an anomaly and should not be emulated.

Note that you *can* add an aspect to a subclass of an *abstract* class without violating the equals contract. This is important for the sort of class hierarchies that you get by following the advice in Item 20, "Replace unions with class hierarchies." For example, you could have an abstract Shape class with no aspects, a Circle subclass that adds a radius field, and a Rectangle subclass that adds length and width fields. Problems of the sort just shown will not occur as long as it is impossible to create an instance of the superclass.

Consistency—The fourth requirement of the equals contract says that if two objects are equal, they must remain equal for all time, unless one (or both) of them is modified. This isn't so much a true requirement as a reminder that mutable objects can be equal to different objects at different times while immutable objects can't. When you write a class, think hard about whether it should be immutable (Item 13). If you conclude that it should, make sure that your equals method enforces the restriction that equal objects remain equal and unequal objects remain unequal for all time.

"Non-nullity"—The final requirement, which in the absence of a name I have taken the liberty of calling "non-nullity," says that all objects must be unequal to null. While it is hard to imagine accidentally returning true in response to the invocation o.equals(null), it isn't hard to imagine accidentally throwing a NullPointerException. The general contract does not allow this. Many classes have equals methods that guard against it with an explicit test for null:

```
public boolean equals(Object o) {
    if (o == null)
        return false;
    ...
}
```

This test is not necessary. To test its argument for equality, the equals method must first cast the argument to an appropriate type so its accessors may be invoked or its fields accessed. Before doing the cast, the method must use the instanceof operator to check that its argument is of the correct type:

```
public boolean equals(Object o) {
    if (!(o instanceof MyType))
        return false;
    ...
}
```

If this type check were missing and the equals method were passed an argument of the wrong type, the equals method would throw a ClassCastException, which violates the equals contract. But the instanceof operator is specified to return false if its first operand is null, regardless of what type appears in the second operand [JLS, 15.19.2]. Therefore the type check will return false if null is passed in, so you don't need a separate null check. Putting it all together, here's a recipe for a high-quality equals method:

1. **Use the == operator to check if the argument is a reference to this object.** If so, return `true`. This is just a performance optimization, but one that is worth doing if the comparison is potentially expensive.

2. **Use the `instanceof` operator to check if the argument is of the correct type.** If not, return `false`. Typically, the correct type is the class in which the method occurs. Occasionally, it is some interface implemented by this class. Use an interface if the class implements an interface that refines the `equals` contract to permit comparisons across classes that implement the interface. The collection interfaces `Set`, `List`, `Map`, and `Map.Entry` have this property.

3. **Cast the argument to the correct type.** Because this cast was preceded by an `instanceof` test, it is guaranteed to succeed.

4. **For each "significant" field in the class, check to see if that field of the argument matches the corresponding field of this object.** If all these tests succeed, return `true`; otherwise, return `false`. If the type in Step 2 is an interface, you must access the argument's significant fields via interface methods; if the type is a class, you may be able to access the fields directly, depending on their accessibility. For primitive fields whose type is not `float` or `double`, use the `==` operator for comparisons; for object reference fields, invoke the `equals` method recursively; for `float` fields, translate to `int` values using `Float.floatToIntBits` and compare the `int` values using the `==` operator; for `double` fields, translate to `long` values using `Double.doubleToLongBits` and compare the `long` values using the `==` operator. (The special treatment of `float` and `double` fields is made necessary by the existence of `Float.NaN`, `-0.0f`, and the analogous `double` constants; see the `Float.equals` documentation for details.) For array fields, apply these guidelines to each element. Some object reference fields may legitimately contain `null`. To avoid the possibility of a `NullPointerException`, use the following idiom to compare such fields:

   ```
   (field == null ? o.field == null : field.equals(o.field))
   ```

This alternative may be faster if `field` and `o.field` are often identical object references:

   ```
   (field == o.field || (field != null && field.equals(o.field)))
   ```

For some classes, like `CaseInsensitiveString` shown earlier, the field comparisons are more complex than simple equality tests. It should be apparent from the specification for a class if this is the case. If so, you may want to store a *canonical form* in each object, so that the `equals` method can do cheap exact comparisons on these canonical forms rather than more costly inexact comparisons. This technique is most appropriate for *immutable* classes (Item 13), as the canonical form would have to be kept up to date if the object could change.

The performance of the `equals` method may be affected by the order in which fields are compared. For best performance, you should first compare fields that are more likely to differ, less expensive to compare, or, ideally, both. You must not compare fields that are not part of an object's logical state, such as `Object` fields used to synchronize operations. You need not compare *redundant fields*, which can be calculated from "significant fields," but doing so may improve the performance of the `equals` method. If a redundant field amounts to a summary description of the entire object, comparing this field will save you the expense of comparing the actual data if the comparison fails.

5. **When you are finished writing your equals method, ask yourself three questions: Is it symmetric, is it transitive, and is it consistent?** (The other two properties generally take care of themselves.) If not, figure out why these properties fail to hold, and modify the method accordingly.

For a concrete example of an `equals` method constructed according to the above recipe, see `PhoneNumber.equals` in Item 8. Here are a few final caveats:

- **Always override `hashCode` when you override `equals`** (Item 8).

- **Don't try to be too clever.** If you simply test fields for equality, it's not hard to adhere to the `equals` contract. If you are overly aggressive in searching for equivalence, it's easy to get into trouble. It is generally a bad idea to take any form of aliasing into account. For example, the `File` class shouldn't attempt to equate symbolic links referring to the same file. Thankfully, it doesn't.

- **Don't write an `equals` method that relies on unreliable resources.** It's extremely difficult to satisfy the consistency requirement if you do this. For example, `java.net.URL`'s `equals` method relies on the IP addresses of the hosts in URLs being compared. Translating a host name to an IP address can require network access, and it isn't guaranteed to yield the same results over time. This can cause the `URL` `equals` method to violate the `equals` contract, and it has caused problems in practice. (Unfortunately, this behavior cannot be changed due to compatibility requirements.) With few exceptions, `equals` methods should perform deterministic computations on memory-resident objects.

- **Don't substitute another type for `Object` in the `equals` declaration.** It is not uncommon for a programmer to write an `equals` method that looks like the following, and then spend hours puzzling over why it doesn't work properly:

```
public boolean equals(MyClass o) {
    ...
}
```

The problem is that this method does not *override* `Object.equals`, whose argument is of type `Object`, but *overloads* it instead (Item 26). It is acceptable to provide such a "strongly typed" `equals` method *in addition* to the normal one as long as the two methods return the same result but there is no compelling reason to do so. It may provide minor performance gains under certain circumstances, but it isn't worth the added complexity (Item 37).

Item 8:   Always override `hashCode` when you override `equals`

A common source of bugs is the failure to override the `hashCode` method. **You must override `hashCode` in every class that overrides `equals`.** Failure to do so will result in a violation of the general contract for `Object.hashCode`, which will prevent your class from functioning properly in conjunction with all hash-based collections, including `HashMap`, `HashSet`, and `Hashtable`.

Here is the contract, copied from the `java.lang.Object` specification:

- Whenever it is invoked on the same object more than once during an execution of an application, the `hashCode` method must consistently return the same integer, provided no information used in `equals` comparisons on the object is modified. This integer need not remain consistent from one execution of an application to another execution of the same application.

- If two objects are equal according to the `equals(Object)` method, then calling the `hashCode` method on each of the two objects must produce the same integer result.

- It is not required that if two objects are unequal according to the `equals(Object)` method, then calling the `hashCode` method on each of the two objects must produce distinct integer results. However, the programmer should be aware that producing distinct integer results for unequal objects may improve the performance of hash tables.

The key provision that is violated when you fail to override `hashCode` is the second one: Equal objects must have equal hash codes. Two distinct instances may be logically equal according to the class's `equals` method, but to the `Object` class's `hashCode` method, they're just two objects with nothing much in common. Therefore object's `hashCode` method returns two seemingly random numbers instead of two equal numbers as required by the contract.

For example, consider the following simplistic `PhoneNumber` class, whose `equals` method is constructed according to the recipe in Item 7:

```
public final class PhoneNumber {
    private final short areaCode;
    private final short exchange;
    private final short extension;

    public PhoneNumber(int areaCode, int exchange,
                       int extension) {
        rangeCheck(areaCode,    999, "area code");
        rangeCheck(exchange,    999, "exchange");
        rangeCheck(extension, 9999, "extension");
```

```
        this.areaCode  = (short) areaCode;
        this.exchange  = (short) exchange;
        this.extension = (short) extension;
    }

    private static void rangeCheck(int arg, int max,
                                        String name) {
        if (arg < 0 || arg > max)
            throw new IllegalArgumentException(name +": " + arg);
    }

    public boolean equals(Object o) {
        if (o == this)
            return true;
        if (!(o instanceof PhoneNumber))
            return false;
        PhoneNumber pn = (PhoneNumber)o;
        return pn.extension == extension &&
               pn.exchange  == exchange  &&
               pn.areaCode  == areaCode;
    }

    // No hashCode method!

    ... // Remainder omitted
}
```

Suppose you attempt to use this class with a `HashMap`:

```
Map m = new HashMap();
m.put(new PhoneNumber(408, 867, 5309), "Jenny");
```

At this point, you might expect `m.get(new PhoneNumber(408, 867, 5309))` to return "Jenny", but it returns `null`. Notice that two `PhoneNumber` instances are involved: One is used for insertion into the `HashMap`, and a second, equal, instance is used for (attempted) retrieval. The `PhoneNumber` class's failure to override `hashCode` causes the two equal instances to have unequal hash codes, in violation of the `hashCode` contract. Therefore the `get` method looks for the phone number in a different hash bucket from the one in which it was stored by the `put` method. Fixing this problem is as simple as providing a proper `hashCode` method for the `PhoneNumber` class.

So what should a hashCode method look like? It's trivial to write one that is legal but not good. This one, for example, is always legal, but it should never be used:

```
// The worst possible legal hash function - never use!
public int hashCode() { return 42; }
```

It's legal because it ensures that equal objects have the same hash code. It's atrocious because it ensures that *every* object has the same hash code. Therefore every object hashes to the same bucket, and hash tables degenerate to linked lists. Programs that should run in linear time run instead in quadratic time. For large hash tables, this is the difference between working and not working.

A good hash function tends to produce unequal hash codes for unequal objects. This is exactly what is meant by the third provision of the hashCode contract. Ideally, a hash function should distribute any reasonable collection of unequal instances uniformly across all possible hash values. Achieving this ideal can be extremely difficult. Luckily it is not too difficult to achieve a fair approximation. Here is a simple recipe:

1. Store some constant nonzero value, say 17, in an int variable called result.

2. For each significant field f in your object (each field taken into account by the equals method, that is), do the following:

   a. Compute an int hash code c for the field:

      i.   If the field is a boolean, compute (f ? 0 : 1).

      ii. If the field is a byte, char, short, or int, compute (int)f.

      iii. If the field is a long, compute (int)(f ^ (f >>> 32)).

      iv. If the field is a float compute Float.floatToIntBits(f).

      v.   If the field is a double, compute Double.doubleToLongBits(f), and then hash the resulting long as in step 2.a.iii.

      vi. If the field is an object reference and this class's equals method compares the field by recursively invoking equals, recursively invoke hashCode on the field. If a more complex comparison is required, compute a "canonical representation" for this field and invoke hashCode on the canonical representation. If the value of the field is null, return 0 (or some other constant, but 0 is traditional).

vii. If the field is an array, treat it as if each element were a separate field. That is, compute a hash code for each significant element by applying these rules recursively, and combine these values as described in step 2.b.

b. Combine the hash code c computed in step a into result as follows:

```
result = 37*result + c;
```

3. Return result.

4. When you are done writing the hashCode method, ask yourself whether equal instances have equal hash codes. If not, figure out why and fix the problem.

It is acceptable to exclude *redundant fields* from the hash code computation. In other words, it is acceptable to exclude any field whose value can be computed from fields that are included in the computation. It is *required* that you exclude any fields that are not used in equality comparisons. Failure to exclude these fields may result in a violation of the second provision of the hashCode contract.

A nonzero initial value is used in step 1, so the hash value will be affected by initial fields whose hash value, as computed in step 2.a, is zero. If zero was used as the initial value in step 1, the overall hash value would be unaffected by any such initial fields, which could increase collisions. The value 17 is arbitrary.

The multiplication in step 2.b makes the hash value depend on the order of the fields, which results in a much better hash function if the class contains multiple similar fields. For example, if the multiplication were omitted from a String hash function built according to this recipe, all anagrams would have identical hash codes. The multiplier 37 was chosen because it is an odd prime. If it was even and the multiplication overflowed, information would be lost because multiplication by two is equivalent to shifting. The advantages of using a prime number are less clear, but it is traditional to use primes for this purpose.

Let's apply this recipe to the PhoneNumber class. There are three significant fields, all of type short. A straightforward application of the recipe yields this hash function:

```
public int hashCode() {
    int result = 17;
    result = 37*result + areaCode;
    result = 37*result + exchange;
    result = 37*result + extension;
    return result;
}
```

Because this method returns the result of a simple deterministic computation whose only inputs are the three significant fields in a PhoneNumber instance, it should be clear that equal PhoneNumber instances have equal hash codes. This method is, in fact, a perfectly reasonable hashCode implementation for Phone-Number, on a par with those in the Java platform libraries as of release 1.4. It is simple, is reasonably fast, and does a reasonable job of dispersing unequal phone numbers into different hash buckets.

If a class is immutable and the cost of computing the hash code is significant, you might consider caching the hash code in the object rather than recalculating it each time it is requested. If you believe that most objects of this type will be used as hash keys, then you should calculate the hash code when the instance is created. Otherwise, you might choose to *lazily initialize* it the first time hashCode is invoked (Item 48). It is not clear that our PhoneNumber class merits this treatment, but just to show you how it's done:

```
// Lazily initialized, cached hashCode
private volatile int hashCode = 0;  // (See Item 48)

public int hashCode() {
    if (hashCode == 0) {
        int result = 17;
        result = 37*result + areaCode;
        result = 37*result + exchange;
        result = 37*result + extension;
        hashCode = result;
    }
    return hashCode;
}
```

While the recipe in this item yields reasonably good hash functions, it does not yield state-of-the-art hash functions, nor do the Java platform libraries provide such hash functions as of release 1.4. Writing such hash functions is a topic of active research and an activity best left to mathematicians and theoretical computer scientists. Perhaps a later release of the Java platform will provide state-of-the-art hash functions for its classes and utility methods to allow average programmers to construct such hash functions. In the meantime, the techniques described in this item should be adequate for most applications.

Do not be tempted to exclude significant parts of an object from the hash code computation to improve performance. While the resulting hash function may run faster, its quality may degrade to the point where hash tables become unusably slow. In particular, the hash function may, in practice, be confronted with a large collection of instances that differ largely in the regions that you've chosen to ignore. If this happens, the hash function will map all of the instances to a very few hash codes, and hash-based collections will display quadratic performance. This is not just a theoretical problem. The `String` hash function implemented in all Java platform releases prior to release 1.2 examined at most sixteen characters, evenly spaced throughout the string, starting with the first character. For large collections of hierarchical names such as URLs, this hash function displayed exactly the pathological behavior noted here.

Many classes in the Java platform libraries, such as `String`, `Integer`, and `Date`, specify the exact value returned by their `hashCode` method as a function of the instance value. This is generally *not* a good idea, as it severely limits your ability to improve the hash function in future releases. If you leave the details of a hash function unspecified and a flaw is found in it, you can fix the hash function in the next release without fear of breaking compatibility with clients who depend on the exact values returned by the hash function.

Item 9:   Always override `toString`

While `java.lang.Object` provides an implementation of the `toString` method, the string that it returns is generally not what the user of your class wants to see. It consists of the class name followed by an "at" sign (@) and the unsigned hexadecimal representation of the hash code, for example, "PhoneNumber@163b91." The general contract for `toString` says that the returned string should be "a concise but informative representation that is easy for a person to read." While it could be argued that "PhoneNumber@163b91" is concise and easy to read, it isn't very informative when compared to "(408) 867-5309". The `toString` contract goes on to say, "It is recommended that all subclasses override this method." Good advice, indeed.

While it isn't as important as obeying the `equals` and `hashCode` contracts (Item 7, Item 8), **providing a good `toString` implementation makes your class much more pleasant to use**. The `toString` method is automatically invoked when your object is passed to `println`, the string concatenation operator (+), or, as of release 1.4, `assert`. If you've provided a good `toString` method, generating a useful diagnostic message is as easy as:

```
System.out.println("Failed to connect: " + phoneNumber);
```

Programmers will generate diagnostic messages in this fashion whether or not you override `toString`, but the messages won't be intelligible unless you do. The benefits of providing a good `toString` method extend beyond instances of the class to objects containing references to these instances, especially collections. Which would you rather see when printing a map, "{Jenny=PhoneNumber@163b91}" or "{Jenny=(408) 867-5309}"?

When practical, the `toString` method should return *all* of the interesting information contained in the object, as in the phone number example just shown. It is impractical if the object is large or if it contains state that is not conducive to string representation. Under these circumstances, `toString` should return a summary such as "Manhattan white pages (1487536 listings)" or "Thread[main, 5,main]". Ideally, the string should be self-explanatory. (The `Thread` example flunks this test.)

One important decision you'll have to make when implementing a `toString` method is whether to specify the format of the return value in the documentation. It is recommended that you do this for *value classes*, such as phone numbers or matrices. The advantage of specifying the format is that it serves as a standard, unambiguous, human-readable representation of the object. This representation can be used for input and output and in persistent human-readable data objects such as XML documents. If you specify the format, it's usually a good idea to provide a matching `String` constructor (or static factory, see Item 1), so programmers can easily translate back and forth between the object and its string representation. This approach is taken by many value classes in the Java platform libraries, including `BigInteger`, `BigDecimal`, and most of the primitive wrapper classes.

The disadvantage of specifying the format of the `toString` return value is that once you've specified it, you're stuck with it for life, assuming your class is widely used. Programmers will write code to parse the representation, to generate it, and to embed it into persistent data. If you change the representation in a future release, you'll break their code and data, and they will yowl. By failing to specify a format, you preserve the flexibility to add information or improve the format in a subsequent release.

Whether or not you decide to specify the format, you should clearly document your intentions. If you specify the format, you should do so precisely. For example, here's a `toString` method to go with the `PhoneNumber` class in Item 8:

```
/**
 * Returns the string representation of this phone number.
 * The string consists of fourteen characters whose format
 * is "(XXX) YYY-ZZZZ", where XXX is the area code, YYY is
 * the extension, and ZZZZ is the exchange.  (Each of the
 * capital letters represents a single decimal digit.)
 *
 * If any of the three parts of this phone number is too small
 * to fill up its field, the field is padded with leading zeros.
 *  For example, if the value of the exchange is 123, the last
 * four characters of the string representation will be "0123".
 *
 * Note that there is a single space separating the closing
 * parenthesis after the area code from the first digit of the
 * exchange.
 */
public String toString() {
    return "(" + toPaddedString(areaCode, 3) + ") " +
            toPaddedString(exchange,  3) + "-" +
            toPaddedString(extension, 4);
}
```

```
/**
 * Translates an int to a string of the specified length,
 * padded with leading zeros.  Assumes i >= 0,
 * 1 <= length <= 10, and Integer.toString(i) <= length.
 */
private static String toPaddedString(int i, int length) {
    String s = Integer.toString(i);
    return ZEROS[length - s.length()] + s;
}

private static String[] ZEROS =
    {"", "0", "00", "000", "0000", "00000",
     "000000", "0000000", "00000000", "000000000"};
```

If you decide not to specify a format, the documentation comment should read something like this:

```
/**
 * Returns a brief description of this potion. The exact details
 * of the representation are unspecified and subject to change,
 * but the following may be regarded as typical:
 *
 * "[Potion #9: type=love, smell=turpentine, look=india ink]"
 */
public String toString() { ... }
```

After reading this comment, programmers who produce code or persistent data that depend on the details of the format will have no one but themselves to blame when the format is changed.

Whether or not you specify the format, **it is always a good idea to provide programmatic access to all of the information contained in the value returned by toString.** For example, the PhoneNumber class should contain accessors for the area code, exchange, and extension. If you fail to do this, you *force* programmers who need this information to parse the string. Besides reducing performance and making unnecessary work for programmers, this process is error prone and results in fragile systems that break if you change the format. By failing to provide accessors, you turn the string format into a de facto API, even if you've specified that it's subject to change.

Item 10: Override clone judiciously

The Cloneable interface was intended as a *mixin interface* (Item 16) for objects to advertise that they permit cloning. Unfortunately, it fails to serve this purpose. Its primary flaw is that it lacks a clone method, and Object's clone method is protected. You cannot, without resorting to *reflection* (Item 35), invoke the clone method on an object merely because it implements Cloneable. Even a reflective invocation may fail, as there is no guarantee that the object has an accessible clone method. Despite this flaw and others, the facility is in sufficiently wide use that it pays to understand it. This item tells you how to implement a well-behaved clone method, discusses when it is appropriate to do so, and briefly discusses alternatives.

So what *does* Cloneable do, given that it contains no methods? It determines the behavior of Object's protected clone implementation: If a class implements Cloneable, Object's clone method returns a field-by-field copy of the object; otherwise it throws CloneNotSupportedException. This is a highly atypical use of interfaces and not one to be emulated. Normally, implementing an interface says something about what a class can do for its clients. In the case of Cloneable, however, it modifies the behavior of a protected method on a superclass.

In order for implementing the Cloneable interface to have any effect on a class, it and all of its superclasses must obey a fairly complex, unenforceable, and largely undocumented protocol. The resulting mechanism is *extralinguistic*: It creates an object without calling a constructor.

The general contract for the clone method is weak. Here it is, copied from the specification for java.lang.Object:

> Creates and returns a copy of this object. The precise meaning of "copy" may depend on the class of the object. The general intent is that, for any object x, the expression
>
>   x.clone() != x
>
> will be true, and the expression
>
>   x.clone().getClass() == x.getClass()
>
> will be true, but these are not absolute requirements. While it is typically the case that
>
>   x.clone().equals(x)
>
> will be true, this is not an absolute requirement. Copying an object will typically entail creating a new instance of its class, but it may require copying of internal data structures as well. No constructors are called.

There are a number of problems with this contract. The provision that "no constructors are called" is too strong. A well-behaved clone method can call constructors to create objects internal to the clone under construction. If the class is final, clone can even return an object created by a constructor.

The provision that x.clone().getClass() should generally be identical to x.getClass(), however, is too weak. In practice, programmers assume that if they extend a class and invoke super.clone from the subclass, the returned object will be an instance of the subclass. The *only* way a superclass can provide this functionality is to return an object obtained by calling super.clone. If a clone method returns an object created by a constructor, it will have the wrong class. Therefore, **if you override the clone method in a nonfinal class, you should return an object obtained by invoking super.clone.** If all of a class's superclasses obey this rule, then invoking super.clone will eventually invoke Object's clone method, creating an instance of the right class. This mechanism is vaguely similar to automatic constructor chaining, except that it isn't enforced.

The Cloneable interface does not, as of Release 1.3, spell out the responsibilities that a class takes on when it implements this interface. The specification says nothing beyond the manner in which implementing the interface affects the behavior of Object's clone implementation. **In practice, a class that implements Cloneable is expected to provide a properly functioning public clone method.** It is not, in general, possible to do so unless all of the class's superclasses provide a well-behaved clone implementation, whether public or protected.

Suppose you want to implement Cloneable in a class whose superclasses provide well-behaved clone methods. The object you get from super.clone() may or may not be close to what you'll eventually return, depending on the nature of the class. This object will be, from the standpoint of each superclass, a fully functional clone of the original object The fields declared in your class (if any) will have values identical to those of the object being cloned. If every field contains a primitive value or a reference to an immutable object, the returned object may be exactly what you need, in which case no further processing is necessary. This is the case, for example, for the PhoneNumber class in Item 8. In this case, all you need do is provide public access to Object's protected clone method:

```
public Object clone() {
    try {
        return super.clone();
    } catch(CloneNotSupportedException e) {
        throw new Error("Assertion failure");  // Can't happen
    }
}
```

If, however, your object contains fields that refer to mutable objects, using this clone implementation can be disastrous. For example, consider the Stack class in Item 5:

```
public class Stack {
    private Object[] elements;
    private int size = 0;

    public Stack(int initialCapacity) {
        this.elements = new Object[initialCapacity];
    }

    public void push(Object e) {
        ensureCapacity();
        elements[size++] = e;
    }

    public Object pop() {
        if (size == 0)
            throw new EmptyStackException();
        Object result = elements[--size];
        elements[size] = null; // Eliminate obsolete reference
        return result;
    }

    // Ensure space for at least one more element.
    private void ensureCapacity() {
        if (elements.length == size) {
            Object oldElements[] = elements;
            elements = new Object[2 * elements.length + 1];
            System.arraycopy(oldElements, 0, elements, 0, size);
        }
    }
}
```

Suppose you want to make this class cloneable. If its clone method merely returns super.clone(), the resulting Stack instance will have the correct value in its size field, but its elements field will refer to the same array as the original Stack instance. Modifying the original will destroy the invariants in the clone and vice versa. You will quickly find that your program produces nonsensical results or throws ArrayIndexOutOfBoundsException.

This situation could never occur as a result of calling the sole constructor in the Stack class. **In effect, the clone method functions as another constructor; you must ensure that it does no harm to the original object and that it properly establishes invariants on the clone**. In order for the clone method on Stack to work properly, it must copy the internals of the stack. The easiest way to do this is by calling clone recursively on the elements array:

```
public Object clone() throws CloneNotSupportedException {
    Stack result = (Stack) super.clone();
    result.elements = (Object[]) elements.clone();
    return result;
}
```

Note that this solution would not work if the buckets field were final because the clone method would be prohibited from assigning a new value to the field. This is a fundamental problem: **the clone architecture is incompatible with normal use of final fields referring to mutable objects**, except in cases where the mutable objects may be safely shared between an object and its clone. In order to make a class cloneable, it may be necessary to remove final modifiers from some fields.

It is not always sufficient to call clone recursively. For example, suppose you are writing a clone method for a hash table whose internals consist of an array of buckets, each of which references the first entry in a linked list of key-value pairs or is null if the bucket is empty. For performance, the class implements its own lightweight singly linked list instead of using java.util.LinkedList internally:

```
public class HashTable implements Cloneable {
    private Entry[] buckets = ...;

    private static class Entry {
        Object key;
        Object value;
        Entry  next;

        Entry(Object key, Object value, Entry next) {
            this.key   = key;
            this.value = value;
            this.next  = next;
        }
    }

    ... // Remainder omitted
}
```

Suppose you merely clone the bucket array recursively, as we did for Stack:

```
// Broken - results in shared internal state!
public Object clone() throws CloneNotSupportedException {
    HashTable result = (HashTable) super.clone();
    result.buckets = (Entry[]) buckets.clone();
    return result;
}
```

Though the clone has its own bucket array, this array references the same linked lists as the original, which can easily cause nondeterministic behavior in both the clone and the original. To fix this problem, you'll have to copy the linked list that comprises each bucket individually. Here is one common approach:

```
public class HashTable implements Cloneable {
    private Entry[] buckets = ...;

    private static class Entry {
        Object key;
        Object value;
        Entry  next;

        Entry(Object key, Object value, Entry next) {
            this.key   = key;
            this.value = value;
            this.next  = next;
        }

        // Recursively copy the linked list headed by this Entry
        Entry deepCopy() {
            return new Entry(key, value,
                next == null ? null : next.deepCopy());
        }
    }

    public Object clone() throws CloneNotSupportedException {
        HashTable result = (HashTable) super.clone();
        result.buckets = new Entry[buckets.length];
        for (int i = 0; i < buckets.length; i++)
            if (buckets[i] != null)
                result.buckets[i] = (Entry)
                    buckets[i].deepCopy();

        return result;
    }
    ... // Remainder omitted
}
```

The private class `HashTable.Entry` has been augmented to support a "deep copy" method. The `clone` method on `HashTable` allocates a new `buckets` array of the proper size and iterates over the original `buckets` array, deep-copying each nonempty bucket. The deep-copy method on `Entry` invokes itself recursively to copy the entire linked list headed by the entry. While this technique is cute and works fine if the buckets aren't too long, it is not a good way to clone a linked list because it consumes one stack frame for each element in the list. If the list is long, this could easily cause a stack overflow. To prevent this from happening, you can replace the recursion in `deepCopy` with iteration:

```
// Iteratively copy the linked list headed by this Entry
Entry deepCopy() {
    Entry result = new Entry(key, value, next);

    for (Entry p = result; p.next != null; p = p.next)
        p.next = new Entry(p.next.key, p.next.value, p.next.next);

    return result;
}
```

A final approach to cloning complex objects is to call `super.clone`, set all of the fields in the resulting object to their virgin state, and then call higher-level methods to regenerate the state of the object. In the case of our `Hashtable` example, the `buckets` field would be initialized to a new bucket array, and the `put(key, value)` method (not shown) would be invoked for each key-value mapping in the hash table being cloned. This approach typically yields a simple, reasonably elegant `clone` method that doesn't run quite as fast as one that directly manipulates the innards of the object and its clone.

Like a constructor, a `clone` method should not invoke any nonfinal methods on the clone under construction (Item 15). If `clone` invokes an overridden method, this method will execute before the subclass in which it is defined has had a chance to fix its state in the clone, quite possibly leading to corruption in the clone and the original. Therefore the `put(key, value)` method discussed in the previous paragraph should be either final or private. (If it is private, it is presumably the "helper method" for a nonfinal public method.)

Object's `clone` method is declared to throw `CloneNotSupportedException`, but overriding `clone` methods may omit this declaration. The `clone` methods of final classes should omit the declaration because methods that don't throw checked exceptions are more pleasant to use than those that do (Item 41). If an extendable class, especially one designed for inheritance (Item 15), overrides the clone method, the overriding `clone` method should include the declaration to throw `CloneNotSupportedException`. Doing this allows subclasses to opt out of clonability gracefully, by providing the following `clone` method:

```
// Clone method to guarantee that instances cannot be cloned
public final Object clone() throws CloneNotSupportedException {
    throw new CloneNotSupportedException();
}
```

It is not essential that the foregoing advice be followed, as the `clone` method of a subclass that doesn't want to be cloned can always throw an unchecked exception, such as `UnsupportedOperationException`, if the `clone` method it overrides is not declared to throw `CloneNotSupportedException`. Common practice, however, dictates that `CloneNotSupportedException` is the correct exception to throw under these circumstances.

To recap, all classes that implement `Cloneable` should override `clone` with a public method. This public method should first call `super.clone` and then fix any fields that need fixing. Typically, this means copying any mutable objects that comprise the internal "deep structure" of the object being cloned and replacing the references to these objects with references to the copies. While these internal copies can generally be made by calling `clone` recursively, this is not always the best approach. If the class contains only primitive fields or references to immutable objects, then it is probably the case that no fields need to be fixed. There are exceptions to this rule. For example, a field representing a serial number or other unique ID or a field representing the object's creation time will need to be fixed, even if it is primitive or immutable.

Is all this complexity really necessary? Rarely. If you extend a class that implements `Cloneable`, you have little choice but to implement a well-behaved `clone` method. Otherwise, **you are probably better off providing some alternative means of object copying or simply not providing the capability**. For example, it doesn't make much sense for immutable classes to support object copying, because copies would be virtually indistinguishable from the original.

A fine approach to object copying is to provide a *copy constructor*. A copy constructor is simply a constructor that takes a single argument whose type is the class containing the constructor, for example,

```
public Yum(Yum yum);
```

A minor variant is to provide a static factory in place of a constructor:

```
public static Yum newInstance(Yum yum);
```

The copy constructor approach and its static factory variant have many advantages over Cloneable/clone: They do not rely on a risk-prone extralinguistic object creation mechanism; they do not demand unenforceable adherence to ill-documented conventions; they do not conflict with the proper use of final fields; they do not require the client to catch an unnecessary checked exception; and they provide a statically typed object to the client. While it is impossible to put a copy constructor or static factory in an interface, Cloneable fails to function as an interface because it lacks a public clone method. Therefore you aren't giving up interface functionality by using a copy constructor instead of a clone method.

Furthermore, a copy constructor (or static factory) can take an argument whose type is an appropriate interface implemented by the class. For example, all general-purpose collection implementations, by convention, provide a copy constructor whose argument is of type Collection or Map. Interface-based copy constructors allow the client to choose the implementation of the copy, rather than forcing the client to accept the implementation of the original. For example, suppose you have a LinkedList l, and you want to copy it as an ArrayList. The clone method does not offer this functionality, but it's easy with a copy constructor: new ArrayList(l).

Given all of the problems associated with Cloneable, it is safe to say that other interfaces should not extend it and that classes designed for inheritance (Item 15) should not implement it. Because of its many shortcomings, some expert programmers simply choose never to override the clone method and never to invoke it except, perhaps, to copy arrays cheaply. Be aware that if you do not at least provide a well-behaved *protected* clone method on a class designed for inheritance, it will be impossible for subclasses to implement Cloneable.

Item 11: Consider implementing `Comparable`

Unlike the other methods discussed in this chapter, the `compareTo` method is not declared in `Object`. Rather, it is the sole method in the `java.lang.Comparable` interface. It is similar in character to `Object`'s `equals` method, except that it permits order comparisons in addition to simple equality comparisons. By implementing `Comparable`, a class indicates that its instances have a *natural ordering.* Sorting an array of objects that implement `Comparable` is as simple as this:

```
Arrays.sort(a);
```

It is similarly easy to search, compute extreme values, and maintain automatically sorted collections of `Comparable` objects. For example, the following program, which relies on the fact that `String` implements `Comparable`, prints an alphabetized list of its command-line arguments with duplicates eliminated:

```
public class WordList {
    public static void main(String[] args) {
        Set s = new TreeSet();
        s.addAll(Arrays.asList(args));
        System.out.println(s);
    }
}
```

By implementing `Comparable`, you allow your class to interoperate with all of the many generic algorithms and collection implementations that depend on this interface. You gain a tremendous amount of power for a small amount of effort. Virtually all of the value classes in the Java platform libraries implement `Comparable`. If you are writing a value class with an obvious natural ordering, such as alphabetical order, numerical order, or chronological order, you should strongly consider implementing this interface. This item tells you how to go about it.

The general contract for the `compareTo` method is similar in character to that of the `equals` method. Here it is, copied from the specification for `Comparable`:

Compares this object with the specified object for order. Returns a negative integer, zero, or a positive integer as this object is less than, equal to, or greater than the specified object. Throws `ClassCastException` if the specified object's type prevents it from being compared to this object.

In the following description, the notation sgn(*expression*) designates the mathematical *signum* function, which is defined to return -1, 0, or 1, according to whether the value of *expression* is negative, zero, or positive.

The implementor must ensure sgn(x.compareTo(y)) == -sgn(y.compareTo(x)) for all x and y. (This implies that x.compareTo(y) must throw an exception if and only if y.compareTo(x) throws an exception.)

- The implementor must also ensure that the relation is transitive: (x.compareTo(y)>0 && y.compareTo(z)>0) implies x.compareTo(z)>0.

- Finally, the implementor must ensure that x.compareTo(y) == 0 implies that sgn(x.compareTo(z)) == sgn(y.compareTo(z)), for all z.

- It is strongly recommended, but not strictly required, that (x.compareTo(y)==0) == (x.equals(y)). Generally speaking, any class that implements the Comparable interface and violates this condition should clearly indicate this fact. The recommended language is "Note: This class has a natural ordering that is inconsistent with equals."

Do not be put off by the mathematical nature of this contract. Like the equals contract (Item 7), the compareTo contract isn't as complicated as it looks. Within a class, any reasonable ordering relation will satisfy the compareTo contract. Across classes, compareTo, unlike equals, doesn't have to work: It is permitted to throw ClassCastException if the two object references being compared refer to objects of different classes. Usually, that is exactly what compareTo should do under these circumstances. While the contract does not preclude interclass comparisons, there are, as of release 1.4, no classes in the Java platform libraries that support them.

Just as a class that violates the hashCode contract can break other classes that depend on hashing, a class that violates the compareTo contract can break other classes that depend on comparison. Classes that depend on comparison include the sorted collections, TreeSet and TreeMap, and the utility classes Collections and Arrays, which contain searching and sorting algorithms.

Let's go over the provisions of the compareTo contract. The first provision says that if you reverse the direction of a comparison between two object references, the expected thing happens: If the first object is less than the second, then the second must be greater than the first; if the first object is equal to the second, then the second must be equal to the first; and if the first object is greater than the second, then the second must be less than the first. The second provision says that if one object is greater than a second and the second is greater than a third, then the first must be greater than the third. The final provision says that all objects that compare as equal must yield the same results when compared to any other object.

One consequence of these three provisions is that the equality test imposed by a `compareTo` method must obey the same restrictions imposed by the `equals` contract: reflexivity, symmetry, transitivity, and non-nullity. Therefore the same caveat applies: There is simply no way to extend an instantiable class with a new aspect while preserving the `compareTo` contract (Item 7). The same workaround applies too. If you want to add a significant aspect to a class that implements `Comparable`, don't extend it; write an unrelated class that contains a field of the first class. Then provide a "view" method that returns this field. This frees you to implement whatever `compareTo` method you like on the second class, while allowing its client to view an instance of the second class as an instance of the first class when needed.

The final paragraph of the `compareTo` contract, which is a strong suggestion rather than a true provision, simply states that the equality test imposed by the `compareTo` method should generally return the same results as the `equals` method. If this provision is obeyed, the ordering imposed by the `compareTo` method is said to be *consistent with equals*. If it's violated, the ordering is said to be *inconsistent with equals*. A class whose `compareTo` method imposes an order that is inconsistent with equals will still work, but sorted collections containing elements of the class may not obey the general contract of the appropriate collection interfaces (`Collection`, `Set`, or `Map`). This is because the general contracts for these interfaces are defined in terms of the `equals` method, but sorted collections use the equality test imposed by `compareTo` in place of `equals`. It is not a catastrophe if this happens, but it's something to be aware of.

For example, consider the `Float` class, whose `compareTo` method is inconsistent with equals. If you create a `HashSet` and add `new Float(-0.0f)` and `new Float(0.0f)`, the set will contain two elements because the two `Float` instances added to the set are unequal when compared using the `equals` method. If, however, you perform the same procedure using a `TreeSet` instead of a `HashSet`, the set will contain only one element because the two `Float` instances are equal when compared using the `compareTo` method. (See the `Float` documentation for details.)

Writing a `compareTo` method is similar to writing an `equals` method, but there are a few key differences. You don't need to type check the argument prior to casting. If the argument is not of the appropriate type, the `compareTo` method *should* throw a `ClassCastException`. If the argument is `null`, the `compareTo` method *should* throw a `NullPointerException`. This is precisely the behavior that you get if you just cast the argument to the correct type and then attempt to access its members.

The field comparisons themselves are order comparisons rather than equality comparisons. Compare object reference fields by invoking the compareTo method recursively. If a field does not implement Comparable or you need to use a nonstandard ordering, you can use an explicit Comparator instead. Either write your own or use a preexisting one as in this compareTo method for the CaseInsensitiveString class in Item 7:

```
public int compareTo(Object o) {
    CaseInsensitiveString cis = (CaseInsensitiveString)o;
    return String.CASE_INSENSITIVE_ORDER.compare(s, cis.s);
}
```

Compare primitive fields using the relational operators < and >, and arrays by applying these guidelines to each element. If a class has multiple significant fields, the order in which you compare them is critical. You must start with the most significant field and work your way down. If a comparison results in anything other than zero (which represents equality), you're done; just return the result. If the most significant fields are equal, go on to compare the next-most-significant fields, and so on. If all fields are equal, the objects are equal; return zero. The technique is demonstrated by this compareTo method for the PhoneNumber class in Item 8:

```
public int compareTo(Object o) {
    PhoneNumber pn = (PhoneNumber)o;

    // Compare area codes
    if (areaCode < pn.areaCode)
        return -1;
    if (areaCode > pn.areaCode)
        return  1;

    // Area codes are equal, compare exchanges
    if (exchange < pn.exchange)
        return -1;
    if (exchange > pn.exchange)
        return  1;

    // Area codes and exchanges are equal, compare extensions
    if (extension < pn.extension)
        return -1;
    if (extension > pn.extension)
        return  1;

    return 0;  // All fields are equal
}
```

While this method works fine, it can be improved. Recall that the contract for compareTo does not specify the magnitude of the return value, only the sign. You can take advantage of this to simplify the code and probably make it run a bit faster:

```
public int compareTo(Object o) {
    PhoneNumber pn = (PhoneNumber)o;

    // Compare area codes
    int areaCodeDiff = areaCode - pn.areaCode;
    if (areaCodeDiff != 0)
        return areaCodeDiff;

    // Area codes are equal, compare exchanges
    int exchangeDiff = exchange - pn.exchange;
    if (exchangeDiff != 0)
        return exchangeDiff;

    // Area codes and exchanges are equal, compare extensions
    return extension - pn.extension;
}
```

This trick works fine here but should be used with extreme caution. Don't do it unless you're certain that the field in question cannot be negative or, more generally, that the difference between the lowest and highest possible field values is less than or equal to INTEGER.MAX_VALUE (2^{31}-1). The reason this trick does not work in general is that a signed 32-bit integer is not big enough to represent the difference between two arbitrary signed 32-bit integers. If i is a large positive int and j is a large negative int, (i-j) will overflow and return a negative value. The resulting compareTo method will not work. It will return nonsensical results for some arguments, and it will violate the first and second provisions of the compareTo contract. This is not a purely theoretical problem; it has caused failures in real systems. These failures can be difficult to debug, as the broken compareTo method works properly for many input values.

CHAPTER 4

Classes and Interfaces

CLASSES and interfaces lie at the heart of the Java programming language. They are its basic units of abstraction. The language provides many powerful elements that you can use to design classes and interfaces. This chapter contains guidelines to help you make the best use of these elements so that your classes and interfaces are usable, robust, and flexible.

Item 12: Minimize the accessibility of classes and members

The single most important factor that distinguishes a well-designed module from a poorly designed one is the degree to which the module hides its internal data and other implementation details from other modules. A well-designed module hides all of its implementation details, cleanly separating its API from its implementation. Modules then communicate with one another only through their APIs and are oblivious to each others' inner workings. This concept, known as *information hiding* or *encapsulation*, is one of the fundamental tenets of software design [Parnas72].

Information hiding is important for many reasons, most of which stem from the fact that it effectively *decouples* the modules that comprise a system, allowing them to be developed, tested, optimized, used, understood, and modified individually. This speeds up system development because modules can be developed in parallel. It eases the burden of maintenance because modules can be understood quickly and debugged with little fear of harming other modules. While information hiding does not, in and of itself, cause good performance, it enables effective performance tuning. Once a system is complete and profiling has determined which modules are causing performance problems (Item 37), those modules can be optimized without affecting the correctness of other modules. Information hiding increases software reuse because individual modules do not depend on one another and frequently prove useful in contexts other than the one for which they were developed. Finally, information hiding decreases the risk in building large systems; individual modules may prove successful even if the system does not.

The Java programming language has many facilities to aid information hiding. One such facility is the *access control* mechanism [JLS, 6.6], which determines the *accessibility* of classes, interfaces, and members. The accessibility of an entity is determined by the location where it is declared and by which, if any, of the access modifiers (`private`, `protected`, and `public`) is present in the entity's declaration. Proper use of these modifiers is essential to information hiding.

The rule of thumb is that you should make each class or member as inaccessible as possible. In other words, you should use the lowest possible access level consistent with the proper functioning of the software that you are writing.

For top-level (non-nested) classes and interfaces, there are only two possible access levels: *package-private* and *public*. If you declare a top-level class or interface with the `public` modifier, it will be public; otherwise, it will be package-private. If a top-level class or interface can be made package-private, it should be. By making it package-private, you make it part of the package's implementation rather than its exported API, and you can modify it, replace it, or eliminate it in a subsequent release without fear of harming existing clients. If you make it public, you are obligated to support it forever to maintain compatibility.

If a package-private top-level class or interface is used only from within a single class, you should consider making it a private nested class (or interface) of the class in which it is used (Item 18). This further reduces its accessibility. It is, however, not as important to do this as it is to make an unnecessarily public class package-private because a package-private class is already part of the package's implementation rather than its API.

For members (fields, methods, nested classes, and nested interfaces) there are four possible access levels, listed here in order of increasing accessibility:

- **private**—The member is accessible only inside the top-level class where it is declared.

- **package-private**—The member is accessible from any class in the package where it is declared. Technically known as *default* access, this is the access level you get if no access modifier is specified.

- **protected**—The member is accessible from subclasses of the class where it is declared (subject to a few restrictions [JLS, 6.6.2]) and from any class in the package where it is declared.

- **public**—The member is accessible from anywhere.

After carefully designing your class's public API, your reflex should be to make all other members private. Only if another class in the same package really needs to access a member should you remove the `private` modifier, making the member package-private. If you find yourself doing this often, you should reexamine the design of your system to see if another decomposition might yield classes that are better decoupled from one another. That said, both private and package-private members are part of a class's implementation and do not normally impact its exported API. These fields can, however, "leak" into the exported API if the class implements `Serializable` (Item 54, Item 55).

For members of public classes, a huge increase in accessibility occurs when the access level goes from package-private to protected. A protected member is part of the class's exported API and must be supported forever. Furthermore, a protected member of an exported class represents a public commitment to an implementation detail (Item 15). The need for protected members should be relatively rare.

There is one rule that restricts your ability to reduce the accessibility of methods. If a method overrides a superclass method, it is not permitted to have a lower access level in the subclass than it does in the superclass [JLS, 8.4.6.3]. This is necessary to ensure that an instance of the subclass is usable anywhere that an instance of the superclass is usable. If you violate this rule, the compiler will generate an error message when you try to compile the subclass. A special case of this rule is that if a class implements an interface, all of the class methods that are also present in the interface must be declared public. This is so because all methods in an interface are implicitly public.

Public classes should rarely, if ever, have public fields (as opposed to public methods). If a field is nonfinal or is a final reference to a mutable object, you give up the ability to limit the values that may be stored in the field by making it public. You also give up the ability to take any action when the field is modified. A simple consequence is that classes with public mutable fields are not thread-safe. Even if a field is final and does not refer to a mutable object, by making the field public, you give up the flexibility to switch to a new internal data representation in which the field does not exist.

There is one exception to the rule that public classes should not have public fields. Classes are permitted to expose constants via public static final fields. By convention, such fields have names consisting of capital letters, with words separated by underscores (Item 38). It is critical that these fields contain either primitive values or references to immutable objects (Item 13). A final field containing a reference to a mutable object has all the disadvantages of a nonfinal field. While the reference cannot be modified, the referenced object can be modified—with disastrous results.

Note that a nonzero-length array is always mutable, so **it is nearly always wrong to have public static final array field**. If a class has such a field, clients will be able to modify the contents of the array. This is a frequent source of security holes:

```
// Potential security hole!
public static final Type[] VALUES =  { ... };
```

The public array should be replaced by a private array and a public immutable list:

```
private static final Type[] PRIVATE_VALUES = { ... };

public static final List VALUES =
    Collections.unmodifiableList(Arrays.asList(PRIVATE_VALUES));
```

Alternatively, if you require compile-time type safety and are willing to tolerate a performance loss, you can replace the public array field with a public method that returns a copy of a private array:

```
private static final Type[] PRIVATE_VALUES = { ... };

public static final Type[] values() {
    return (Type[]) PRIVATE_VALUES.clone();
}
```

To summarize, you should always reduce accessibility as much as possible. After carefully designing a minimal public API, you should prevent any stray classes, interfaces, or members from becoming a part of the API. With the exception of public static final fields, public classes should have no public fields. Ensure that objects referenced by public static final fields are immutable.

Item 13: Favor immutability

An immutable class is simply a class whose instances cannot be modified. All of the information contained in each instance is provided when it is created and is fixed for the lifetime of the object. The Java platform libraries contain many immutable classes, including `String`, the primitive wrapper classes, and `BigInteger` and `Big-Decimal`. There are many good reasons for this: Immutable classes are easier to design, implement, and use than mutable classes. They are less prone to error and are more secure.

To make a class immutable, follow these five rules:

1. **Don't provide any methods that modify the object** (known as *mutators*).

2. **Ensure that no methods may be overridden.** This prevents careless or malicious subclasses from compromising the immutable behavior of the class. Preventing method overrides is generally done by making the class final, but there are alternatives that we'll discuss later.

3. **Make all fields final.** This clearly expresses your intentions in a manner that is enforced by the system. Also, it may be necessary to ensure correct behavior if a reference to a newly created instance is passed from one thread to another without synchronization, depending on the results of ongoing efforts to rework the *memory model* [Pugh01a].

4. **Make all fields private.** This prevents clients from modifying fields directly. While it is technically permissible for immutable classes to have public final fields containing primitive values or references to immutable objects, it is not recommended because it precludes changing the internal representation in a later release (Item 12).

5. **Ensure exclusive access to any mutable components.** If your class has any fields that refer to mutable objects, ensure that clients of the class cannot obtain references to these objects. Never initialize such a field to a client-provided object reference nor return the object reference from an accessor. Make *defensive copies* (Item 24) in contructors, accessors, and `readObject` methods (Item 56).

Many of the example classes in previous items are immutable. One such class is PhoneNumber in Item 8, which has accessors for each attribute but no corresponding mutators. Here is a slightly more complex example:

```java
public final class Complex {
    private final float re;
    private final float im;

    public Complex(float re, float im) {
        this.re = re;
        this.im = im;
    }

    // Accessors with no corresponding mutators
    public float realPart()      { return re; }
    public float imaginaryPart() { return im; }

    public Complex add(Complex c) {
        return new Complex(re + c.re, im + c.im);
    }

    public Complex subtract(Complex c) {
        return new Complex(re - c.re, im - c.im);
    }

    public Complex multiply(Complex c) {
        return new Complex(re*c.re - im*c.im,
                           re*c.im + im*c.re);
    }

    public Complex divide(Complex c) {
        float tmp = c.re*c.re + c.im*c.im;
        return new Complex((re*c.re + im*c.im)/tmp,
                           (im*c.re - re*c.im)/tmp);
    }

    public boolean equals(Object o) {
        if (o == this)
            return true;
        if (!(o instanceof Complex))
            return false;
        Complex c = (Complex)o;
        return (Float.floatToIntBits(re) ==      // See page 33 to
                Float.floatToIntBits(c.re)) &&    // find out why
               (Float.floatToIntBits(im) ==       // floatToIntBits
                Float.floatToIntBits(im)));        // is used.
    }
```

```
    public int hashCode() {
        int result = 17 + Float.floatToIntBits(re);
        result = 37*result + Float.floatToIntBits(im);
        return result;
    }

    public String toString() {
        return "(" + re + " + " + im + "i)";
    }
}
```

This class represents a *complex number* (a number with both real and imaginary parts). In addition to the standard `Object` methods, it provides accessors for the real and imaginary parts and provides the four basic arithmetic operations: addition, subtraction, multiplication, and division. Notice how the arithmetic operations create and return a new `Complex` instance rather than modifying this instance. This pattern is used in most nontrivial immutable classes. It is known as the *functional* approach because methods return the result of applying a function to their operand without modifying it. Contrast this to the more common *procedural* approach in which methods apply a procedure to their operand causing its state to change.

The functional approach may appear unnatural if you're not familiar with it, but it enables immutability, which has many advantages. **Immutable objects are simple.** An immutable object can be in exactly one state, the state in which it was created. If you make sure that all constructors establish class invariants, then it is guaranteed that these invariants will remain true for all time, with no further effort on your part or on the part of the programmer who uses the class. Mutable objects, on the other hand, can have arbitrarily complex state spaces. If the documentation does not provide a precise description of the state transitions performed by mutator methods, it can be difficult or impossible to use a mutable class reliably.

Immutable objects are inherently thread-safe; they require no synchronization. They cannot be corrupted by multiple threads accessing them concurrently. This is far and away the easiest approach to achieving thread safety. In fact, no thread can ever observe any effect of another thread on an immutable object. Therefore **immutable objects can be shared freely.** Immutable classes should take advantage of this by encouraging clients to reuse existing instances wherever possible. One easy way to do this is to provide public static final constants for frequently used values. For example, the Complex class might provide the following constants:

```
public static final Complex ZERO = new Complex(0, 0);
public static final Complex ONE  = new Complex(1, 0);
public static final Complex I  =   new Complex(0, 1);
```

This approach can be taken one step further. An immutable object can provide static factories that cache frequently requested instances and avoid creating new instances whenever a preexisting instance is requested. The BigInteger and Boolean classes both have such static factories. Using such static factories causes clients to share preexisting instances rather than creating new ones, reducing memory footprint and garbage collection costs.

A consequence of the fact that immutable objects can be shared freely is that you never have to make *defensive copies* (Item 24). In fact, you never have to make any copies at all because the copies would be forever equivalent to the originals. Therefore you need not and should not provide a clone method or *copy constructor* (Item 10) on an immutable class. This was not well understood in the early days of the Java platform, so the String class does have a copy constructor, but it should rarely, if ever, be used (Item 4).

Not only can you share immutable objects, but you can share their internals. For example, the BigInteger class uses a sign-magnitude representation internally. The sign is represented by an int, and the magnitude is represented by an int array. The negate method produces a new BigInteger of like magnitude and opposite sign. It does not need to copy the array; the newly created BigInteger points to the same internal array as the original.

Immutable objects make great building blocks for other objects, whether mutable or immutable. It's much easier to maintain the invariants of a complex object if you know that its component objects will not change underneath it. A special case of this principle is that immutable objects make great map keys and set elements; you don't have to worry about their values changing once they're in the map or set, which would destroy the map or set's invariants.

The only real disadvantage of immutable classes is that they require a separate object for each distinct value. Creating these objects can be costly, especially if they are large. For example, suppose that you have a million-bit BigInteger and you want to complement its low-order bit:

```
BigInteger moby = ...;
moby = moby.flipBit(0);
```

The `flipBit` method creates a new `BigInteger` instance, also a million bits long, that differs from the original in only one bit. The operation requires time and space proportional to the size of the `BigInteger`. Contrast this to `java.util.BitSet`. Like `BigInteger`, `BitSet` represents an arbitrarily long sequence of bits, but unlike `BigInteger`, `BitSet` is mutable. The `BitSet` class provides a method that allows you to change the state of a single bit of a million-bit instance in constant time.

The performance problem is magnified if you perform a multistep operation that generates a new object at every step, eventually discarding all objects except the final result. There are two approaches to coping with this problem. The first is to guess which multistep operations will be commonly required and provide them as primitives. If a multistep operation is provided as a primitive, the immutable class does not have to create a separate object at each step. Internally, the immutable class can be arbitrarily clever. For example, `BigInteger` has a package-private mutable "companion class" that it uses to speed up multistep operations such as modular exponentiation. It is much harder to use the mutable companion class for all of the reasons outlined earlier, but luckily you don't have to. The implementors of `BigInteger` did all the hard work for you.

This approach works fine if you can accurately predict which complex multistage operations clients will want to perform on your immutable class. If not, then your best bet is to provide a *public* mutable companion class. The main example of this approach in the Java platform libraries is the `String` class, whose mutable companion is `StringBuffer`. Arguably, `BitSet` plays the role of mutable companion to `BigInteger` under certain circumstances.

Now that you know how to make an immutable class and you understand the pros and cons of immutability, let's discuss a few design alternatives. Recall that to guarantee immutability, a class must not permit any of its methods to be overridden. In addition to making a class final, there are two other ways to guarantee this. One way is to make each method of the class, but not the class itself, final. The sole advantage of this approach is that it allows programmers to extend the class by adding new methods built atop the old ones. It is equally effective to provide the new methods as static methods in a separate, noninstantiable utility class (Item 3), so this approach isn't recommended.

A second alternative to making an immutable class final is to make all of its constructors private or package-private, and to add public *static factories* in place of the public constructors (Item 1). To make this concrete, here's how `Complex` would look if this approach were used:

```
// Immutable class with static factories instead of constructors
public class Complex {
    private final float re;
    private final float im;

    private Complex(float re, float im) {
        this.re = re;
        this.im = im;
    }

    public static Complex valueOf(float re, float im) {
        return new Complex(re, im);
    }

    ... // Remainder unchanged
}
```

While this approach is not commonly used, it is often the best of the three alternatives. It is the most flexible because it allows the use of multiple package-private implementation classes. To its clients that reside outside its package, the immutable class is effectively final because it is impossible to extend a class that comes from another package and that lacks a public or protected constructor. Besides allowing the flexibility of multiple implementation classes, this approach makes it possible to tune the performance of the class in subsequent releases by improving the object-caching capabilities of the static factories.

Static factories have many other advantages over constructors, as discussed in Item 1. For example, suppose that you want to provide a means of creating a complex number based on its polar coordinates. This would be very messy using constructors because the natural constructor would have the same signature that we already used: `Complex(float, float)`. With static factories it's easy; just add a second static factory with a name that clearly identifies its function:

```
public static Complex valueOfPolar(float r, float theta) {
    return new Complex((float) (r * Math.cos(theta)),
                       (float) (r * Math.sin(theta)));
}
```

It was not widely understood that immutable classes had to be effectively final when `BigInteger` and `BigDecimal` were written, so all of their methods may be overridden. Unfortunately, this could not be corrected after the fact while preserving upward compatibility. If you write a class whose security depends on the immutability of a `BigInteger` or `BigDecimal` argument from an untrusted client, you must check to see that the argument is a "real" `BigInteger` or `BigDecimal`, rather than an instance of an untrusted subclass. If it is the latter, you must defensively copy it under the assumption that it might be mutable (Item 24):

```
public void foo(BigInteger b) {
    if (b.getClass() != BigInteger.class)
        b = new BigInteger(b.toByteArray());
    ...
}
```

The list of rules for immutable classes at the beginning of this item says that no methods may modify the object and that all fields must be final. In fact these rules are a bit stronger than necessary and can be relaxed to improve performance. In truth, no method may produce an *externally visible* change in the object's state. However, many immutable classes have one or more nonfinal redundant fields in which they cache the results of expensive computations the first time they are required. If the same computation is required in future, the cached value is returned, saving the cost of recalculation. This trick works precisely because the object is immutable; its immutability guarantees that the computation would yield the same result if it were performed again.

For example, the `hashCode` method for `PhoneNumber` (Item 8, page 40) computes the hash code the first time it is invoked and caches it in case it is needed again. This technique, which is a classic example of *lazy initialization* (Item 48), is also used by the `String` class. No synchronization is necessary, as it is not a problem if the hash value is recalculated once or twice. Here is the general idiom to return a cached, lazily initialized function of an immutable object:

```
// Cached, lazily initialized function of an immutable object
private volatile Foo cachedFooVal = UNLIKELY_FOO_VALUE;

public Foo foo() {
    int result = cachedFooVal;
    if (result == UNLIKELY_FOO_VALUE)
        result = cachedFooVal = fooValue();
    return result;
}

// Private helper function to calculate our foo value
private Foo fooVal() { ... }
```

One caveat should be added concerning serializability. If you choose to have your immutable class implement Serializable and it contains one or more fields that refer to mutable objects, you must provide an explicit readObject or readResolve method, even if the default serialized form is acceptable. The default readObject method would allow an attacker to create a mutable instance of your otherwise immutable class. This topic is covered in detail in Item 56.

To summarize, resist the urge to write a set method for every get method. **Classes should be immutable unless there's a very good reason to make them mutable.** Immutable classes provide many advantages, and their only disadvantage is the potential for performance problems under certain circumstances. You should always make small value objects, such as PhoneNumber and Complex, immutable. (There are several classes in the Java platform libraries, such as java.util.Date and java.awt.Point, that should have been immutable but aren't.) You should seriously consider making larger value objects, such as String and BigInteger, immutable as well. You should provide a public mutable companion class for your immutable class *only* once you've confirmed that it's necessary to achieve satisfactory performance (Item 37).

There are some classes for which immutability is impractical, including "process classes" such as Thread and TimerTask. **If a class cannot be made immutable, you should still limit its mutability as much as possible.** Reducing the number of states in which an object can exist makes it easier to reason about the object and reduces the likelihood of errors. Therefore **constructors should create fully initialized objects with all of their invariants established** and they should not pass partially constructed instances to other methods. You should not provide a public initialization method separate from the constructor unless there is an extremely good reason to do so. Similarly, you should not provide a "reinitialize" method, which enables an object to be reused as if it had been constructed with a different initial state. A reinitialize method generally provides little if any performance benefit at the expense of increased complexity.

The TimerTask class exemplifies these principles. It is mutable, but its state space is kept intentionally small. You create an instance, schedule it for execution, and optionally cancel it. Once a timer task has run to completion or has been cancelled, you may not reschedule it.

A final note should be added concerning the Complex class in this item. This example was meant only to illustrate immutability. It is not an industrial strength complex number implementation. It uses the standard formulas for complex multiplication and division, which are not correctly rounded and provide poor semantics for complex NaNs and infinities [Kahan91, Smith62, Thomas94].

Item 14: Favor composition over inheritance

Inheritance is a powerful way to achieve code reuse, but it is not always the best tool for the job. Used inappropriately, it leads to fragile software. It is safe to use inheritance within a package, where the subclass and the superclass implementation are under the control of the same programmers. It is also safe to use inheritance when extending classes specifically designed and documented for extension (Item 15). Inheriting from ordinary concrete classes across package boundaries, however, is dangerous. As a reminder, this book uses the word "inheritance" to mean *implementation inheritance* (when one class extends another). The problems discussed in this item do not apply to *interface inheritance* (when a class implements an interface or where one interface extends another).

Unlike method invocation, inheritance breaks encapsulation [Snyder86]. In other words, a subclass depends on the implementation details of its superclass for its proper function. The superclass's implementation may change from release to release, and if it does, the subclass may break, even though its code has not been touched. As a consequence, a subclass must evolve in tandem with its superclass, unless the superclass's authors have designed and documented it specifically for the purpose of being extended.

To make this concrete, let's suppose we have a program that uses a HashSet. To tune the performance of our program, we need to query the HashSet as to how many elements have been added since it was created (not to be confused with its current size, which goes down when an element is removed). To provide this functionality, we write a HashSet variant that keeps count of the number of attempted element insertions and exports an accessor for this count. The HashSet class contains two methods capable of adding elements, add and addAll, so we override both of these methods:

```
// Broken - Inappropriate use of inheritance!
public class InstrumentedHashSet extends HashSet {
    // The number of attempted element insertions
    private int addCount = 0;

    public InstrumentedHashSet() {
    }

    public InstrumentedHashSet(Collection c) {
        super(c);
    }
```

```
public InstrumentedHashSet(int initCap, float loadFactor) {
    super(initCap, loadFactor);
}

public boolean add(Object o) {
    addCount++;
    return super.add(o);
}

public boolean addAll(Collection c) {
    addCount += c.size();
    return super.addAll(c);
}

public int getAddCount() {
    return addCount;
}
}
```

This class looks reasonable, but it doesn't work. Suppose we create an instance and add three elements using the addAll method:

```
InstrumentedHashSet s = new InstrumentedHashSet();
s.addAll(Arrays.asList(new String[] {"Snap","Crackle","Pop"}));
```

We would expect the getAddCount method to return three at this point, but it returns six. What went wrong? Internally, HashSet's addAll method is implemented on top of its add method, although HashSet, quite reasonably, does not document this implementation detail. The addAll method in InstrumentedHash-Set added three to addCount and then invoked HashSet's addAll implementation using super.addAll. This in turn invoked the add method, as overridden in InstrumentedHashSet, once for each element. Each of these three invocations added one more to addCount, for a total increase of six: Each element added with the addAll method is double-counted.

We could "fix" the subclass by eliminating its override of the addAll method. While the resulting class would work, it would depend for its proper function on the fact that HashSet's addAll method is implemented on top of its add method. This "self-use" is an implementation detail, not guaranteed to hold in all implementations of the Java platform and subject to change from release to release. Therefore, the resulting InstrumentedHashSet class would be fragile.

It would be slightly better to override the addAll method to iterate over the specified collection, calling the add method once for each element. This would guarantee the correct result whether or not HashSet's addAll method were implemented atop its add method because HashSet's addAll implementation would no longer be invoked. This technique, however, does not solve all our problems. It amounts to reimplementing superclass methods that may or may not result in self-use, which is difficult, time-consuming, and error prone. Additionally, it isn't always possible, as some methods cannot be implemented without access to private fields inaccessible to the subclass.

A related cause of fragility in subclasses is that their superclass can acquire new methods in subsequent releases. Suppose a program depends for its security on the fact that all elements inserted into some collection satisfy some predicate. This can be guaranteed by subclassing the collection and overriding each method capable of adding an element to ensure that the predicate is satisfied before adding the element. This works fine until a new method capable of adding an element is added to the superclass in a subsequent release. Once this happens, it becomes possible to add an "illegal" element to an instance of the subclass merely by invoking the new method, which is not overridden in the subclass. This is not a purely theoretical problem. Several security holes of this nature had to be fixed when Hashtable and Vector were retrofitted to participate in the Collections Framework.

Both of the above problems stem from overriding methods. You might think that it is safe to extend a class if you merely add new methods and refrain from overriding existing methods. While this sort of extension is much safer, it is not without risk. If the superclass acquires a new method in a subsequent release and you have the bad luck to have given the subclass a method with the same signature and a different return type, your subclass will no longer compile [JLS, 8.4.6.3]. If you've given the subclass a method with exactly the same signature as the new superclass method, then you're now overriding it, so you're subject to the two problems described above. Furthermore, it is doubtful that your method will fulfill the contract of the new superclass method, as that contract had not yet been written when you wrote the subclass method.

Luckily, there is a way to avoid all of the problems described earlier. Instead of extending an existing class, give your new class a private field that references an instance of the existing class. This design is called *composition* because the existing class becomes a component of the new one. Each instance method in the new class invokes the corresponding method on the contained instance of the existing class and returns the results. This is known as *forwarding*, and the methods in the new class are known as *forwarding methods*. The resulting class will be rock solid, with no dependencies on the implementation details of the existing class. Even adding new methods to the existing class will have no impact on the new class. To make this concrete, here's a replacement for `InstrumentedHashSet` that uses the composition/forwarding approach:

```
// Wrapper class - uses composition in place of inheritance
public class InstrumentedSet implements Set {
    private final Set s;
    private int addCount = 0;

    public InstrumentedSet(Set s) {
        this.s = s;
    }

    public boolean add(Object o) {
        addCount++;
        return s.add(o);
    }

    public boolean addAll(Collection c) {
        addCount += c.size();
        return s.addAll(c);
    }

    public int getAddCount() {
        return addCount;
    }

    // Forwarding methods
    public void clear()                 { s.clear();             }
    public boolean contains(Object o) { return s.contains(o); }
    public boolean isEmpty()          { return s.isEmpty();   }
    public int size()                 { return s.size();      }
    public Iterator iterator()        { return s.iterator();  }
    public boolean remove(Object o)   { return s.remove(o);   }
    public boolean containsAll(Collection c)
                                { return s.containsAll(c); }
    public boolean removeAll(Collection c)
                                { return s.removeAll(c);   }
    public boolean retainAll(Collection c)
                                { return s.retainAll(c);   }
    public Object[] toArray()           { return s.toArray();  }
    public Object[] toArray(Object[] a) { return s.toArray(a); }
    public boolean equals(Object o)   { return s.equals(o);  }
    public int hashCode()             { return s.hashCode(); }
    public String toString()          { return s.toString(); }
}
```

The design of the `InstrumentedSet` class is enabled by the existence of the `Set` interface, which captures the functionality of the `HashSet` class. Besides being robust, this design is extremely flexible. The `InstrumentedSet` class implements the `Set` interface and has a single constructor whose argument is also of type `Set`. In essence, the class transforms one `Set` into another, adding the instrumentation functionality. Unlike the inheritance-based approach, which works only for a single concrete class and requires a separate constructor for each supported constructor in the superclass, the wrapper class can be used to instrument any Set implementation and will work in conjunction with any preexisting constructor. For example,

```
Set s1 = new InstrumentedSet(new TreeSet(list));
Set s2 = new InstrumentedSet(new HashSet(capacity, loadFactor));
```

The `InstrumentedSet` class can even be used to temporarily instrument a set instance that has already been used without instrumentation:

```
static void f(Set s) {
    InstrumentedSet sInst = new InstrumentedSet(s);
    ... // Within this method use sInst instead of s
}
```

The `InstrumentedSet` class is known as a *wrapper* class because each `InstrumentedSet` instance wraps another `Set` instance. This is also known as the *Decorator* pattern [Gamma98, p. 175] because the `InstrumentedSet` class "decorates" a set by adding instrumentation. Sometimes the combination of composition and forwarding is erroneously referred to as *delegation*. Technically, it's not delegation unless the wrapper object passes itself to the wrapped object [Gamma98, p. 20].

The disadvantages of wrapper classes are few. One caveat is that wrapper classes are not suited for use in *callback frameworks*, wherein objects pass self-references to other objects for later invocations ("callbacks"). Because the wrapped object doesn't know of its wrapper, it passes a reference to itself (`this`) and callbacks elude the wrapper. This is known as the *SELF problem* [Lieberman86]. Some people worry about the performance impact of forwarding method invocations or the memory footprint impact of wrapper objects. Neither of these things turns out to have much impact in practice. It is a bit tedious to write forwarding methods, but the tedium is partially offset by the fact that you have to write only one constructor.

Inheritance is appropriate only in circumstances where the subclass really is a *subtype* of the superclass. In other words, a class *B* should extend a class only *A* if an "is-a" relationship exists between the two classes. If you are tempted to have a class *B* extend a class *A*, ask yourself the question: "Is every *B* really an *A*?" If you cannot truthfully answer yes to this question, *B* should not extend *A*. If the answer is no, it is often the case that *B* should contain a private instance of *A* and expose a smaller and simpler API: *A* is not an essential part of *B*, merely a detail of its implementation.

There are a number of obvious violations of this principle in the Java platform libraries. For example, a stack is not a vector, so `Stack` should not extend `Vector`. Similarly, a property list is not a hash table so `Properties` should not extend `Hashtable`. In both cases, composition would have been appropriate.

If you use inheritance where composition is appropriate, you needlessly expose implementation details. The resulting API ties you to the original implementation, forever limiting the performance of your class. More seriously, by exposing the internals you let the client access them directly. At the very least, this can lead to confusing semantics. For example, if p refers to a `Properties` instance, then `p.getProperty(key)` may yield different results from `p.get(key)`: The former method takes defaults into account, while the latter method, which is inherited from `Hashtable`, does not. Most seriously, the client may be able to corrupt invariants of the subclass by modifying the superclass directly. In the case of `Properties`, the designers intended that only strings be allowed as keys and values, but direct access to the underlying `Hashtable` allows this invariant to be violated. Once this invariant is violated, it is no longer possible to use other parts of the `Properties` API (`load` and `store`). By the time this problem was discovered, it was too late to correct it because clients depended on the use of nonstring keys and values.

There is one last set of questions you should ask yourself before deciding to use inheritance rather than composition. Does the class that you're contemplating extending have any flaws in its API? If so, are you comfortable propagating those flaws into the API of your class? Inheritance propagates any flaws in the superclass's API, while composition allows you to design a new API that hides these flaws.

To summarize, inheritance is powerful, but it is problematic because it violates encapsulation. It is appropriate only when a genuine subtype relationship exists between the subclass and the superclass. Even then, inheritance may lead to fragility if the subclass is in a different package from the superclass and the superclass is not designed for extension. To avoid this fragility, use composition and forwarding instead of inheritance, especially if an appropriate interface to implement a wrapper class exists. Not only are wrapper classes more robust than subclasses, they are also more powerful.

Item 15: Design and document for inheritance or else prohibit it

Item 14 alerted you to the dangers of subclassing a "foreign" class that was not designed and documented for inheritance. So what does it mean for a class to be designed and documented for inheritance?

First, **the class must document precisely the effects of overriding any method**. In other words, the class must document its *self-use* of overridable methods: For each public or protected method or constructor, its documentation must indicate which overridable methods it invokes, in what sequence, and how the results of each invocation affect subsequent processing. (By *overridable*, we mean nonfinal and either public or protected.) More generally, a class must document any circumstances under which it might invoke an overridable method. For example, invocations might come from background threads or static initializers.

By convention, a method that invokes overridable methods contains a description of these invocations at the end of its doc comment. The description begins with the phrase, "This implementation." This phrase should not be taken to indicate that the behavior may change from release to release. It connotes that the description concerns the inner workings of the method. Here's an example, copied from the specification for `java.util.AbstractCollection`:

```
public boolean remove(Object o)
```

> Removes a single instance of the specified element from this collection, if it is present (optional operation). More formally, removes an element e such that `(o==null ? e==null : o.equals(e))`, if the collection contains one or more such elements. Returns `true` if the collection contained the specified element (or equivalently, if the collection changed as a result of the call).

> This implementation iterates over the collection looking for the specified element. If it finds the element, it removes the element from the collection using the iterator's `remove` method. Note that this implementation throws an `UnsupportedOperationException` if the iterator returned by this collection's `iterator` method does not implement the `remove` method.

This documentation leaves no doubt that overriding the `iterator` method will affect the behavior of the `remove` method. Furthermore, it describes exactly how the behavior of the `Iterator` returned by the `iterator` method will affect the behavior of the `remove` method. Contrast this to the situation in Item 14, wherein the programmer subclassing HashSet simply could not say whether overriding the add method would affect the behavior of the addAll method.

But doesn't this violate the dictum that good API documentation should describe *what* a given method does and not *how* it does it? Yes it does! This is an unfortunate consequence of the fact that inheritance violates encapsulation. To document a class so that it can be safely subclassed, you must describe implementation details that should otherwise be left unspecified.

Design for inheritance involves more than just documenting patterns of self-use. To allow programmers to write efficient subclasses without undue pain, **a class may have to provide hooks into its internal workings in the form of judiciously chosen protected methods** or, in rare instances, protected fields. For example, consider the removeRange method from java.util.AbstractList:

> protected void removeRange(int fromIndex, int toIndex)
>
> > Removes from this list all of the elements whose index is between fromIndex, inclusive, and toIndex, exclusive. Shifts any succeeding elements to the left (reduces their index). This call shortens the ArrayList by (toIndex - fromIndex) elements. (If toIndex==fromIndex, this operation has no effect.)
> >
> > This method is called by the clear operation on this list and its sublists. Overriding this method to take advantage of the internals of the list implementation can substantially improve the performance of the clear operation on this list and its subLists.
> >
> > This implementation gets a list iterator positioned before fromIndex and repeatedly calls ListIterator.next followed by ListIterator.remove, until the entire range has been removed. Note: If ListIterator.remove requires linear time, this implementation requires quadratic time.
> >
> > Parameters:
> >
> > > fromIndex   index of first element to be removed.
> > >
> > > toIndex   index after last element to be removed.

This method is of no interest to end users of a List implementation. It is provided solely to make it easy for subclasses to provide a fast clear method on sublists. In the absence of the removeRange method, subclasses would have to make do with quadratic performance when the clear method was invoked on sublists or rewrite the entire subList mechanism from scratch—not an easy task!

So how do you decide what protected methods or fields to expose when designing a class for inheritance? Unfortunately, there is no magic bullet. The best you can do is to think hard, take your best guess, and then test it by writing some subclasses. You should provide as few protected methods and fields as possible because each one represents a commitment to an implementation detail. On the other hand, you must not provide too few, as a missing protected method can render a class practically unusable for inheritance.

When you design for inheritance a class that is likely to achieve wide use, realize that you are committing *forever* to the self-use patterns that you document and to the implementation decisions implicit in its protected methods and fields. These commitments can make it difficult or impossible to improve the performance or functionality of the class in a subsequent release.

Also, note that the special documentation required for inheritance clutters up the normal documentation, which is designed for programmers who create instances of your class and invoke methods on them. As of this writing, there is little in the way of tools or commenting conventions to separate ordinary API documentation from information of interest only to programmers implementing subclasses.

There are a few more restrictions that a class must obey to allow inheritance. **Constructors must not invoke overridable methods**, directly or indirectly. If this rule is violated, it is likely that program failure will result. The superclass constructor runs before the subclass constructor, so the overriding method in the subclass will get invoked before the subclass constructor has run. If the overriding method depends on any initialization performed by the subclass constructor, then the method will not behave as expected. To make this concrete, here's a tiny class that violates this rule:

```
public class Super {
    // Broken - constructor invokes overridable method
    public Super() {
        m();
    }

    public void m() {
    }
}
```

Here's a subclass that overrides m, which is erroneously invoked by Super's sole constructor:

```
final class Sub extends Super {
    private final Date date; // Blank final, set by constructor

    Sub() {
        date = new Date();
    }

    // Overrides Super.m, invoked by the constructor Super()
    public void m() {
        System.out.println(date);
    }

    public static void main(String[] args) {
        Sub s = new Sub();
        s.m();
    }
}
```

You might expect this program to print out the date twice, but it prints out null the first time because the method m is invoked by the constructor Super() before the constructor Sub() has a chance to initialize the date field. Note that this program observes a final field in two different states.

The Cloneable and Serializable interfaces present special difficulties when designing for inheritance. It is generally not a good idea for a class designed for inheritance to implement either of these interfaces, as they place a substantial burden on programmers who extend the class. There are, however, special actions that you can take to allow subclasses to implement these interfaces without mandating that they do so. These actions are described in Item 10 and Item 54.

If you do decide to implement Cloneable or Serializable in a class designed for inheritance, you should be aware that because the clone and readObject methods behave a lot like constructors, a similar restriction applies: **Neither clone nor readObject may invoke an overridable method, directly or indirectly**. In the case of the readObject method, the overriding method will run before the subclass's state has been deserialized. In the case of the clone method, the overriding method will run before the subclass's clone methods has a chance to fix the clone's state. In either case, a program failure is likely to follow. In the case of the clone method, the failure can do damage to the object being cloned as well as to the clone itself.

Finally, if you decide to implement `Serializable` in a class designed for inheritance and the class has a `readResolve` or `writeReplace` method, **you must make the `readResolve` or `writeReplace` method protected rather than private**. If these methods are private, they will be silently ignored by subclasses. This is one more case where an implementation detail becomes part of a class's API to permit inheritance.

By now, it should be apparent that **designing a class for inheritance places substantial limitations on the class**. This is not a decision to be undertaken lightly. There are some situations where it is clearly the right thing to do, such as abstract classes, including *skeletal implementations* of interfaces (Item 16). There are other situations where it is clearly the wrong thing to do, such as immutable classes (Item 13).

But what about ordinary concrete classes? Traditionally, they are neither final nor designed and documented for subclassing, but this state of affairs is dangerous. Each time a change is made in such a class, there is a chance that client classes that extend the class will break. This is not just a theoretical problem. It is not uncommon to receive subclassing-related bug reports after modifying the internals of a nonfinal concrete class that was not designed and documented for inheritance.

The best solution to this problem is to prohibit subclassing in classes that are not designed and documented to be safely subclassed. There are two ways to prohibit subclassing. The easier of the two is to declare the class final. The alternative is to make all the constructors private or package-private and to add public *static* factories in place of the constructors. This alternative, which provides the flexibility to use subclasses internally, is discussed in Item 13. Either approach is acceptable.

This advice may be somewhat controversial, as many programmers have grown accustomed to subclassing ordinary concrete classes to add facilities such as instrumentation, notification, and synchronization or to limit functionality. If a class implements some interface that captures its essence, such as `Set`, `List`, or `Map`, then you should feel no compunction about prohibiting subclassing. The *wrapper class* pattern, described in Item 14, provides a superior alternative to inheritance for altering the functionality.

If a concrete class does not implement a standard interface, then you may inconvenience some programmers by prohibiting inheritance. If you feel that you must allow inheritance from such a class, one reasonable approach is to ensure that the class never invokes any of its overridable methods and to document this fact. In other words, eliminate the class's self-use of overridable methods entirely.

In doing so, you'll create a class that is reasonably safe to subclass. Overriding a method will never affect the behavior of any other method.

You can eliminate a class's self-use of overridable methods mechanically, without changing its behavior. Move the body of each overridable method to a private "helper method" and have each overridable method invoke its private helper method. Then replace each self-use of an overridable method with a direct invocation of the overridable method's private helper method.

Item 16: Prefer interfaces to abstract classes

The Java programming language provides two mechanisms for defining a type that permits multiple implementations: interfaces and abstract classes. The most obvious difference between the two mechanisms is that abstract classes are permitted to contain implementations for some methods while interfaces are not. A more important difference is that to implement the type defined by an abstract class, a class must be a subclass of the abstract class. Any class that defines all of the required methods and obeys the general contract is permitted to implement an interface, regardless of where the class resides in the class hierarchy. Because Java permits only single inheritance, this restriction on abstract classes severely constrains their use as type definitions.

Existing classes can be easily retrofitted to implement a new interface. All you have to do is add the required methods if they don't yet exist and add an `implements` clause to the class declaration. For example, many existing classes were retrofitted to implement the `Comparable` interface when it was introduced into the platform. Existing classes cannot, in general, be retrofitted to extend a new abstract class. If you want to have two classes extend the same abstract class, you have to place the abstract class high up in the type hierarchy where it subclasses an ancestor of both classes. Unfortunately, this causes great collateral damage to the type hierarchy, forcing all descendants of the common ancestor to extend the new abstract class whether or not it is appropriate for them to do so.

Interfaces are ideal for defining mixins. A *mixin* is a type that a class can implement in addition to its "primary type" to declare that it provides some optional behavior. For example, `Comparable` is a mixin interface that allows a class to declare that its instances are ordered with respect to other mutually comparable objects. Such an interface is called a mixin because it allows the optional functionality to be "mixed in" to the type's primary functionality. Abstract classes cannot be used to define mixins for the same reason that they can't be retrofitted onto existing classes: A class cannot have more than one parent, and there is no reasonable place in the class hierarchy to put a mixin.

Interfaces allow the construction of nonhierarchical type frameworks. Type hierarchies are great for organizing some things, but other things don't fall neatly into a rigid hierarchy. For example, suppose we have an interface representing a singer and another representing a songwriter:

```
public interface Singer {
    AudioClip Sing(Song s);
}
```

```
public interface Songwriter {
    Song compose(boolean hit);
}
```

In real life, some singers are also songwriters. Because we used interfaces rather than abstract classes to define these types, it is perfectly permissible for a single class to implement both Singer and Songwriter. In fact, we can define a third interface that extends both Singer and Songwriter and adds new methods that are appropriate to the combination:

```
public interface SingerSongwriter extends Singer, Songwriter {
    AudioClip strum();
    void actSensitive();
}
```

You don't always need this level of flexibility, but when you do, interfaces are a lifesaver. The alternative is a bloated class hierarchy containing a separate class for every supported combination of attributes. If there are n attributes in the type system, there are 2^n possible combinations that you might have to support. This is what's known as a *combinatorial explosion*. Bloated class hierarchies can lead to bloated classes containing many methods that differ only in the type of their arguments, as there are no types in the class hierarchy to capture common behaviors.

Interfaces enable safe, powerful functionality enhancements via the *wrapper class* idiom, described in Item 14. If you use abstract classes to define types, you leave the programmer who wants to add functionality with no alternative but to use inheritance. The resulting classes are less powerful and more fragile than wrapper classes.

While interfaces are not permitted to contain method implementations, using interfaces to define types does not prevent you from providing implementation assistance to programmers. **You can combine the virtues of interfaces and abstract classes by providing an abstract *skeletal implementation* class to go with each nontrivial interface that you export.** The interface still defines the type, but the skeletal implementation takes all of the work out of implementing it.

By convention, skeletal implementations are called Abstract*Interface*, where *Interface* is the name of the interface they implement. For example, the Collections Framework provides a skeletal implementation to go along with each main collection interface: AbstractCollection, AbstractSet, AbstractList, and AbstractMap.

When properly designed, skeletal implementations make it *very* easy for programmers to provide their own implementations of your interfaces. For example, here's a static factory method containing a complete, fully functional List implementation:

```
// List adapter for int array
static List intArrayAsList(final int[] a) {
    if (a == null)
        throw new NullPointerException();

    return new AbstractList() {
        public Object get(int i) {
            return new Integer(a[i]);
        }

        public int size() {
            return a.length;
        }

        public Object set(int i, Object o) {
            int oldVal = a[i];
            a[i] = ((Integer)o).intValue();
            return new Integer(oldVal);
        }
    };
}
```

When you consider all that a List implementation does for you, this example is an impressive demonstration of the power of skeletal implementations. Incidentally, the example is an *Adapter* [Gamma98, p. 139] that allows an int array to be viewed as a list of Integer instances. Because of all the translation back and forth between int values and Integer instances, the performance is not terribly good. Note that a static factory is provided and that the class is an inaccessible *anonymous class* (Item 18) hidden inside the static factory.

The beauty of skeletal implementations is that they provide the implementation assistance of abstract classes without imposing the severe constraints that abstract classes impose when they serve as type definitions. For most implementors of an interface, extending the skeletal implementation is the obvious choice, but it is strictly optional. If a preexisting class cannot be made to extend the skeletal implementation, the class can always implement the interface manually. Furthermore, the skeletal implementation can still aid the implementor's task. The class implementing the interface can forward invocations of interface methods to a contained instance of a private inner class that extends the skeletal implementation. This technique, known as *simulated multiple inheritance*, is closely related to the wrapper class idiom discussed in Item 14. It provides most of the benefits of multiple inheritance, while avoiding the pitfalls.

Writing a skeletal implementation is a relatively simple, if somewhat tedious, matter. First you must study the interface and decide which methods are the primitives in terms of which the others can be implemented. These primitives will be the abstract methods in your skeletal implementation. Then you must provide concrete implementations of all the other methods in the interface. For example, here's a skeletal implementation of the Map.Entry interface. As of this writing, this class is not included in the Java platform libraries, but it probably should be:

```java
// Skeletal Implementation
public abstract class AbstractMapEntry implements Map.Entry {
    // Primitives
    public abstract Object getKey();
    public abstract Object getValue();

    // Entries in modifiable maps must override this method
    public Object setValue(Object value) {
        throw new UnsupportedOperationException();
    }

    // Implements the general contract of Map.Entry.equals
    public boolean equals(Object o) {
        if (o == this)
            return true;
        if (! (o instanceof Map.Entry))
            return false;
        Map.Entry arg = (Map.Entry)o;

        return eq(getKey(),   arg.getKey()) &&
               eq(getValue(), arg.getValue());
    }

    private static boolean eq(Object o1, Object o2) {
        return (o1 == null ? o2 == null : o1.equals(o2));
    }

    // Implements the general contract of Map.Entry.hashcode
    public int hashCode() {
        return
            (getKey()   == null ? 0 :   getKey().hashCode()) ^
            (getValue() == null ? 0 : getValue().hashCode());
    }
}
```

Because skeletal implementations are designed for inheritance, you should follow all of the design and documentation guidelines in Item 15. For brevity's sake, the documentation comments were omitted from the previous example, but good documentation is absolutely essential for skeletal implementations.

Using abstract classes to define types that permit multiple implementations has one great advantage over using interfaces: **It is far easier to evolve an abstract class than it is to evolve an interface.** If, in a subsequent release, you want to add a new method to an abstract class, you can always add a concrete method containing a reasonable default implementation. All existing implementations of the abstract class will then provide the new method. This does not work for interfaces.

It is, generally speaking, impossible to add a method to a public interface without breaking all existing programs that use the interface. Classes that previously implemented the interface will be missing the new method and won't compile anymore. You could limit the damage somewhat by adding the new method to the skeletal implementation at the same time as you added it to the interface, but this really doesn't solve the problem. Any implementation that didn't inherit from the skeletal implementation would still be broken.

Public interfaces, therefore, must be designed carefully. Once an interface is released and widely implemented, it is almost impossible to change it. You really must get it right the first time. If an interface contains a minor flaw, it will irritate you and its users forever. If an interface is severely deficient, it can doom the API. The best thing to do when releasing a new interface is to have as many programmers as possible implement the interface in as many ways as possible *before* the interface is "frozen." This will allow you to discover any flaws while you can still correct them.

To summarize, an interface is generally the best way to define a type that permits multiple implementations. An exception to this rule is the case where ease of evolution is deemed more important than flexibility and power. Under these circumstances, you should use an abstract class to define the type, but only if you understand and can accept the limitations. If you export a nontrivial interface, you should strongly consider providing a skeletal implementation to go with it. Finally, you should design all of your public interfaces with the utmost care and test them thoroughly by writing multiple implementations.

Item 17: Use interfaces only to define types

When a class implements an interface, the interface serves as a *type* that can be used to refer to instances of the class. That a class implements an interface should therefore say something about what a client can do with instances of the class. It is inappropriate to define an interface for any other purpose.

One kind of interface that fails this test is the so-called *constant interface*. Such an interface contains no methods; it consists solely of static final fields, each exporting a constant. Classes using these constants implement the interface to avoid the need to qualify constant names with a class name. Here is an example:

```
// Constant interface pattern - do not use!
public interface PhysicalConstants {
    // Avogadro's number (1/mol)
    static final double AVOGADROS_NUMBER    = 6.02214199e23;

    // Boltzmann constant (J/K)
    static final double BOLTZMANN_CONSTANT = 1.3806503e-23;

    // Mass of the electron (kg)
    static final double ELECTRON_MASS       = 9.10938188e-31;
}
```

The constant interface pattern is a poor use of interfaces. That a class uses some constants internally is an implementation detail. Implementing a constant interface causes this implementation detail to leak into the class's exported API. It is of no consequence to the users of a class that the class implements a constant interface. In fact, it may even confuse them. Worse, it represents a commitment: if in a future release the class is modified so that it no longer needs to use the constants, it still must implement the interface to ensure binary compatibility. If a nonfinal class implements a constant interface, all of its subclasses will have their namespaces polluted by the constants in the interface.

There are several constant interfaces in the java platform libraries, such as `java.io.ObjectStreamConstants`. These interfaces should be regarded as anomalies and should not be emulated.

If you want to export constants, there are several reasonable choices. If the constants are strongly tied to an existing class or interface, you should add them to the class or interface. For example, all of the numerical wrapper classes in the Java platform libraries, such as `Integer` and `Float`, export `MIN_VALUE` and `MAX_VALUE` constants. If the constants are best viewed as members of an enumerated type, you should export them with a *typesafe enum* class (Item 21). Otherwise, you should export the constants with a noninstantiable *utility class* (Item 3). Here is a utility class version of the PhysicalConstants example above:

```
// Constant utility class
public class PhysicalConstants {
    private PhysicalConstants() { }  // Prevents instantiation

    public static final double AVOGADROS_NUMBER   = 6.02214199e23;
    public static final double BOLTZMANN_CONSTANT = 1.3806503e-23;
    public static final double ELECTRON_MASS      = 9.10938188e-31;
}
```

While the utility class version of PhysicalConstants does require clients to qualify constant names with a class name, this is a small price to pay for sensible APIs. It is possible that the language may eventually allow the importation of static fields. In the meantime, you can minimize the need for excessive typing by storing frequently used constants in local variables or private static fields, for example:

```
private static final double PI = Math.PI;
```

In summary, interfaces should be used only to define types. They should not be used to export constants.

Item 18: Favor static member classes over nonstatic

A *nested class* is a class defined within another class. A nested classes should exist only to serve its enclosing class. If a nested class would be useful in some other context, then it should be a top-level class. There are four kinds of nested classes: *static member classes*, *nonstatic member classes*, *anonymous classes*, and *local classes*. All but the first kind are known as *inner classes*. This item tells you when to use which kind of nested class and why.

A static member class is the simplest kind of nested class. It is best thought of as an ordinary class that happens to be declared inside another class and has access to all of the enclosing class's members, even those declared private. A static member class is a static member of its enclosing class and obeys the same accessibility rules as other static members. If it is declared private, it is accessible only within the enclosing class, and so forth.

One common use of a static member class is as a public auxiliary class, useful only in conjunction with its outer class. For example, consider a typesafe enum describing the operations supported by a calculator (Item 21). The `Operation` class should be a public static member class of the `Calculator` class. Clients of the `Calculator` class could then refer to operations using names like `Calculator.Operation.PLUS` and `Calculator.Operation.MINUS`. This use is demonstrated later in this item.

Syntactically, the only difference between static and nonstatic member classes is that static member classes have the modifier `static` in their declarations. Despite the syntactic similarity, these two kinds of nested classes are very different. Each instance of a nonstatic member class is implicitly associated with an *enclosing instance* of its containing class. Within instance methods of a nonstatic member class, it is possible to invoke methods on the enclosing instance. Given a reference to an instance of a nonstatic member class, it is possible to obtain a reference to the enclosing instance. If an instance of a nested class can exist in isolation from an instance of its enclosing class, then the nested class *cannot* be a nonstatic member class: It is impossible to create an instance of a nonstatic member class without an enclosing instance.

The association between a nonstatic member class instance and its enclosing instance is established when the former is created; it cannot be modified thereafter. Normally, the association is established automatically by invoking a nonstatic member class constructor from within an instance method of the enclosing class. It is possible, although rare, to establish the association manually using the expression `enclosingInstance.new MemberClass(args)`. As you would expect, the association takes up space in the nonstatic member class instance and adds time to its construction.

One common use of a nonstatic member class is to define an *Adapter* [Gamma98, p. 139] that allows an instance of the outer class to be viewed as an instance of some unrelated class. For example, implementations of the Map interface typically use nonstatic member classes to implement their *collection views*, which are returned by Map's keySet, entrySet, and values methods. Similarly, implementations of the collection interfaces, such as Set and List, typically use nonstatic member classes to implement their iterators:

```
// Typical use of a nonstatic member class
public class MySet extends AbstractSet {
    ... // Bulk of the class omitted

    public Iterator iterator() {
        return new MyIterator();
    }

    private class MyIterator implements Iterator {
        ...
    }
}
```

If you declare a member class that does not require access to an enclosing instance, remember to put the static modifier in the declaration, making it a static rather than a nonstatic member class. If you omit the static modifier, each instance will contain an extraneous reference to the enclosing object. Maintaining this reference costs time and space with no corresponding benefits. Should you ever need to allocate an instance without an enclosing instance, you'll be unable to do so, as nonstatic member class instances are required to have an enclosing instance.

A common use of private static member classes is to represent components of the object represented by their enclosing class. For example, consider a Map instance, which associates keys with values. Map instances typically have an internal Entry object for each key-value pair in the map. While each entry is associated with a map, the methods on an entry (getKey, getValue, and setValue) do not need access to the map. Therefore it would be wasteful to use a nonstatic member class to represent entries; a private static member class is best. If you accidentally omit the static modifier in the entry declaration, the map will still work, but each entry will contain a superfluous reference to the map, which wastes space and time.

It is doubly important to choose correctly between a static and nonstatic member class if the class in question is a public or protected member of an exported class. In this case, the member class is an exported API element and may not be changed from a nonstatic to a static member class in a subsequent release without violating binary compatibility.

Anonymous classes are unlike anything else in the Java programming language. As you would expect, an anonymous class has no name. It is not a member of its enclosing class. Rather than being declared along with other members, it is simultaneously declared and instantiated at the point of use. Anonymous classes are permitted at any point in the code where an expression is legal. Anonymous classes behave like static or nonstatic member classes depending on where they occur: They have enclosing instances if they occur in a nonstatic context.

There are several limitations on the applicability of anonymous classes. Because they are simultaneously declared and instantiated, an anonymous class may be used only if it is to be instantiated at a single point in the code. Because anonymous classes have no name, they may be used only if there is no need to refer to them after they are instantiated. Anonymous classes typically implement only methods in their interface or superclass. They do not declare any new methods, as there is no nameable type to access new methods. Because anonymous classes occur in the midst of expressions, they should be very short, perhaps twenty lines or less. Longer anonymous classes would harm the readability of the program.

One common use of an anonymous class is to create a *function object*, such as a `Comparator` instance. For example, the following method invocation sorts an array of strings according to their length:

```
// Typical use of an anonymous class
Arrays.sort(args, new Comparator() {
    public int compare(Object o1, Object o2) {
        return  ((String)o1).length() - ((String)o2).length();
    }
});
```

Another common use of an anonymous class is to create a *process object*, such as a `Thread`, `Runnable`, or `TimerTask` instance. A third common use is within a static factory method (see the `intArrayAsList` method in Item 16). A fourth common use is in the public static final field initializers of sophisticated typesafe enums that require a separate subclass for each instance (see the `Operation` class in Item 21). If the `Operation` class is a static member class of `Calcu-`

lator, as recommended earlier, then the individual Operation constants are doubly nested classes:

```java
// Typical use of a public static member class
public class Calculator {
    public static abstract class Operation {
        private final String name;

        Operation(String name)    { this.name = name; }

        public String toString() { return this.name; }

        // Perform arithmetic op represented by this constant
        abstract double eval(double x, double y);

        // Doubly nested anonymous classes
        public static final Operation PLUS = new Operation("+") {
            double eval(double x, double y) { return x + y; }
        };
        public static final Operation MINUS = new Operation("-") {
            double eval(double x, double y) { return x - y; }
        };
        public static final Operation TIMES = new Operation("*") {
            double eval(double x, double y) { return x * y; }
        };
        public static final Operation DIVIDE = new Operation("/") {
            double eval(double x, double y) { return x / y; }
        };
    }

    // Return the results of the specified calculation
    public double calculate(double x, Operation op, double y) {
        return op.eval(x, y);
    }
}
```

Local classes are probably the least frequently used of the four kinds of nested classes. A local class may be declared anywhere that a local variable may be declared and obeys the same scoping rules. Local classes have some attributes in common with each of the other three kinds of nested classes. Like member classes, they have names and may be used repeatedly. Like anonymous classes, they have enclosing instances if and only if they are used in a nonstatic context. Like anonymous classes, they should be short so as not to harm the readability of the enclosing method or initializer.

To recap, there are four different kinds of nested classes, and each has its place. If a nested class needs to be visible outside of a single method or is too long to fit comfortably inside a method, use a member class. If each instance of the member class needs a reference to its enclosing instance, make it nonstatic; otherwise make it static. Assuming the class belongs inside a method, if you need to create instances from only one location and there is a preexisting type that characterizes the class, make it an anonymous class; otherwise, make it a local class.

CHAPTER 5

Substitutes for C Constructs

THE Java programming language shares many similarities with the C programming language, but several C constructs have been omitted. In most cases, it's obvious why a C construct was omitted and how to make do without it. This chapter suggests replacements for several omitted C constructs whose replacements are not so obvious.

The common thread that connects the items in this chapter is that all of the omitted constructs are data-oriented rather than object-oriented. The Java programming language provides a powerful type system, and the suggested replacements take full advantage of that type system to deliver a higher quality abstraction than the C constructs they replace.

Even if you choose to skip this chapter, it's probably worth reading Item 21, which discusses the *typesafe enum* pattern, a replacement for C's enum construct. This pattern is not widely known at the time of this writing, and it has several advantages over the methods currently in common use.

Item 19: Replace structures with classes

The C struct construct was omitted from the Java programming language because a class does everything a structure does and more. A structure merely groups multiple data fields into a single object; a class associates operations with the resulting object and allows the data fields to be hidden from users of the object. In other words, a class can *encapsulate* its data into an object that is accessed solely by its methods, allowing the implementor the freedom to change the representation over time (Item 12).

Upon first exposure to the Java programming language, some C programmers believe that classes are too heavyweight to replace structures under some circumstances, but this is not the case. Degenerate classes consisting solely of data fields are loosely equivalent to C structures:

```
// Degenerate classes like this should not be public!
class Point {
    public float x;
    public float y;
}
```

Because such classes are accessed by their data fields, they do not offer the benefits of encapsulation. You cannot change the representation of such a class without changing its API, you cannot enforce any invariants, and you cannot take any auxiliary action when a field is modified. Hard-line object-oriented programmers feel that such classes are anathema and should always be replaced by classes with private fields and public *accessor methods*:

```
// Encapsulated structure class
class Point {
    private float x;
    private float y;

    public Point(float x, float y) {
        this.x = x;
        this.y = y;
    }

    public float getX() { return x; }
    public float getY() { return y; }

    public void setX(float x) { this.x = x; }
    public void setY(float y) { this.y = y; }
}
```

Certainly, the hard-liners are correct when it comes to public classes: If a class is accessible outside the confines of its package, the prudent programmer will provide accessor methods to preserve the flexibility to change the class's internal representation. If a public class were to expose its data fields, all hope of changing the representation would be lost, as client code for public classes can be distributed all over the known universe.

If, however, a class is package-private, or it is a private nested class, there is nothing inherently wrong with directly exposing its data fields—assuming they really do describe the abstraction provided by the class. This approach generates less visual clutter than the access method approach, both in the class definition and in the client code that uses the class. While the client code is tied to the internal representation of the class, this code is restricted to the package that contains the class. In the unlikely event that a change in representation becomes desirable, it is possible to effect the change without touching any code outside the package. In the case of a private nested class, the scope of the change is further restricted to the enclosing class.

Several classes in the Java platform libraries violate the advice that public classes should not expose fields directly. Prominent examples include the `Point` and `Dimension` classes in the `java.awt` package. Rather than examples to be emulated, these classes should be regarded as cautionary tales. As described in Item 37, the decision to expose the internals of the Dimension class resulted in a serious performance problem that could not be solved without affecting clients.

Item 20: Replace unions with class hierarchies

The C union construct is most frequently used to define structures capable of holding more than one type of data. Such a structure typically contains at least two fields: a union and a *tag*. The tag is just an ordinary field used to indicate which of the possible types is held by the union. The tag is generally of some enum type. A structure containing a union and a tag is sometimes called a *discriminated union*.

In the C example below, the shape_t type is a discriminated union that can be used to represent either a rectangle or a circle. The area function takes a pointer to a shape_t structure and returns its area, or -1.0, if the structure is invalid:

```
/* Discriminated union */
#include "math.h"
typedef enum {RECTANGLE, CIRCLE} shapeType_t;

typedef struct {
    double length;
    double width;
} rectangleDimensions_t;

typedef struct {
    double radius;
} circleDimensions_t;

typedef struct {
    shapeType_t tag;
    union {
        rectangleDimensions_t rectangle;
        circleDimensions_t    circle;
    } dimensions;
} shape_t;

double area(shape_t *shape) {
    switch(shape->tag) {
      case RECTANGLE: {
        double length = shape->dimensions.rectangle.length;
        double width  = shape->dimensions.rectangle.width;
        return length * width;
      }
      case CIRCLE: {
        double r = shape->dimensions.circle.radius;
        return M_PI * (r*r);
      }
      default: return -1.0; /* Invalid tag */
    }
}
```

The designers of the Java programming language chose to omit the union construct because there is a much better mechanism for defining a single data type capable of representing objects of various types: subtyping. A discriminated union is really just a pallid imitation of a class hierarchy.

To transform a discriminated union into a class hierarchy, define an abstract class containing an abstract method for each operation whose behavior depends on the value of the tag. In the earlier example, there is only one such operation, area. This abstract class is the root of the class hierarchy. If there are any operations whose behavior does not depend on the value of the tag, turn these operations into concrete methods in the root class. Similarly, if there are any data fields in the discriminated union besides the tag and the union, these fields represent data common to all types and should be added to the root class. There are no such type-independent operations or data fields in the example.

Next, define a concrete subclass of the root class for each type that can be represented by the discriminated union. In the earlier example, the types are circle and rectangle. Include in each subclass the data fields particular to its type. In the example, radius is particular to circle, and length and width are particular to rectangle. Also include in each subclass the appropriate implementation of each abstract method in the root class. Here is the class hierarchy corresponding to the discriminated union example:

```
abstract class Shape {
    abstract double area();
}

class Circle extends Shape {
    final double radius;

    Circle(double radius) { this.radius = radius; }

    double area() { return Math.PI * radius*radius; }
}

class Rectangle extends Shape {
    final double length;
    final double width;

    Rectangle(double length, double width) {
        this.length = length;
        this.width  = width;
    }
    double area() { return length * width; }
}
```

A class hierarchy has numerous advantages over a discriminated union. Chief among these is that the class hierarchy provides type safety. In the example, every Shape instance is either a valid Circle or a valid Rectangle. It is a simple matter to generate a shape_t structure that is complete garbage, as the association between the tag and the union is not enforced by the language. If the tag indicates that the shape_t represents a rectangle but the union has been set for a circle, all bets are off. Even if a discriminated union has been initialized properly, it is possible to pass it to a function that is inappropriate for its tag value.

A second advantage of the class hierarchy is that code is simple and clear. The discriminated union is cluttered with boilerplate: declaring the enum type, declaring the tag field, switching on the tag field, dealing with unexpected tag values, and the like. The discriminated union code is made even less readable by the fact that the operations for the various types are intermingled rather than segregated by type.

A third advantage of the class hierarchy is that it is easily extensible, even by multiple parties working independently. To extend a class hierarchy, simply add a new subclass. If you forget to override one of the abstract methods in the superclass, the compiler will tell you in no uncertain terms. To extend a discriminated union, you need access to the source code. You must add a new value to the enum type, as well as a new case to the switch statement in each operation on the discriminated union. Finally, you must recompile. If you forget to provide a new case for some method, you won't find out until run time, and then only if you're careful to check for unrecognized tag values and generate an appropriate error message.

A fourth advantage of the class hierarchy is that it can be made to reflect natural hierarchical relationships among types, to allow for increased flexibility and better compile-time type checking. Suppose the discriminated union in the original example also allowed for squares. The class hierarchy could be made to reflect the fact a square is a special kind of rectangle (assuming both are immutable):

```
class Square extends Rectangle {
    Square(double side) {
        super(side, side);
    }

    double side() {
        return length; // or equivalently, width
    }
}
```

The class hierarchy in this example is not the only one that could have been written to replace the discriminated union. The hierarchy embodies several design decisions worthy of note. The classes in the hierarchy, with the exception of Square, are accessed by their fields rather than by accessor methods. This was done for brevity and would be unacceptable if the classes were public (Item 19). The classes are immutable, which is not always appropriate, but is generally a good thing (Item 13).

Since the Java programming language does not provide the union construct, you might think there's no danger of implementing a discriminated union, but it is possible to write code with many of the same disadvantages. Whenever you're tempted to write a class with an explicit tag field, think about whether the tag could be eliminated and the class replaced by a class hierarchy.

Another use of C's union construct, completely unrelated to discriminated unions, involves looking at the internal representation of a piece of data, intentionally violating the type system. This usage is demonstrated by the following C code fragment, which prints the machine-specific hex representation of a float:

```
union {
    float f;
    int   bits;
} sleaze;

sleaze.f = 6.699e-41;    /* Put data in one field of union... */
printf("%x\n", sleaze.bits); /* ...and read it out the other. */
```

While it can be useful, especially for system programming, this nonportable usage has no counterpart in the Java programming language. In fact, it is antithetical to the spirit of the language, which guarantees type safety and goes to great lengths to insulate programmers from machine-specific internal representations.

The java.lang package does contain methods to translate floating point numbers into bit representations, but these methods are defined in terms of a precisely specified bit representation to ensure portability. The code fragment that follows, which is loosely equivalent to the earlier C fragment, is guaranteed to print the same result, no matter where it's run:

```
System.out.println(
    Integer.toHexString(Float.floatToIntBits(6.699e-41f)));
```

Item 21: Replace enum constructs with classes

The C enum construct was omitted from the Java programming language. Nominally, this construct defines an *enumerated type*: a type whose legal values consist of a fixed set of constants. Unfortunately, the enum construct doesn't do a very good job of defining enumerated types. It just defines a set of named integer constants, providing nothing in the way of type safety and little in the way of convenience. Not only is the following legal C:

```
typedef enum {FUJI, PIPPIN, GRANNY_SMITH} apple_t;
typedef enum {NAVEL, TEMPLE, BLOOD} orange_t;
orange_t myFavorite = PIPPIN;     /* Mixing apples and oranges */
```

but so is this atrocity:

```
orange_t x = (FUJI - PIPPIN)/TEMPLE;     /* Applesauce! */
```

The enum construct does not establish a name space for the constants it generates. Therefore the following declaration, which reuses one of the names, conflicts with the orange_t declaration:

```
typedef enum {BLOOD, SWEAT, TEARS} fluid_t;
```

Types defined with the enum construct are brittle. Adding constants to such a type without recompiling its clients causes unpredictable behavior, unless care is taken to preserve all of the preexisting constant values. Multiple parties cannot add constants to such a type independently, as their new enumeration constants are likely to conflict. The enum construct provides no easy way to translate enumeration constants into printable strings or to enumerate over the constants in a type.

Unfortunately, the most commonly used pattern for enumerated types in the Java programming language, shown here, shares the shortcomings of the C enum construct:

```
// The int enum pattern - problematic!!
public class PlayingCard {
    public static final int SUIT_CLUBS    = 0;
    public static final int SUIT_DIAMONDS = 1;
    public static final int SUIT_HEARTS   = 2;
    public static final int SUIT_SPADES   = 3;
    ...
}
```

You may encounter a variant of this pattern in which `String` constants are used in place of `int` constants. This variant should never be used. While it does provide printable strings for its constants, it can lead to performance problems because it relies on string comparisons. Furthermore, it can lead naive users to hard-code string constants into client code instead of using the appropriate field names. If such a hard-coded string constant contains a typographical error, the error will escape detection at compile time and result in bugs at run time.

Luckily, the Java programming language presents an alternative that avoids all the shortcomings of the common `int` and `String` patterns and provides many added benefits. It is called the *typesafe enum* pattern. Unfortunately, it is not yet widely known. The basic idea is simple: Define a class representing a single element of the enumerated type, and don't provide any public constructors. Instead, provide public static final fields, one for each constant in the enumerated type. Here's how the pattern looks in its simplest form:

```
// The typesafe enum pattern
public class Suit {
    private final String name;

    private Suit(String name) { this.name = name; }

    public String toString()  { return name; }

    public static final Suit CLUBS    = new Suit("clubs");
    public static final Suit DIAMONDS = new Suit("diamonds");
    public static final Suit HEARTS   = new Suit("hearts");
    public static final Suit SPADES   = new Suit("spades");
}
```

Because there is no way for clients to create objects of the class or to extend it, there will never be any objects of the type besides those exported via the public static final fields. Even though the class is not declared final, there is no way to extend it: Subclass constructors must invoke a superclass constructor, and no such constructor is accessible.

As its name implies, the typesafe enum pattern provides compile-time type safety. If you declare a method with a parameter of type `Suit`, you are guaranteed that any non-null object reference passed in represents one of the four valid suits. Any attempt to pass an incorrectly typed object will be caught at compile time, as will any attempt to assign an expression of one enumerated type to a variable of another. Multiple typesafe enum classes with identically named enumeration constants coexist peacefully because each class has its own name space.

Constants may be added to a typesafe enum class without recompiling its clients because the public static object reference fields containing the enumeration constants provide a layer of insulation between the client and the enum class. The constants themselves are never compiled into clients as they are in the more common int pattern and its String variant.

Because typesafe enums are full-fledged classes, you can override the toString method as shown earlier, allowing values to be translated into printable strings. You can, if you desire, go one step further and internationalize typesafe enums by standard means. Note that string names are used only by the toString method; they are not used for equality comparisons, as the equals implementation, which is inherited from Object, performs a reference identity comparison.

More generally, you can augment a typesafe enum class with any method that seems appropriate. Our Suit class, for example, might benefit from the addition of a method that returns the color of the suit or one that returns an image representing the suit. A class can start life as a simple typesafe enum and evolve over time into a full-featured abstraction.

Because arbitrary methods can be added to typesafe enum classes, they can be made to implement any interface. For example, suppose that you want Suit to implement Comparable so clients can sort bridge hands by suit. Here's a slight variant on the original pattern that accomplishes this feat. A static variable, nextOrdinal, is used to assign an ordinal number to each instance as it is created. These ordinals are used by the compareTo method to order instances:

```java
// Ordinal-based typesafe enum
public class Suit implements Comparable {
    private final String name;

    // Ordinal of next suit to be created
    private static int nextOrdinal = 0;

    // Assign an ordinal to this suit
    private final int ordinal = nextOrdinal++;

    private Suit(String name) { this.name = name; }

    public String toString()  { return name; }

    public int compareTo(Object o) {
        return ordinal - ((Suit)o).ordinal;
    }
```

```
        public static final Suit CLUBS    = new Suit("clubs");
        public static final Suit DIAMONDS = new Suit("diamonds");
        public static final Suit HEARTS   = new Suit("hearts");
        public static final Suit SPADES   = new Suit("spades");
    }
```

Because typesafe enum constants are objects, you can put them into collections. For example, suppose you want the Suit class to export an immutable list of the suits in standard order. Merely add these two field declarations to the class:

```
    private static final Suit[] PRIVATE_VALUES =
        { CLUBS, DIAMONDS, HEARTS, SPADES };
    public static final List VALUES =
        Collections.unmodifiableList(Arrays.asList(PRIVATE_VALUES));
```

Unlike the simplest form of the typesafe enum pattern, classes of the ordinal-based form above can be made serializable (Chapter 10) with a little care. It is not sufficient merely to add implements Serializable to the class declaration. You must also provide a readResolve method (Item 57):

```
    private Object readResolve() throws ObjectStreamException {
        return PRIVATE_VALUES[ordinal]; // Canonicalize
    }
```

This method, which is invoked automatically by the serialization system, prevents duplicate constants from coexisting as a result of deserialization. This maintains the guarantee that only a single object represents each enum constant, avoiding the need to override Object.equals. Without this guarantee, Object.equals would report a false negative when presented with two equal but distinct enumeration constants. Note that the readResolve method refers to the PRIVATE_VALUES array, so you must declare this array even if you choose not to export VALUES. Note also that the name field is not used by the readResolve method, so it can and should be made transient.

The resulting class is somewhat brittle; constructors for any new values must appear after those of all existing values, to ensure that previously serialized instances do not change their value when they're deserialized. This is so because the serialized form (Item 55) of an enumeration constant consists solely of its ordinal. If the enumeration constant pertaining to an ordinal changes, a serialized constant with that ordinal will take on the new value when it is deserialized.

There may be one or more pieces of behavior associated with each constant that are used only from within the package containing the typesafe enum class.

Such behaviors are best implemented as package-private methods on the class. Each enum constant then carries with it a hidden collection of behaviors that allows the package containing the enumerated type to react appropriately when presented with the constant.

If a typesafe enum class has methods whose behavior varies significantly from one class constant to another, you should use a separate private class or anonymous inner class for each constant. This allows each constant to have its own implementation of each such method and automatically invokes the correct implementation. The alternative is to structure each such method as a multiway branch that behaves differently depending on the constant on which it's invoked. This alternative is ugly, error prone, and likely to provide performance that is inferior to that of the virtual machine's automatic method dispatching.

The two techniques described in the previous paragraphs are illustrated in the typesafe enum class that follows. The class, Operation, represents an operation performed by a basic four-function calculator. Outside of the package in which the class is defined, all you can do with an Operation constant is to invoke the Object methods (toString, hashCode, equals, and so forth). Inside the package, however, you can perform the arithmetic operation represented by the constant. Presumably, the package would export some higher-level calculator object that exported one or more methods that took an Operation constant as a parameter. Note that Operation itself is an abstract class, containing a single package-private abstract method, eval, that performs the appropriate arithmetic operation. An anonymous inner class is defined for each constant so that each constant can define its own version of the eval method:

```java
// Typesafe enum with behaviors attached to constants
public abstract class Operation {
    private final String name;

    Operation(String name)   { this.name = name; }

    public String toString() { return this.name; }

    // Perform arithmetic operation represented by this constant
    abstract double eval(double x, double y);

    public static final Operation PLUS = new Operation("+") {
        double eval(double x, double y) { return x + y; }
    };
    public static final Operation MINUS = new Operation("-") {
        double eval(double x, double y) { return x - y; }
    };
```

```
        public static final Operation TIMES = new Operation("*") {
            double eval(double x, double y) { return x * y; }
        };
        public static final Operation DIVIDED_BY =
            new Operation("/") {
                double eval(double x, double y) { return x / y; }
        };
    }
```

Typesafe enums are, generally speaking, comparable in performance to `int` enumeration constants. Two distinct instances of a typesafe enum class can never represent the same value, so reference identity comparisons, which are fast, are used to check for logical equality. Clients of a typesafe enum class can use the `==` operator instead of the `equals` method; the results are guaranteed to be identical, and the `==` operator may be even faster.

If a typesafe enum class is generally useful, it should be a top-level class; if its use is tied to a specific top-level class, it should be a static member class of that top-level class (Item 18). For example, the `java.math.BigDecimal` class contains a collection of `int` enumeration constants representing *rounding modes* for decimal fractions. These rounding modes provide a useful abstraction that is not fundamentally tied to the `BigDecimal` class; they would been better implemented as a freestanding `java.math.RoundingMode` class. This would have encouraged any programmer who needed rounding modes to reuse those rounding modes, leading to increased consistency across APIs.

The basic typesafe enum pattern, as exemplified by both `Suit` implementations shown earlier, is *fixed*: It is impossible for users to add new elements to the enumerated type, as its class has no user-accessible constructors. This makes the class effectively final, whether or not it is declared with the `final` access modifier. This is normally what you want, but occasionally you may want to make a typesafe enum class *extensible*. This might be the case, for example, if you used a typesafe enum to represent image encoding formats and you wanted third parties to be able to add support for new formats.

To make a typesafe enum extensible, merely provide a protected constructor. Others can then extend the class and add new constants to their subclasses. You needn't worry about enumeration constant conflicts as you would if you were using the `int` enum pattern. The extensible variant of the typesafe enum pattern takes advantage of the package namespace to create a "magically administered" namespace for the extensible enumeration. Multiple organizations can extend the enumeration without knowledge of one another, and their extensions will never conflict.

Merely adding an element to an extensible enumerated type does not ensure that the new element is fully supported: Methods that take an element of the enumerated type must contend with the possibility of being passed an element unknown to the programmer. Multiway branches on fixed enumerated types are questionable; on extensible enumerated types they're lethal, as they won't magically grow a branch each time a programmer extends the type.

One way to cope with this problem is to outfit the typesafe enum class with all of the methods necessary to describe the behavior of a constant of the class. Methods that are not useful to clients of the class should be protected to hide them from clients while allowing subclasses to override them. If such a method has no reasonable default implementation, it should be abstract as well as protected.

It is a good idea for extensible typesafe enum classes to override the equals and hashCode methods with final methods that invoke the Object methods. This ensures that no subclass accidentally overrides these methods, maintaining the guarantee that all equal objects of the enumerated type are also identical (a.equals(b) if and only if a==b):

```
//Override-prevention methods
public final boolean equals(Object that) {
    return super.equals(that);
}

public final int hashCode() {
    return super.hashCode();
}
```

Note that the extensible variant is not compatible with the comparable variant; if you tried to combine them, the ordering among the elements of the subclasses would be a function of the order in which the subclasses were initialized, which could vary from program to program and run to run.

The extensible variant of the typesafe enum pattern is compatible with the serializable variant, but combining these variants demands some care. Each subclass must assign its own ordinals and provide its own readResolve method. In essence, each class is responsible for serializing and deserializing its own instances. To make this concrete, here is a version of the Operation class that has been modified to be both extensible and serializable:

```java
// Serializable, extensible typesafe enum
public abstract class Operation implements Serializable {
    private final transient String name;
    protected Operation(String name) { this.name = name; }

    public static Operation PLUS = new Operation("+") {
        protected double eval(double x, double y) { return x+y; }
    };
    public static Operation MINUS = new Operation("-") {
        protected double eval(double x, double y) { return x-y; }
    };
    public static Operation TIMES = new Operation("*") {
        protected double eval(double x, double y) { return x*y; }
    };
    public static Operation DIVIDE = new Operation("/") {
        protected double eval(double x, double y) { return x/y; }
    };

    // Perform arithmetic operation represented by this constant
    protected abstract double eval(double x, double y);

    public String toString() { return this.name; }
    // Prevent subclasses from overriding Object.equals
    public final boolean equals(Object that) {
        return super.equals(that);
    }
    public final int hashCode() {
        return super.hashCode();
    }

    // The 4 declarations below are necessary for serialization
    private static int nextOrdinal = 0;
    private final int ordinal = nextOrdinal++;
    private static final Operation[] VALUES =
        { PLUS, MINUS, TIMES, DIVIDE };
    Object readResolve() throws ObjectStreamException {
        return VALUES[ordinal];  // Canonicalize
    }
}
```

Here is a subclass of Operation that adds logarithm and exponential operations. This subclass could exist outside of the package containing the revised

Operation class. It could be public, and it could itself be extensible. Multiple independently written subclasses can coexist peacefully:

```
// Subclass of extensible, serializable typesafe enum
abstract class ExtendedOperation extends Operation {
    ExtendedOperation(String name) { super(name); }

    public static Operation LOG = new ExtendedOperation("log") {
        protected double eval(double x, double y) {
            return Math.log(y) / Math.log(x);
        }
    };
    public static Operation EXP = new ExtendedOperation("exp") {
        protected double eval(double x, double y) {
            return Math.pow(x, y);
        }
    };

    // The 4 declarations below are necessary for serialization
    private static int nextOrdinal = 0;
    private final int ordinal = nextOrdinal++;
    private static final Operation[] VALUES = { LOG, EXP };
    Object readResolve() throws ObjectStreamException {
        return VALUES[ordinal];  // Canonicalize
    }
}
```

Note that the readResolve methods in the classes just shown are package-private rather than private. This is necessary because the instances of Operation and ExtendedOperation are, in fact, instances of anonymous subclasses, so private readResolve methods would have no effect (Item 57).

The typesafe enum pattern has few disadvantages when compared to the int pattern. Perhaps the only serious disadvantage is that it is more awkward to aggregate typesafe enum constants into sets. With int-based enums, this is traditionally done by choosing enumeration constant values, each of which is a distinct positive power of two, and representing a set as the bitwise OR of the relevant constants:

```
// Bit-flag variant of int enum pattern
public static final int SUIT_CLUBS    = 1;
public static final int SUIT_DIAMONDS = 2;
public static final int SUIT_HEARTS   = 4;
public static final int SUIT_SPADES   = 8;

public static final int SUIT_BLACK = SUIT_CLUBS | SUIT_SPADES;
```

Representing sets of enumerated type constants in this fashion is concise and extremely fast. For sets of typesafe enum constants, you can use a general purpose set implementation from the Collections Framework, but this is neither as concise nor as fast:

```
Set blackSuits = new HashSet();
blackSuits.add(Suit.CLUBS);
blackSuits.add(Suit.SPADES);
```

While sets of typesafe enum constants probably cannot be made as concise or as fast as sets of int enum constants, it is possible to reduce the disparity by providing a special-purpose Set implementation that accepts only elements of one type and represents the set internally as a bit vector. Such a set is best implemented in the same package as its element type to allow access, via a package-private field or method, to a bit value internally associated with each typesafe enum constant. It makes sense to provide public constructors that take short sequences of elements as parameters so that idioms like this are possible:

```
hand.discard(new SuitSet(Suit.CLUBS, Suit.SPADES));
```

A minor disadvantage of typesafe enums, when compared with int enums, is that typesafe enums can't be used in switch statements because they aren't integral constants. Instead, you use an if statement, like this:

```
if (suit == Suit.CLUBS) {
    ...
} else if (suit == Suit.DIAMONDS) {
    ...
} else if (suit == Suit.HEARTS) {
    ...
} else if (suit == Suit.SPADES) {
    ...
} else {
    throw new NullPointerException("Null Suit"); // suit == null
}
```

The if statement may not perform quite as well as the switch statement, but the difference is unlikely to be very significant. Furthermore, the need for multiway branches on typesafe enum constants should be rare because they're amenable to automatic method dispatching by the JVM, as in the Operator example.

Another minor performance disadvantage of typesafe enums is that there is a space and time cost to load enum type classes and construct the constant objects. Except on resource-constrained devices like cell phones and toasters, this problem in unlikely to be noticeable in practice.

In summary, the advantages of typesafe enums over int enums are great, and none of the disadvantages seem compelling unless an enumerated type is to be used primarily as a set element or in a severely resource constrained environment. Thus **the typesafe enum pattern should be what comes to mind when circumstances call for an enumerated type**. APIs that use typesafe enums are far more programmer friendly than those that use int enums. The only reason that typesafe enums are not used more heavily in the Java platform APIs is that the typesafe enum pattern was unknown when many of those APIs were written. Finally, it's worth reiterating that the need for enumerated types of any sort should be relatively rare, as a major use of these types has been made obsolete by subclassing (Item 20).

Item 22: Replace function pointers with classes and interfaces

C supports *function pointers*, which allow a program to store and transmit the ability to invoke a particular function. Function pointers are typically used to allow the caller of a function to specialize its behavior by passing in a pointer to a second function, sometimes referred to as a *callback*. For example, the qsort function in C's standard library takes a pointer to a *comparator* function, which it uses to compare the elements to be sorted. The comparator function takes two parameters, each of which is a pointer to an element. It returns a negative integer if the element pointed to by the first parameter is less than the one pointed to by the second, zero if the two elements are equal, and a positive integer if the element pointed to by the first parameter is greater than the one pointed to by the second. Different sort orders can be obtained by passing in different comparator functions. This is an example of the *Strategy* pattern [Gamma98, p. 315]; the comparator function represents a strategy for sorting elements.

Function pointers were omitted from the Java programming language because object references can be used to provide the same functionality. Invoking a method on an object typically performs some operation on *that object*. However, it is possible to define an object whose methods perform operations on *other objects*, passed explicitly to the methods. An instance of a class that exports exactly one such method is effectively a pointer to that method. Such instances are known as *function objects*. For example, consider the following class:

```
class StringLengthComparator {
    public int compare(String s1, String s2) {
        return s1.length() - s2.length();
    }
}
```

This class exports a single method that takes two strings and returns a negative integer if the first string is shorter than the second, zero if the two strings are of equal length, and a positive integer if the first string is longer. This method is a comparator that orders strings based on their length instead of the more typical lexicographic ordering. A reference to a StringLengthComparator object serves as a "function pointer" to this comparator, allowing it to be invoked on arbitrary pairs of strings. In other words, a StringLengthComparator instance is a *concrete strategy* for string comparison.

As is typical for concrete strategy classes, the StringLengthComparator class is *stateless*: It has no fields, hence all instances of the class are functionally equivalent to one another. Thus it could just as well be a singleton to save on unnecessary object creation costs (Item 4, Item 2):

```
class StringLengthComparator {
    private StringLengthComparator() { }

    public static final StringLengthComparator
        INSTANCE = new StringLengthComparator();

    public int compare(String s1, String s2) {
        return s1.length() - s2.length();
    }
}
```

To pass a StringLengthComparator instance to a method, we need an appropriate type for the parameter. It would do no good to use StringLengthComparator because clients would be unable to pass any other comparison strategy. Instead, we need to define a Comparator interface and modify StringLengthComparator to implement this interface. In other words, we need to define a *strategy interface* to go with the concrete strategy class. Here it is:

```
// Strategy interface
public interface Comparator {
    public int compare(Object o1, Object o2);
}
```

This definition of the Comparator interface happens to come from the java.util package, but there's nothing magic about it; you could just as well have defined it yourself. So that it is applicable to comparators for objects other than strings, its compare method takes parameters of type Object rather than String. Therefore, the StringLengthComparator class shown earlier must be modified slightly to implement Comparator: The Object parameters must be cast to String prior to invoking the length method.

Concrete strategy classes are often declared using anonymous classes (Item 18). The following statement sorts an array of strings according to length:

```
Arrays.sort(stringArray, new Comparator() {
    public int compare(Object o1, Object o2) {
        String s1 = (String)o1;
        String s2 = (String)o2;
        return s1.length() - s2.length();
    }
});
```

Because the strategy interface serves as a type for all of its concrete strategy instances, a concrete strategy class needn't be made public to export a concrete strategy. Instead, a "host class" can export a public static field (or static factory method) whose type is the strategy interface, and the concrete strategy class can be a private nested class of the host. In the example that follows, a static member class is used in preference to an anonymous class to allow the concrete strategy class to implement a second interface, Serializable:

```
// Exporting a concrete strategy
class Host {
    ...  // Bulk of class omitted

    private static class StrLenCmp
            implements Comparator, Serializable {
        public int compare(Object o1, Object o2) {
            String s1 = (String)o1;
            String s2 = (String)o2;
            return s1.length() - s2.length();
        }
    }

    // Returned comparator is serializable
    public static final Comparator
        STRING_LENGTH_COMPARATOR = new StrLenCmp();
}
```

The String class uses this pattern to export a case-independent string comparator via its CASE_INSENSITIVE_ORDER field.

To summarize, the primary use of C's function pointers is to implement the Strategy pattern. To implement this pattern in the Java programming language, declare an interface to represent the strategy and a class that implements this interface for each concrete strategy. When a concrete strategy is used only once, its class is typically declared and instantiated using an anonymous class. When a concrete strategy is exported for repeated use, its class is generally a private static member class, and it is exported via a public static final field whose type is the strategy interface.

CHAPTER 6

Methods

THIS chapter discusses several aspects of method design: how to treat parameters and return values, how to design method signatures, and how to document methods. Much of the material in this chapter applies to constructors as well as to methods. Like Chapter 5, this chapter focuses on usability, robustness, and flexibility.

Item 23: Check parameters for validity

Most methods and constructors have some restrictions on what values may be passed into their parameters. For example, it is not uncommon that index values must be nonnegative and object references must be non-null. You should clearly document all such restrictions and enforce them with checks at the beginning of the method body. This is a special case of the general principle, and you should attempt to detect errors as soon as possible after they occur. Failing to do so makes it less likely that an error will be detected and makes it harder to determine the source of an error once it has been detected.

If an invalid parameter value is passed to a method and the method checks its parameters before execution, it will fail quickly and cleanly with an appropriate exception. If the method fails to check its parameters, several things could happen. The method could fail with a confusing exception in the midst of processing. Worse, the method could return normally but silently compute the wrong result. Worst of all, the method could return normally but leave some object in a compromised state, causing an error at some unrelated point in the code at some undetermined time in the future.

For public methods, use the Javadoc @throws tag to document the exception that will be thrown if a restriction on parameter values is violated (Item 44). Typically the exception will be `IllegalArgumentException`, `IndexOutOfBounds-Exception`, or `NullPointerException` (Item 42). Once you've documented the restrictions on a method's parameters and you've documented the exceptions that will be thrown if these restrictions are violated, it is a simple matter to enforce the restrictions. Here's a typical example:

```
/**
 * Returns a BigInteger whose value is (this mod m).  This method
 * differs from the remainder method in that it always returns a
 * nonnegative BigInteger.
 *
 * @param  m the modulus, which must be positive.
 * @return this mod m.
 * @throws ArithmeticException if m <= 0.
 */
public BigInteger mod(BigInteger m) {
    if (m.signum() <= 0)
        throw new ArithmeticException("Modulus not positive");

    ... // Do the computation
}
```

For an unexported method, you as the package author control the circumstances under which the method is called, so you can and should ensure that only valid parameter values are ever passed in. Therefore nonpublic methods should generally check their parameters using *assertions* rather than normal checks. If you are using a release of the platform that supports assertions (1.4 or later), you should use the assert construct; otherwise you should use a makeshift assertion mechanism.

It is particularly important to check the validity of parameters that are not used by a method but are stored away for later use. For example, consider the static factory method on page 86, which takes an int array and returns a List view of the array. If a client of this method were to pass in null, the method would throw a NullPointerException because the method contains an explicit check. If the check had been omitted, the method would return a reference to a newly created List instance that would throw a NullPointerException as soon as a client attempted to use it. By that time, unfortunately, the origin of the List instance might be very difficult to determine, which could greatly complicate the task of debugging.

Constructors represent a special case of the principle that you should check the validity of parameters that are to be stored away for later use. It is very important to check the validity of parameters to constructors to prevent the construction of an object that violates class invariants.

There are exceptions to the rule that you should check a method's parameters before performing its computation. An important exception is the case in which the validity check would be expensive or impractical *and* the validity check is performed implicitly in the process of doing the computation. For example, consider a method that sorts a list of objects, such as `Collections.sort(List)`. All of the objects in the list must be mutually comparable. In the process of sorting the list, every object in the list will be compared to some other object in the list. If the objects aren't mutually comparable, one of these comparisons will throw a `Class-CastException`, which is exactly what the sort method should do. Therefore there would be little point in checking ahead of time that the elements in the list were mutually comparable. Note, however, that indiscriminate application of this technique can result in a loss of failure atomicity (Item 46).

Occasionally, a computation implicitly performs the required validity check on some parameter but throws the wrong exception if the check fails. That is to say, the exception that the computation would naturally throw as the result of an invalid parameter value does not match the exception that you have documented the method to throw. Under these circumstances, you should use the *exception translation* idiom described in Item 43 to translate the natural exception into the correct one.

Do not infer from this item that arbitrary restrictions on parameters are a good thing. On the contrary, you should design methods to be as general as it is practical to make them. The fewer restrictions that you place on parameters, the better, assuming the method can do something reasonable with all of the parameter values that it accepts. Often, however, some restrictions are intrinsic to the abstraction being implemented.

To summarize, each time you write a method or constructor, you should think about what restrictions exist on its parameters. You should document these restrictions and enforce them with explicit checks at the beginning of the method body. It is important to get into the habit of doing this; the modest work that it entails will be paid back with interest the first time a validity check fails.

Item 24: Make defensive copies when needed

One thing that makes the Java programming language such a pleasure to use is that it is a *safe language*. This means that in the absence of native methods it is immune to buffer overruns, array overruns, wild pointers, and other memory corruption errors that plague unsafe languages such as C and C++. In a safe language it is possible to write classes and to know with certainty that their invariants will remain true, no matter what happens in any other part of the system. This is not possible in languages that treat all of memory as one giant array.

Even in a safe language, you aren't insulated from other classes without some effort on your part. **You must program defensively with the assumption that clients of your class will do their best to destroy its invariants.** This may actually be true if someone tries to break the security of your system, but more likely your class will have to cope with unexpected behavior resulting from honest mistakes on the part of the programmer using your API. Either way, it is worth taking the time to write classes that are robust in the face of ill-behaved clients.

While it is impossible for another class to modify an object's internal state without some assistance from the object, it is surprisingly easy to provide such assistance without meaning to do so. For example, consider the following class, which purports to represent an immutable time period:

```java
// Broken "immutable" time period class
public final class Period {
    private final Date start;
    private final Date end;

    /**
     * @param  start the beginning of the period.
     * @param  end the end of the period; must not precede start.
     * @throws IllegalArgumentException if start is after end.
     * @throws NullPointerException if start or end is null.
     */
    public Period(Date start, Date end) {
        if (start.compareTo(end) > 0)
            throw new IllegalArgumentException(start + " after "
                                                     + end);
        this.start = start;
        this.end   = end;
    }

    public Date start() {
        return start;
    }
```

```
    public Date end() {
        return end;
    }

    ...  // Remainder omitted
}
```

At first glance, this class may appear to be immutable and to enforce the invariant that the start of a period does not follow its end. It is, however, easy to violate this invariant by exploiting the fact that Date is mutable:

```
// Attack the internals of a Period instance
Date start = new Date();
Date end = new Date();
Period p = new Period(start, end);
end.setYear(78);  // Modifies internals of p!
```

To protect the internals of a Period instance from this sort of attack, **it is essential to make a *defensive copy* of each mutable parameter to the constructor** and to use the copies as components of the Period instance in place of the originals:

```
// Repaired constructor - makes defensive copies of parameters
public Period(Date start, Date end) {
    this.start = new Date(start.getTime());
    this.end   = new Date(end.getTime());

    if (this.start.compareTo(this.end) > 0)
        throw new IllegalArgumentException(start +" after "+ end);
}
```

With the new constructor in place, the previous attack will have no effect on the Period instance. Note that **defensive copies are made *before* checking the validity of the parameters (Item 23), and the validity check is performed on the copies rather than on the originals.** While this may seem unnatural, it is necessary. It protects the class against changes to the parameters from another thread during the "window of vulnerability" between the time the parameters are checked and the time they are copied.

Note also that we did not use Date's clone method to make the defensive copies. Because Date is nonfinal, the clone method is not guaranteed to return an object whose class is java.util.Date; it could return an instance of an untrusted subclass specifically designed for malicious mischief. Such a subclass could, for example, record a reference to each instance in a private static list at the time of its creation and allow the attacker access to this list. This would give the attacker free reign over all instances. To prevent this sort of attack, **do not use the `clone` method to make a defensive copy of a parameter whose type is subclassable by untrusted parties.**

While the replacement constructor successfully defends against the previous attack, it is still possible to mutate a `Period` instance because its accessors offer access to its mutable internals:

```
// Second attack on the internals of a Period instance
Date start = new Date();
Date end = new Date();
Period p = new Period(start, end);
p.end().setYear(78);   // Modifies internals of p!
```

To defend against the second attack, merely modify the accessors to **return defensive copies of mutable internal fields**:

```
// Repaired accessors - make defensive copies of internal fields
public Date start() {
    return (Date) start.clone();
}

public Date end() {
    return (Date) end.clone();
}
```

With the new constructor and the new accessors in place, `Period` is truly immutable. No matter how malicious or incompetent a programmer, there is simply no way he can violate the invariant that the start of a period does not follow its end. This is true because there is no way for any class other than `Period` itself to gain access to either of the mutable fields in a `Period` instance. These fields are truly encapsulated within the object.

Note that the new accessors, unlike the new constructor, do use the `clone` method to make defensive copies. This is acceptable (although not required), as we know with certainty that the class of `Period`'s internal `Date` objects is `java.util.Date` rather than some potentially untrusted subclass.

Defensive copying of parameters is not just for immutable classes. Anytime you write a method or constructor that enters a client-provided object into an internal data structure, think about whether the client-provided object is potentially mutable. If it is, think about whether your class could tolerate a change in the object after it was entered into the data structure. If the answer is no, you must defensively copy the object and enter the copy into the data structure in place of the original. For example, if you are considering using a client-provided object reference as an element in an internal Set instance or as a key in an internal Map instance, you should be aware that the invariants of the set or map would be destroyed if the object were modified after it were inserted.

The same is true for defensive copying of internal components prior to returning them to clients. Whether or not your class is immutable, you should think twice before returning a reference to an internal component that is mutable. Chances are you should be returning a defensive copy. Also, it is critical to remember that nonzero-length arrays are always mutable. Therefore you should always make a defensive copy of an internal array before returning it to a client. Alternatively, you could return an immutable view of the array to the user. Both of these techniques are shown in Item 12.

Arguably, the real lesson in all of this is that you should, where possible, use immutable objects as components of your objects so that you that don't have to worry about defensive copying (Item 13). In the case of our Period example, it is worth pointing out that experienced programmers often use the primitive long returned by Date.getTime() as an internal time representation rather than using a Date object reference. They do this primarily because Date is mutable.

It is not always appropriate to make a defensive copy of a mutable parameter before integrating it into an object. There are some methods and constructors whose invocation indicates an explicit *handoff* of the object referenced by a parameter. When invoking such a method, the client promises that it will no longer modify the object directly. A method or constructor that expects to take control of a client-provided mutable object must make this clear in its documentation.

Classes containing methods or constructors whose invocation indicates a transfer of control cannot defend themselves against malicious clients. Such classes are acceptable only when there is mutual trust between the class and its client or when damage to the class's invariants would harm no one but the client. An example of the latter situation is the wrapper class pattern (Item 14). Depending on the nature of the wrapper class, the client could destroy the class's invariants by directly accessing an object after it has been wrapped, but this typically would harm only the client.

Item 25: Design method signatures carefully

This item is a grab bag of API design hints that don't quite deserve items of their own. Taken together, they'll help make your API easier to learn and use and less prone to errors.

Choose method names carefully. Names should always obey the standard naming conventions (Item 38). Your primary goal should be to choose names that are understandable and consistent with other names in the same package. Your secondary goal should be to choose names consistent with the broader consensus, where it exists. When in doubt, look to the Java library APIs for guidance. While there are plenty of inconsistencies—inevitable, given the size and scope of the libraries—there is also consensus. An invaluable resource is Patrick Chan's *The Java Developers Almanac* [Chan00], which contains the method declarations for every single method in the Java platform libraries, indexed alphabetically. If, for example, you were wondering whether to name a method `remove` or `delete`, a quick look at the index of this book would tell you that `remove` was the obvious choice. There are hundreds of methods whose names begin with `remove` and a small handful whose names begin with `delete`.

Don't go overboard in providing convenience methods. Every method should "pull its weight." Too many methods make a class difficult to learn, use, document, test, and maintain. This is doubly true for interfaces, where too many methods complicate life for implementors as well as for users. For each action supported by your type, provide a fully functional method. Consider providing a "shorthand" for an operation only when it will be used frequently. **When in doubt, leave it out.**

Avoid long parameter lists. As a rule, three parameters should be viewed as a practical maximum, and fewer is better. Most programmers can't remember longer parameter lists. If many of your methods exceed this limit, your API won't be usable without constant reference to its documentation. **Long sequences of identically typed parameters are especially harmful.** Not only won't the users of your API be able to remember the order of the parameters, but when they transpose parameters by mistake, their programs will still compile and run. They just won't do what their authors intended.

There are two techniques for shortening overly long parameter lists. One is to break the method up into multiple methods, each of which requires only a subset of the parameters. If done carelessly, this can lead to too many methods, but it can also help *reduce* the method count by increasing orthogonality. For example, consider the `java.util.List` interface. It does not provide methods to find the first or last index of an element in a sublist, both of which would require three parameters. Instead it provides the `subList` method, which takes two parameters and returns a *view* of a sublist. This method can be combined with the `indexOf` or `lastIndexOf` methods, each of which has a single parameter, to yield the desired functionality. Moreover, the `subList` method can be combined with any other method that operates on a `List` instance to perform arbitrary computations on sublists. The resulting API has a very high power-to-weight ratio.

A second technique for shortening overly long parameter lists is to create *helper classes* to hold aggregates of parameters. Typically these helper classes are static member classes (Item 18). This technique is recommended if a frequently occurring sequence of parameters is seen to represent some distinct entity. For example suppose you are writing a class representing a card game, and you find yourself constantly passing a sequence of two parameters representing a card's rank and its suit. Your API, as well as the internals of your class, would probably be improved if you added a helper class to represent a card and replaced every occurrence of the parameter sequence with a single parameter of the helper class.

For parameter types, favor interfaces over classes. Whenever an appropriate interface to define a parameter exists, use it in favor of a class that implements the interface. For example, there is no reason ever to write a method that takes `Hashtable` on input—use `Map` instead. This lets you pass in a `Hashtable`, a `HashMap`, a `TreeMap`, a submap of a `TreeMap`, or any `Map` implementation yet to be written. By using a class instead of an interface, you restrict your client to a particular implementation and force an unnecessary and potentially expensive copy operation if the input data happen to exist in some other form.

Use *function objects* (Item 22) judiciously. There are some languages, notably Smalltalk and the various Lisp dialects, that encourage a style of programming rich in objects that represent functions to be applied to other objects. Programmers with experience in these languages may be tempted to adopt a similar style in the Java programming language, but it isn't a terribly good fit. The easiest way to create a function object is with an anonymous class (Item 18), but even that involves some syntactic clutter and has limitations in power and performance when compared to inline control constructs. Furthermore, the style of programming wherein you are constantly creating function objects and passing them from method to method is out of the mainstream, so other programmers will have a difficult time understanding your code if you adopt this style. This is not meant to imply that function objects don't have legitimate uses; they are essential to many powerful design patterns, such as *Strategy* [Gamma98, p. 315] and *Visitor* [Gamma98, p. 331]. Rather, function objects should be used only with good reason.

Item 26: Use overloading judiciously

Here is a well-intentioned attempt to classify collections according to whether they are sets, lists, or some other kind of collections:

```
// Broken - incorrect use of overloading!
public class CollectionClassifier {
    public static String classify(Set s) {
        return "Set";
    }

    public static String classify(List l) {
        return "List";
    }

    public static String classify(Collection c) {
        return "Unknown Collection";
    }

    public static void main(String[] args) {
        Collection[] tests = new Collection[] {
            new HashSet(),          // A Set
            new ArrayList(),        // A List
            new HashMap().values()  // Neither Set nor List
        };

        for (int i = 0; i < tests.length; i++)
            System.out.println(classify(tests[i]));
    }
}
```

You might expect this program to print "Set," followed by "List" and "Unknown Collection," but it doesn't; it prints out "Unknown Collection" three times. Why does this happen? Because the classify method is *overloaded*, and **the choice of which overloading to invoke is made at compile time**. For all three iterations of the loop, the compile-time type of the parameter is the same: Collection. The run-time type is different in each iteration, but this does not affect the choice of overloading. Because the compile-time type of the parameter is Collection, the only applicable overloading is the third one, classify(Collection), and this overloading is invoked in each iteration of the loop.

The behavior of this program is counterintuitive because **selection among overloaded methods is static, while selection among overridden methods is dynamic**. The correct version of an *overridden* method is chosen at run time, based on the run-time type of the object on which the method is invoked. As a reminder, a method is overridden when a subclass contains a method declaration with exactly the same signature as a method declaration in an ancestor. If an instance method is overridden in a subclass and this method is invoked on an instance of the subclass, the subclass's *overriding method* executes, regardless of the compile-time type of the subclass instance. To make this concrete, consider the following little program:

```
class A {
    String name() { return "A"; }
}

class B extends A {
    String name() { return "B"; }
}

class C extends A {
    String name() { return "C"; }
}

public class Overriding {
    public static void main(String[] args) {
        A[] tests = new A[] { new A(), new B(), new C() };

        for (int i = 0; i < tests.length; i++)
            System.out.print(tests[i].name());
    }
}
```

The name method is declared in class A and overridden in classes B and C. As you would expect, this program prints out "ABC" even though the compile-time type of the instance is A in each iteration of the loop. The compile-time type of an object has no effect on which method is executed when an overridden method is invoked; the "most specific" overriding method always gets executed. Compare this to overloading, where the run-time type of an object has no effect on which overloading is executed; the selection is made at compile time, based entirely on the compile-time types of the parameters.

In the CollectionClassifier example, the intent of the program was to discern the type of the parameter by dispatching automatically to the appropriate method overloading based on the run-time type of the parameter, just as the name method did in the "ABC" example. Method overloading simply does not provide this functionality. The way to fix the program is to replace all three overloadings of classify with a single method that does an explicit instanceof test:

```
public static String classify(Collection c) {
    return (c instanceof Set ? "Set" :
            (c instanceof List ? "List" : "Unknown Collection"));
}
```

Because overriding is the norm and overloading is the exception, overriding sets people's expectations for the behavior of method invocation. As demonstrated by the CollectionClassifier example, overloading can easily confound these expectations. It is bad practice to write code whose behavior would not be obvious to the average programmer upon inspection. This is especially true for APIs. If the typical user of an API does not know which of several method overloadings will get invoked for a given set of parameters, use of the API is likely to result in errors. These errors will likely manifest themselves as erratic behavior at run time, and many programmers will be unable to diagnose them. Therefore you should **avoid confusing uses of overloading**.

Exactly what constitutes a confusing use of overloading is open to some debate. **A safe, conservative policy is never to export two overloadings with the same number of parameters.** If you adhere to this restriction, programmers will never be in doubt as to which overloading applies to any set of parameters. This restriction is not terribly onerous because you can always give methods different names instead of overloading.

For example, consider the class ObjectOutputStream. It has a variant of its write method for every primitive type and for several reference types. Rather than overloading the write method, these variants have signatures like writeBoolean(boolean), writeInt(int), and writeLong(long). An added benefit of this naming pattern, when compared to overloading, is that it is possible to provide read methods with corresponding names, for example, readBoolean(), readInt(), and readLong(). The ObjectInputStream class does, in fact, provide read methods with these names.

For constructors, you don't have the option of using different names; multiple constructors for a class are always overloaded. You do, in some cases, have the option of exporting static factories instead of constructors (Item 1), but that isn't always practical. On the bright side, with constructors you don't have to worry about interactions between overloading and overriding, as constructors can't be overridden. Because you'll probably have occasion to export multiple constructors with the same number of parameters, it pays to know when it is safe to do so.

Exporting multiple overloadings with the same number of parameters is unlikely to confuse programmers if it is always clear which overloading will apply to any given set of actual parameters. This is the case when at least one corresponding formal parameter in each pair of overloadings has a "radically different" type in the two overloadings. Two types are radically different if it is clearly impossible to cast an instance of either type to the other. Under these circumstances, which overloading applies to a given set of actual parameters is fully determined by the run-time types of the parameters and cannot be affected by their compile-time types, so the major source of confusion evaporates.

For example, `ArrayList` has one constructor that takes an `int` and a second constructor that takes a `Collection`. It is hard to imagine any confusion over which of these two constructors will be invoked under any circumstances because primitive types and reference types are radically different. Similarly, `BigInteger` has one constructor that takes a `byte` array and another that takes a `String`; this causes no confusion. Array types and classes other than `Object` are radically different. Also, array types and interfaces other than `Serializable` and `Cloneable` are radically different. Finally, `Throwable`, as of release 1.4, has one constructor that takes a `String` and another takes a `Throwable`. The classes `String` and `Throwable` are *unrelated*, which is to say that neither class is a descendant of the other. It is impossible for any object to be an instance of two unrelated classes, so unrelated classes are radically different.

There are a few additional examples of pairs of types that can't be converted in either direction [JLS, 5.1.7], but once you go beyond these simple cases, it can become very difficult for the average programmer to discern which, if any, overloading applies to a set of actual parameters. The specification that determines which overloading is selected is complex, and few programmers understand all of its subtleties [JLS, 15.12.1-3].

Occasionally you may be forced to violate the above guidelines when retrofitting existing classes to implement new interfaces. For example, many of the value types in the Java platform libraries had "self-typed" `compareTo` methods prior to the introduction of the `Comparable` interface. Here is the declaration for `String`'s original self-typed `compareTo` method:

```
public int compareTo(String s);
```

With the introduction of the `Comparable` interface, all of the these classes were retrofitted to implement this interface, which involved adding a more general `compareTo` method with this declaration:

```
public int compareTo(Object o);
```

While the resulting overloading is clearly a violation of the above guidelines, it causes no harm as long as both overloaded methods always do exactly the same thing when they are invoked on the same parameters. The programmer may not know which overloading will be invoked, but it is of no consequence as long as both methods return the same result. The standard way to ensure this behavior is to have the more general overloading forward to the more specific:

```
public int compareTo(Object o) {
    return compareTo((String) o);
}
```

A similar idiom is sometimes used for equals methods:

```
public boolean equals(Object o) {
    return o instanceof String && equals((String) o);
}
```

This idiom is harmless and may result in slightly improved performance if the compile-time type of the parameter matches the parameter of the more specific overloading. That said, it probably isn't worth doing as a matter of course (Item 37).

While the Java platform libraries largely adhere to the advice in this item, there are a number of places where it is violated. For example, the `String` class exports two overloaded static factory methods, `valueOf(char[])` and `valueOf(Object)`, that do completely different things when passed the same object reference. There is no real justification for this, and it should be regarded as an anomaly with the potential for real confusion.

To summarize, just because you can overload methods doesn't mean you should. You should generally refrain from overloading methods with multiple signatures that have the same number of parameters. In some cases, especially where constructors are involved, it may be impossible to follow this advice. In that case, you should at least avoid situations where the same set of parameters can be passed to different overloadings by the addition of casts. If such a situation cannot be avoided, for example because you are retrofitting an existing class to implement a new interface, you should ensure that all overloadings behave identically when passed the same parameters. If you fail to do this, programmers will not be able to make effective use of the overloaded method or constructor, and they won't understand why it doesn't work.

Item 27: Return zero-length arrays, not nulls

It is not uncommon to see methods that look something like this:

```
private List cheesesInStock = ...;

/**
 * @return an array containing all of the cheeses in the shop,
 *         or null if no cheeses are available for purchase.
 */
public Cheese[] getCheeses() {
    if (cheesesInStock.size() == 0)
        return null;
    ...
}
```

There is no reason to make a special case for the situation where no cheeses are available for purchase. Doing so requires extra code in the client to handle the null return value, for example:

```
Cheese[] cheeses = shop.getCheeses();
if (cheeses != null &&
    Arrays.asList(shop.getCheeses()).contains(Cheese.STILTON))
    System.out.println("Jolly good, just the thing.");
```

instead of:

```
if (Arrays.asList(shop.getCheeses()).contains(Cheese.STILTON))
    System.out.println("Jolly good, just the thing.");
```

This sort of circumlocution is required in nearly every use of a method that returns null in place of a zero length array. It is error prone, as the programmer writing the client might forget to write the special-case code to handle a null return. Such an error may go unnoticed for years, as such methods usually return one or more objects. Less significant, but still worthy of note, returning null in place of a zero length array also complicates the array-returning method itself.

It is sometimes argued that a null return value is preferable to a zero-length array because it avoids the expense of allocating the array. This argument fails on two counts. First, it is inadvisable to worry about performance at this level unless profiling has shown that the method in question is a real contributor to performance problems (Item 37). Second, it is possible to return the same zero-length array from every invocation that returns no items because zero-length arrays are immutable and immutable objects may be shared freely (Item 13). In fact, this is exactly what happens when you use the standard idiom for dumping items from a collection into a typed array:

```
private List cheesesInStock = ...;

private final static Cheese[] NULL_CHEESE_ARRAY = new Cheese[0];

/**
 * @return an array containing all of the cheeses in the shop.
 */
public Cheese[] getCheeses() {
  return (Cheese[]) cheesesInStock.toArray(NULL_CHEESE_ARRAY);
}
```

In this idiom, a zero-length array constant is passed to the toArray method to indicate the desired return type. Normally the toArray method allocates the returned array, but if the collection is empty, it fits in the input array, and the specification for Collection.toArray(Object[]) guarantees that the input array will be returned if it is large enough to hold the collection. Therefore the idiom never allocates a zero-length array but instead reuses the "type-specifier constant."

In summary, **there is no reason ever to return null from an array-valued method instead of returning a zero-length array.** This idiom is likely a holdover from the C programming language, in which array lengths are returned separately from actual arrays. In C, there is no advantage to allocating an array if zero is returned as the length.

Item 28: Write doc comments for all exposed API elements

If an API is to be usable, it must be documented. Traditionally API documentation was generated manually, and keeping documentation in sync with code was a big chore. The Java programming environment eases this task with a utility called *Javadoc*. This utility generates API documentation automatically from source code in conjunction with specially formatted *documentation comments*, more commonly known as *doc comments*. The Javadoc utility provides an easy and effective way to document your APIs, and its use is widespread.

If you are not already familiar with the doc comment conventions, you should learn them. While these conventions are not part of the Java programming language, they constitute a de facto API that every programmer should know. The conventions are defined *The Javadoc Tool Home Page* [Javadoc-b].

To document your API properly, you must precede every exported class, interface, constructor, method, and field declaration with a doc comment, subject to one exception discussed at the end of this item. In the absence of a doc comment, the best that Javadoc can do is to reproduce the declaration as the sole documentation for the affected API element. It is frustrating and error-prone to use an API with missing documentation comments. To write maintainable code, you should also write doc comments for unexported classes, interfaces, constructors, methods, and fields.

The doc comment for a method should describe succinctly the contract between the method and its client. With the exception of methods in classes designed for inheritance (Item 15), the contract should say *what* the method does rather than *how* it does its job. The doc comment should enumerate all of the method's *preconditions*, which are the things that have to be true in order for a client to invoke it, and its *postconditions*, which are the things that will be true after the invocation has completed successfully. Typically, preconditions are described implicitly by the @throws tags for unchecked exceptions; each unchecked exception corresponds to a precondition violation. Also, preconditions can be specified along with the affected parameters in their @param tags.

In addition to preconditions and postconditions, methods should document any *side effects*. A side effect is an observable change in the state of the system that is not obviously required to achieve the postcondition. For example, if a method starts a background thread, the documentation should make note of it. Finally, documentation comments should describe the *thread safety* of a class, as discussed in Item 52.

To describe its contract fully, the doc comment for a method should have a `@param` tag for every parameter, a `@return` tag unless the method has a void return type, and a `@throws` tag for every exception thrown by the method, whether checked or unchecked (Item 44). By convention the text following a `@param` tag or `@return` tag should be a noun phrase describing the value represented by the parameter or return value. The text following a `@throws` tag should consist of the word "if," followed by a noun phrase describing the conditions under which the exception is thrown. Occasionally, arithmetic expressions are used in place of noun phrases. All of these conventions are illustrated in the following short doc comment, which comes from the `List` interface:

```
/**
 * Returns the element at the specified position in this list.
 *
 * @param  index index of element to return; must be
 *         nonnegative and less than the size of this list.
 * @return the element at the specified position in this list.
 * @throws IndexOutOfBoundsException if the index is out of range
 *         (<tt>index &lt; 0 || index &gt;= this.size()</tt>).
 */
Object get(int index);
```

Notice the use of HTML metacharacters and tags in this doc comment. The Javadoc utility translates doc comments into HTML, and arbitrary HTML elements contained in doc comments end up in the resulting HTML document. Occasionally programmers go so far as to embed HTML tables in their doc comments, although this is uncommon. The most commonly used tags are `<p>` to separate paragraphs; `<code>` and `<tt>`, which are used for code fragments; and `<pre>`, which is used for longer code fragments.

The `<code>` and `<tt>` tags are largely equivalent. The `<code>` tag is more commonly used and, according to the HTML 4.01 specification, is generally preferable because `<tt>` is a *font style element*. (The use of font style elements is discouraged in favor of style sheets [HTML401].) That said, some programmers prefer `<tt>` because it is shorter and less intrusive.

Don't forget that escape sequences are required to generate HTML metacharacters, such as the less than sign (<), the greater than sign (>), and the ampersand (&). To generate a less than sign, use the escape sequence "`&lt;`". To generate a greater than sign, use the escape sequence "`&gt;`". To generate an ampersand, use the escape sequence "`&amp;`". The use of escape sequences is demonstrated in the `@throws` tag of the above doc comment.

Finally, notice the use of word "this" in the doc comment. By convention, the word "this" always refers to the object on which the method is invoked when it is used in the doc comment for an instance method.

The first sentence of each doc comment becomes the *summary description* of the element to which the comment pertains. The summary description must stand on its own to describe the functionality of the entity it summarizes. To avoid confusion, no two members or constructors in a class or interface should have the same summary description. Pay particular attention to overloadings, for which it is often natural to use the same first sentence in a prose description.

Be careful not to include a period within the first sentence of a doc comment. If you do, it will prematurely terminate the summary description. For example, a documentation comment that began with "A college degree, such as B.S., M.S., or Ph.D." would result in a summary description of "A college degree, such as B." The best way avoid this problem is to avoid the use of abbreviations and decimal fractions in summary descriptions. It is, however, possible to include a period in a summary description by replacing the period with its *numeric encoding,* ".". While this works, it doesn't make for pretty source code:

```
/**
 * A college degree, such as B&#46;S&#46;, M&#46;S&#46; or
 * Ph&#46;D.
 */
public class Degree { ... }
```

It is somewhat misleading to say that the summary description is the first *sentence* in a doc comment. Convention dictates that it should seldom be a complete sentence. For methods and constructors, the summary description should be a verb phrase describing the action performed by the method. For example,

- `ArrayList(int initialCapacity)`—Constructs an empty list with the specified initial capacity.

- `Collection.size()`—Returns the number of elements in this collection.

For classes, interfaces, and fields, the summary description should be a noun phrase describing the thing represented by an instance of the class or interface or by the field itself. For example,

- `TimerTask`—A task that can be scheduled for one-time or repeated execution by a `Timer`.

- `Math.PI`—The `double` value that is closer than any other to pi, the ratio of the circumference of a circle to its diameter.

The doc comment conventions described in this item are sufficient to get by, but there are many others. There are several style guides for writing doc comments [Javadoc-a, Vermeulen00]. Also, there are utilities to check adherence to these rules [Doclint].

Since release 1.2.2, Javadoc has had the ability to "automatically reuse" or "inherit" method comments. If a method does not have a doc comment, Javadoc searches for the most specific applicable doc comment, giving preference to interfaces over superclasses. The details of the search algorithm can be found in *The Javadoc Manual.*

This means that classes can now reuse the doc comments from interfaces they implement, rather than copying these comments. This facility has the potential to reduce or eliminate the burden of maintaining multiple sets of nearly identical doc comments, but it does have a limitation. Doc-comment inheritance is all-or-nothing: the inheriting method cannot modify the inherited doc comment in any way. It is not uncommon for a method to specialize the contract inherited from an interface, in which case the method really does need its own doc comment.

A simple way to reduce the likelihood of errors in documentation comments is to run the HTML files generated by Javadoc through an *HTML validity checker.* This will detect many incorrect uses of HTML tags, as well as HTML metacharacters that should have been escaped. Several HTML validity checkers are available for download, such as *weblint* [Weblint].

One caveat should be added concerning documentation comments. While it is necessary to provide documentation comments for all exported API elements, it is not always sufficient. For complex APIs consisting of multiple interrelated classes, it is often necessary to supplement the documentation comments with an external document describing the overall architecture of the API. If such a document exists, the relevant class or package documentation comments should include a link to it.

To summarize, documentation comments are the best, most effective way to document your API. Their use should be considered mandatory for all exported API elements. Adopt a consistent style adhering to standard conventions. Remember that arbitrary HTML is permissible within documentation comments and that HTML metacharacters must be escaped.

CHAPTER 7

General Programming

THIS chapter is largely devoted to the nuts and bolts of the language. It discusses the treatment of local variables, the use of libraries, the use of various data types, and the use of two extralinguistic facilities: *reflection* and *native methods*. Finally, it discusses optimization and naming conventions.

Item 29: Minimize the scope of local variables

This item is similar in nature to Item 12, "Minimize the accessibility of classes and members." By minimizing the scope of local variables, you increase the readability and maintainability of your code and reduce the likelihood of error.

The C programming language mandates that local variables must be declared at the head of a block, and programmers continue to do this out of habit; it's a habit worth breaking. As a reminder, the Java programming language lets you declare variables anywhere a statement is legal.

The most powerful technique for minimizing the scope of a local variable is to declare it where it is first used. If a variable is declared before it is used, it is just clutter—one more thing to distract the reader who is trying to figure out what the program does. By the time the variable is used, the reader might not remember the variable's type or initial value. If the program evolves and the variable is no longer used, it is easy to forget to remove the declaration if it's far removed from the point of first use.

Not only can declaring a local variable prematurely cause its scope to extend too early, but also too late. The scope of a local variable extends from the point of its declaration to the end of the enclosing block. If a variable is declared outside of the block in which it is used, it remains visible after the program exits that block. If a variable is used accidentally before or after its region of intended use, the consequences can be disastrous.

Nearly every local variable declaration should contain an initializer. If you don't yet have enough information to initialize a variable sensibly, you should postpone the declaration until you do. One exception to this rule concerns try-catch statements. If a variable is initialized by a method that throws a checked exception, it must be initialized inside a try block. If the value must be used outside of the try block, then it must be declared before the try block, where it cannot yet be "sensibly initialized." For example, see page 159.

Loops present a special opportunity to minimize the scope of variables. The for loop allows you to declare *loop variables*, limiting their scope to the exact region where they're needed. (This region consists of the body of the loop as well as the initialization, test, and update preceding the body.) Therefore **prefer for loops to while loops**, assuming the contents of the loop variable(s) aren't needed after the loop terminates.

For example, here is the preferred idiom for iterating over a collection:

```
for (Iterator i = c.iterator(); i.hasNext(); ) {
    doSomething(i.next());
}
```

To see why this for loop is preferable to the more obvious while loop, consider the following code fragment, which contains two while loops and one bug:

```
Iterator i = c.iterator();
while (i.hasNext()) {
    doSomething(i.next());
}

    ...

Iterator i2 = c2.iterator();
while (i.hasNext()) {                    // BUG!
    doSomethingElse(i2.next());
}
```

The second loop contains a cut-and-paste error: It initializes a new loop variable, i2, but uses the old one, i, which unfortunately is still in scope. The resulting code compiles without error and runs without throwing an exception, but it does the wrong thing. Instead of iterating over c2, the second loop terminates immediately, giving the false impression that c2 is empty. Because the program errs silently, the error can remain undetected for a long time.

If the analogous cut-and-paste error were made in conjunction with the preferred for loop idiom, the resulting code wouldn't even compile. The loop variable from the first loop would not be in scope at the point where the second loop occurred:

```
for (Iterator i = c.iterator(); i.hasNext(); ) {
    doSomething(i.next());
}
    ...

// Compile-time error - the symbol i cannot be resolved
for (Iterator i2 = c2.iterator(); i.hasNext(); ) {
    doSomething(i2.next());
}
```

Moreover, if you use the for loop idiom, it's much less likely that you'll make the cut-and-paste error, as there's no incentive to use a different variable name in the two loops. The loops are completely independent, so there's no harm in reusing the loop variable name. In fact, it's stylish to do so.

The for loop idiom has one other advantage over the while loop idiom, albeit a minor one. The for loop idiom is one line shorter, which helps the containing method fit in a fixed-size editor window, enhancing readability.

Here is another loop idiom for iterating over a list that minimizes the scope of local variables:

```
// High-performance idiom for iterating over random access lists
for (int i = 0, n = list.size(); i < n; i++) {
    doSomething(list.get(i));
}
```

This idiom is useful for random access List implementations such as Array-List and Vector because it is likely to run faster than the "preferred idiom" above for such lists. The important thing to notice about this idiom is that it has *two* loop variables, i and n, both of which have exactly the right scope. The use of the second variable is essential to the performance of the idiom. Without it, the loop would have to call the size method once per iteration, which would negate the performance advantage of the idiom. Using this idiom is acceptable when you're sure the list really does provide random access; otherwise, it displays quadratic performance.

Similar idioms exist for other looping tasks, for example,

```
for (int i = 0, n = expensiveComputation(); i < n; i++) {
    doSomething(i);
}
```

Again, this idiom uses two loop variables, and the second variable, n, is used to avoid the cost of performing redundant computation on every iteration. As a rule, you should use this idiom if the loop test involves a method invocation and the method invocation is guaranteed to return the same result on each iteration.

A final technique to minimize the scope of local variables is to **keep methods small and focused**. If you combine two activities in the same method, local variables relevant to one activity may be in the scope of the code performing the other activity. To prevent this from happening, simply separate the method into two: one for each activity.

Item 30: Know and use the libraries

Suppose you want to generate random integers between 0 and some upper bound. Faced with this common task, many programmers would write a little method that looks something like this:

```
static Random rnd = new Random();

// Common but flawed!
static int random(int n) {
    return Math.abs(rnd.nextInt()) % n;
}
```

This method isn't bad, but it isn't perfect, either—it has three flaws. The first flaw is that if n is a small power of two, the sequence of random numbers it generates will repeat itself after a fairly short period. The second flaw is that if n is not a power of two, some numbers will, on average, be returned more frequently than others. If n is large, this flaw can be quite pronounced. This is graphically demonstrated by the following program, which generates a million random numbers in a carefully chosen range and then prints out how many of the numbers fell in the lower half of the range:

```
public static void main(String[] args) {
    int n = 2 * (Integer.MAX_VALUE / 3);
    int low = 0;
    for (int i = 0; i < 1000000; i++)
        if (random(n) < n/2)
            low++;

    System.out.println(low);
}
```

If the random method worked properly, the program would print a number close to half a million, but if you run it, you'll find that it prints a number close to 666,666. Two thirds of the numbers generated by the random method fall in the lower half of its range!

The third flaw in the random method is that it can, on rare occasion, fail catastrophically, returning a number outside the specified range. This is so because the method attempts to map the value returned by rnd.nextInt() into a nonnegative integer with Math.abs. If nextInt() returns Integer.MIN_VALUE, Math.abs will also return Integer.MIN_VALUE, and the remainder operator (%) will return a negative number, assuming n is not a power of two. This will almost certainly cause your program to fail, and the failure may be difficult to reproduce.

To write a version of random that corrects these three flaws, you'd have to know a fair amount about linear congruential pseudorandom number generators, number theory, and two's complement arithmetic. Luckily, you don't have to do this—it's already been done for you. It's called Random.nextInt(int), and it was added to the standard library package java.util in release 1.2.

You don't have to concern yourself with the details of how nextInt(int) does its job (although you can study the documentation or the source code if you're morbidly curious). A senior engineer with a background in algorithms spent a good deal of time designing, implementing, and testing this method and then showed it to experts in the field to make sure it was right. Then the library was beta tested, released, and used extensively by thousands of programmers for several years. No flaws have yet been found in the method, but if a flaw were to be discovered, it would get fixed in the next release. **By using a standard library, you take advantage of the knowledge of the experts who wrote it and the experience of those who used it before you.**

A second advantage of using the libraries is that you don't have to waste your time writing ad hoc solutions to problems only marginally related to your work. If you are like most programmers, you'd rather spend your time working on your application than on the underlying plumbing.

A third advantage of using standard libraries is that their performance tends to improve over time, with no effort on your part. Because many people use them and because they're used in industry-standard benchmarks, the organizations that supply these libraries have a strong incentive to make them run faster. For example, the standard multiprecision arithmetic library, java.math, was rewritten in release 1.3, resulting in dramatic performance improvements.

Libraries also tend to gain new functionality over time. If a library class is missing some important functionality, the developer community will make this shortcoming known. The Java platform has always been developed with substantial input from this community. Previously the process was informal; now there is a formal process in place called the Java Community Process (JCP). Either way, missing features tend to get added over time.

A final advantage of using the standard libraries is that you place your code in the mainstream. Such code is more easily readable, maintainable, and reusable by the multitude of developers.

Given all these advantages, it seems only logical to use library facilities in preference to ad hoc implementations, yet a significant fraction of programmers don't. Why? Perhaps they don't know that the library facilities exist. **Nume** **features are added to the libraries in every major release, and it pays to ke** **abreast of these additions.** You can peruse the documentation online or read about the libraries in any number of books [J2SE-APIs, Chan00, Flanagan99, Chan98]. The libraries are too big to study all the documentation, but **every pro-** **grammer should be familiar with the contents of java.lang, java.util, and,** **to a lesser extent, java.io.** Knowledge of other libraries can be acquired on an as-needed basis.

It is beyond the scope of this item to summarize all the facilities in the librar- ies, but a few bear special mention. In the 1.2 release, a *Collections Framework* was added to the java.util package. It should be part of every programmer's basic toolkit. The Collections Framework is a unified architecture for representing and manipulating collections, allowing them to be manipulated independently of the details of their representation. It reduces programming effort while increasing performance. It allows for interoperability among unrelated APIs, reduces effort in designing and learning new APIs, and fosters software reuse.

The framework is based on six collection interfaces (Collection, Set, List, Map, SortedList, and SortedMap). It includes implementations of these interfaces and algorithms to manipulate them. The legacy collection classes, Vector and Hashtable, were retrofitted to participate in the framework, so you don't have to abandon them to take advantage of the framework.

The Collections Framework substantially reduces the amount of code neces- sary to do many mundane tasks. For example, suppose you have a vector of strings, and you want to sort it alphabetically. This one-liner does the job:

```
Collections.sort(v);
```

If you want to do the same thing ignoring case distinctions, use the following:

```
Collections.sort(v, String.CASE_INSENSITIVE_ORDER);
```

Suppose you want to print out all of the elements in an array. Many program- mers use a for loop, but there's no need if you use the following idiom:

```
System.out.println(Arrays.asList(a));
```

Finally, suppose you want to know all of the keys for which two Hashtable instances, h1 and h2, contain the same mappings. Before the Collections

ed, this would have required a fair amount of code, but now it

```
shMap(h1);
tainAll(h2.entrySet());
keySet();
```

egoing examples barely scratch the surface of what you can do with Collections Framework. If you want to know more, see the documentation on Sun's Web site [Collections] or read the tutorial [Bloch99].

A third-party library worthy of note is Doug Lea's `util.concurrent` [Lea01], which provides high-level concurrency utilities to simplify the task of multithreaded programming.

There are many additions to the libraries in the 1.4 release. Notable additions include the following:

- **`java.util.regex`**—A full-blown Perl-like regular expression facility.

- **`java.util.prefs`**—A facility for the persistent storage of user preferences and program configuration data.

- **`java.nio`**—A high-performance I/O facility, including *scalable I/O* (akin to the Unix `poll` call) and *memory-mapped I/O* (akin to the Unix `mmap` call).

- **`java.util.LinkedHashSet, LinkedHashMap, IdentityHashMap`**—New collection implementations.

Occasionally, a library facility may fail to meet your needs. The more specialized your needs, the more likely this is to happen. While your first impulse should be to use the libraries, if you've looked at what they have to offer in some area and it doesn't meet your needs, use an alternate implementation. There will always be holes in the functionality provided by any finite set of libraries. If the functionality that you need is missing, you may have no choice but to implement it yourself.

To summarize, don't reinvent the wheel. If you need to do something that seems reasonably common, there may already be a class in the libraries that does what you want. If there is, use it; if you don't know, check. Generally speaking, library code is likely to be better than code that you'd write yourself and is likely to improve over time. This is no reflection on your abilities as a programmer; economies of scale dictate that library code receives far more attention than the average developer could afford to devote to the same functionality.

Item 31: Avoid `float` and `double` if exact answers are required

The `float` and `double` types are designed primarily for scientific and engineering calculations. They perform *binary floating-point arithmetic*, which was carefully designed to furnish accurate approximations quickly over a broad range of magnitudes. They do not, however, provide exact results and should not be used where exact results are required. **The `float` and `double` types are particularly ill-suited for monetary calculations** because it is impossible to represent 0.1 (or any other negative power of ten) as a `float` or `double` exactly.

For example, suppose you have $1.03 in your pocket, and you spend 42¢. How much money do you have left? Here's a naive program fragment that attempts to answer this question:

```
System.out.println(1.03 - .42);
```

Unfortunately, it prints out 0.6100000000000001. This is not an isolated case. Suppose you have a dollar in your pocket, and you buy nine washers priced at ten cents each. How much change do you get?

```
System.out.println(1.00 - 9*.10);
```

According to this program fragment, you get $0.09999999999999995. You might think that the problem could be solved merely by rounding results prior to printing, but unfortunately this does not always work. For example, suppose you have a dollar in your pocket, and you see a shelf with a row of delicious candies priced at 10¢, 20¢, 30¢, and so forth, up to a dollar. You buy one of each candy, starting with the one that costs 10¢, until you can't afford to buy the next candy on the shelf. How many candies do you buy, and how much change do you get? Here's a naive program designed to solve this problem:

```
// Broken - uses floating point for monetary calculation!
public static void main(String[] args) {
    double funds = 1.00;
    int itemsBought = 0;
    for (double price = .10; funds >= price; price += .10) {
        funds -= price;
        itemsBought++;
    }
    System.out.println(itemsBought + " items bought.");
    System.out.println("Change: $" + funds);
}
```

If you run the program, you'll find that you can afford three pieces of candy, and you have $0.3999999999999999 left. This is the wrong answer! The right way to solve this problem is to **use BigDecimal, int, or long for monetary calculations**. Here's a straightforward transformation of the previous program to use the BigDecimal type in place of double:

```
public static void main(String[] args) {
    final BigDecimal TEN_CENTS = new BigDecimal( ".10");

    int itemsBought = 0;
    BigDecimal funds = new BigDecimal("1.00");
    for (BigDecimal price = TEN_CENTS;
          funds.compareTo(price) >= 0;
          price = price.add(TEN_CENTS)) {
        itemsBought++;
        funds = funds.subtract(price);
    }
    System.out.println(itemsBought + " items bought.");
    System.out.println("Money left over: $" + funds);
}
```

If you run the revised program, you'll find that you can afford four pieces of candy, with $0.00 left over. This is the correct answer. There are, however, two disadvantages to using BigDecimal: It's less convenient than using a primitive arithmetic type, and its slower. The latter disadvantage is irrelevant if you're solving a single short problem, but the former may annoy you.

An alternative to using BigDecimal is to use int or long, depending on the amounts involved, and to keep track of the decimal point yourself. In this example, the obvious approach is to do all computation in pennies instead of dollars. Here's a straightforward transformation of the program just shown that takes this approach:

```
public static void main(String[] args) {
    int itemsBought = 0;
    int funds = 100;
    for (int price = 10; funds >= price; price += 10) {
        itemsBought++;
        funds -= price;
    }
    System.out.println(itemsBought + " items bought.");
    System.out.println("Money left over: "+ funds + " cents");
}
```

In summary, don't use `float` or `double` for any calculations that require an exact answer. Use `BigDecimal` if you want the system to keep track of the decimal point and you don't mind the inconvenience of not using a primitive type. Using `BigDecimal` has the added advantage that it gives you full control over rounding, letting you select from eight rounding modes whenever an operation that entails rounding is performed. This comes in handy if you're performing business calculations with legally mandated rounding behavior. If performance is of the essence, if you don't mind keeping track of the decimal point yourself, and if the quantities aren't too big, use `int` or `long`. If the quantities don't exceed nine decimal digits, you can use `int`; if they don't exceed eighteen digits, you can use `long`. If the quantities exceed eighteen digits, you must use `BigDecimal`.

Item 32: Avoid strings where other types are more appropriate

Strings are designed to represent text, and they do a fine job of it. Because strings are so common and so well supported by the language, there is a natural tendency to use strings for purposes other than those for which they were designed. This item discusses a few things that you shouldn't do with strings.

Strings are poor substitutes for other value types. When a piece of data comes into a program from a file, from the network, or from keyboard input, it is often in string form. There is a natural tendency to leave it that way, but this tendency is justified only if it really is textual in nature. If it's numeric, it should be translated into the appropriate numeric type, such as `int`, `float`, or `BigInteger`. If it's the answer to a yes-or-no question, it should be translated into a `boolean`. More generally, if there's an appropriate value type, whether primitive or object reference, you should use it; if there isn't, you should write one. While this advice may seem obvious, it is often violated.

Strings are poor substitutes for enumerated types. As discussed in Item 21, both typesafe enums and `int` values make far better enumerated type constants than strings.

Strings are poor substitutes for aggregate types. If an entity has multiple components, it is usually a bad idea to represent it as a single string. For example, here's a line of code that comes from a real system—identifier names have been changed to protect the guilty:

```
// Inappropriate use of string as aggregate type
String compoundKey = className + "#" + i.next();
```

This approach has many disadvantages. If the character used to separate fields occurs in one of the fields, chaos may result. To access individual fields, you have to parse the string, which is slow, tedious, and error-prone. You can't provide `equals`, `toString`, or `compareTo` methods but are forced to accept the behavior that `String` provides. A better approach is simply to write a class to represent the aggregate, often a private static member class (Item 18).

Strings are poor substitutes for *capabilities*. Occasionally, strings are used to grant access to some functionality. For example, consider the design of a thread-local variable facility. Such a facility provides variables for which each thread has its own value. When confronted with designing such a facility several

```
          BOSTON BEER WORKS-Fenway
               617-536-BEER

   0400b  Table 998  #Party 1
   MAIN BAR M  SvrCk:461  7:02p 10/01/09

   1 BACK BAY BURGER, medium,
     classic fries                    10.45
   1 CHARLESTOWN BURG, medium,
     $ubo-ring                        11.40
   1 CASK-22oz                         5.75


                   Sub Total:  27.60
   (MA   21.85, 0thr  5.75)  MA :   1.37
                        Cit:   0.16
   (Incl Tax:   0.38)
                   Sub Total:  29.13
   10/01 7:59pTOTAL =        29.13

             BOLD AMERICAN FOOD
             AWARD WINNING BEER


             VISIT OUR BEER WORKS AT
       112 CANAL STREET BEFORE OR AFTER
          ALL FLEET CENTER EVENTS
```

years ago, several people independently came up with the same design in which
client-provided string keys grant access to the contents of a thread-local variable:

```
// Broken - inappropriate use of String as capability!
public class ThreadLocal {
    private ThreadLocal() { } // Noninstantiable

    // Sets the current thread's value for the named variable.
    public static void set(String key, Object value);

    // Returns the current thread's value for the named variable.
    public static Object get(String key);
}
```

The problem with this approach is that the keys represent a shared global
namespace. If two independent clients of the package decide to use the same name
for their thread-local variable, they unintentionally share the variable, which will
generally cause both clients to fail. Also, the security is poor; a malicious client
could intentionally use the same key as another client to gain illicit access to the
other client's data.

This API can be fixed by replacing the string with an unforgeable key (sometimes called a *capability*):

```
public class ThreadLocal {
    private ThreadLocal() { } // Noninstantiable

    public static class Key {
        Key() { }
    }

    // Generates a unique, unforgeable key
    public static Key getKey() {
        return new Key();
    }

    public static void set(Key key, Object value);
    public static Object get(Key key);
}
```

While this solves both of the problems with the string-based API, you can do
better. You don't really need the static methods any more. They can instead
become instance methods on the key, at which point the key is no longer a key: it
is a thread-local variable. At this point, the noninstantiable top-level class isn't

doing anything for you any more, so you might as well get rid of it and rename the nested class to `ThreadLocal`:

```
public class ThreadLocal {
    public ThreadLocal() { }
    public void set(Object value);
    public Object get();
}
```

This is, roughly speaking, the API that `java.util.ThreadLocal` provides. In addition to solving the problems with the string-based API, it's faster and more elegant than either of the key-based APIs.

To summarize, avoid the natural tendency to represent objects as strings when better data types exist or can be written. Used inappropriately, strings are more cumbersome, less flexible, slower, and more error-prone than other types. Types for which strings are commonly misused include primitive types, enumerated types, and aggregate types.

Item 33: Beware the performance of string concatenation

The string concatenation operator (+) is a convenient way to combine a few strings into one. It is fine for generating a single line of output or for constructing the string representation of a small, fixed-size object, but it does not scale. **Using the string concatenation operator repeatedly to concatenate *n* strings requires time quadratic in *n*.** It is an unfortunate consequence of the fact that strings are *immutable* (Item 13). When two strings are concatenated, the contents of both are copied.

For example, consider the following method that constructs a string representation of a billing statement by repeatedly concatenating a line for each item:

```
// Inappropriate use of string concatenation - Performs horribly!
public String statement() {
    String s = "";
    for (int i = 0; i < numItems(); i++)
        s += lineForItem(i);  // String concatenation
    return s;
}
```

This method performs abysmally if the number of items is large. **To achieve acceptable performance, use a `StringBuffer` in place of a `String`** to store the statement under construction:

```
public String statement() {
    StringBuffer s = new StringBuffer(numItems() * LINE_WIDTH);
    for (int i = 0; i < numItems(); i++)
        s.append(lineForItem(i));
    return s.toString();
}
```

The difference in performance is dramatic. If `numItems` returns 100 and `lineForItem` returns a constant 80-character string, the second method is ninety times faster on my machine than the first. Because the first method is quadratic in the number of items and the second is linear, the performance difference is even more dramatic for larger numbers of items. Note that the second method preallocates a `StringBuffer` large enough to hold the result. Even if it is detuned to use a default-sized `StringBuffer`, it is still forty-five times faster than the first.

The moral is simple: Don't use the string concatenation operator to combine more than a few strings unless performance is irrelevant. Use `StringBuffer`'s append method instead. Alternatively, use a character array, or process the strings one at a time instead of combining them.

Item 34: Refer to objects by their interfaces

Item 25 contains the advice that you should use interfaces rather than classes as parameter types. More generally, you should favor the use of interfaces rather than classes to refer to objects. **If appropriate interface types exist, parameters, return values, variables, and fields should all be declared using interface types.** The only time you really need to refer to an object's class is when you're creating it. To make this concrete, consider the case of Vector, which is an implementation of the List interface. Get in the habit of typing this:

```
// Good - uses interface as type
List subscribers = new Vector();
```

rather than this:

```
// Bad - uses class as type!
Vector subscribers = new Vector();
```

If you get into the habit of using interfaces as types, your program will be much more flexible. If you decide that you want to switch implementations, all you have to do is change the class name in the constructor (or use a different static factory). For example, the first declaration could be changed to read

```
List subscribers = new ArrayList();
```

and all of the surrounding code would continue to work. The surrounding code was unaware of the old implementation type, so it would be oblivious to the change.

There is one caveat: If the original implementation offered some special functionality not required by the general contract of the interface and the code depended on that functionality, then it is critical that the new implementation provide the same functionality. For example, if the code surrounding the first declaration depended on the fact that Vector is synchronized, then it would be incorrect to substitute ArrayList for Vector in the declaration.

So why would you want to change implementations? Because the new implementation offers better performance or because it offers desirable extra functionality. A real-world example concerns the ThreadLocal class. Internally, this class uses a package-private Map field in Thread to associate per-thread values with ThreadLocal instances. In the 1.3 release, this field was initialized to a HashMap instance. In the 1.4 release, a new, special-purpose Map implementation, called

IdentityHashMap, was added to the platform. By changing a single line of code to initialize the field to an IdentityHashMap instead of a HashMap, the ThreadLocal facility was made faster.

Had the field been declared as a HashMap instead of a Map, there is no guarantee that a single-line change would have been sufficient. If the client code had used HashMap operations outside of the Map interface or passed the map to a method that demanded a HashMap, the code would no longer compile if the field were changed to an IdentityHashMap. Declaring the field with the interface type "keeps you honest."

It is entirely appropriate to refer to an object by a class rather than an interface if no appropriate interface exists. For example, consider *value classes,* such as String and BigInteger. Value classes are rarely written with multiple implementations in mind. They are often final and rarely have corresponding interfaces. It is perfectly appropriate to use a value class as a parameter, variable, field, or return type. More generally, if a concrete class has no associated interface, then you have no choice but to refer to it by its class whether or not it represents a value. The Random class falls into this category.

A second case in which there is no appropriate interface type is that of objects belonging to a framework whose fundamental types are classes rather than interfaces. If an object belongs to such a *class-based framework*, it is preferable to refer to it by the relevant *base class*, which is typically abstract, rather than by its implementation class. The java.util.TimerTask class falls into this category.

A final case in which there is no appropriate interface type is that of classes that implement an interface but provide extra methods not found in the interface— for example, LinkedList. Such a class should be used only to refer to its instances if the program relies on the extra methods: it should never be used as a parameter type (Item 25).

These cases are not meant to be exhaustive but merely to convey the flavor of situations where it is appropriate to refer to an object by its class. In practice, it should be apparent whether a given object has an appropriate interface. If it does, your program will be more flexible if you use the interface to refer to the object; if not, just use the highest class in the class hierarchy that provides the required functionality.

Item 35: Prefer interfaces to reflection

The reflection facility, `java.lang.reflect`, offers programmatic access to information about loaded classes. Given a `Class` instance, you can obtain `Constructor`, `Method`, and `Field` instances representing the constructors, methods, and fields of the class represented by the `Class` instance. These objects provide programmatic access to the class's member names, field types, method signatures, and so on.

Moreover, `Constructor`, `Method`, and `Field` instances let you manipulate their underlying counterparts *reflectively*: You can construct instances, invoke methods, and access fields of the underlying class by invoking methods on the `Constructor`, `Field`, and `Method` instances. For example, `Method.invoke` lets you invoke any method on any object of any class (subject to the usual security constraints). Reflection allows one class to use another, even if the latter class did not exist when the former was compiled. This power, however, comes at a price:

- **You lose all the benefits of compile-time type checking**, including exception checking. If a program attempts to invoke a nonexistent or inaccessible method reflectively, it will fail at run time unless you've taken special precautions.

- **The code required to perform reflective access is clumsy and verbose**. It is tedious to write and difficult to read.

- **Performance suffers**. As of release 1.3, reflective method invocation was forty times slower on my machine than normal method invocation. Reflection was rearchitected in release 1.4 for greatly improved performance, but it is still twice as slow as normal access, and the gap is unlikely to narrow.

The reflection facility was originally designed for component-based application builder tools. Such tools generally load classes on demand and use reflection to find out what methods and constructors they support. The tools let their users interactively construct applications that access these classes, but the generated applications access the classes normally, not reflectively. Reflection is used only at *design time*. **As a rule, objects should not be accessed reflectively in normal applications at run time.**

There are a few sophisticated applications that demand the use of reflection. Examples include class browsers, object inspectors, code analysis tools, and interpretive embedded systems. Reflection is also appropriate for use in RPC systems to eliminate the need for stub compilers. If you have any doubts as to whether your application falls into one of these categories, it probably doesn't.

You can obtain many of the benefits of reflection while incurring few of its costs by using it only in a very limited form. For many programs that must use a class unavailable at compile time, there exists at compile time an appropriate interface or superclass by which to refer to the class (Item 34). If this is the case, you can **create instances reflectively and access them normally via their interface or superclass**. If the appropriate constructor has no parameters, as is usually the case, then you don't even need to use the java.lang.reflect package; the Class.newInstance method provides the required functionality.

For example, here's a program that creates a Set instance whose class is specified by the first command line argument. The program inserts the remaining command line arguments into the set and prints it. Regardless of the first argument, the program prints the remaining arguments with duplicates eliminated. The order in which these arguments are printed depends on the class specified in the first argument. If you specify "java.util.HashSet," they're printed in apparently random order; if you specify "java.util.TreeSet," they're printed in alphabetical order, as the elements in a TreeSet are sorted:

```
// Reflective instantiation with interface access
public static void main(String[] args) {
    // Translate the class name into a class object
    Class cl = null;
    try {
        cl = Class.forName(args[0]);
    } catch(ClassNotFoundException e) {
        System.err.println("Class not found.");
        System.exit(1);
    }

    // Instantiate the class
    Set s = null;
    try {
        s = (Set) cl.newInstance();
    } catch(IllegalAccessException e) {
        System.err.println("Class not accessible.");
        System.exit(1);
    } catch(InstantiationException e) {
        System.err.println("Class not instantiable.");
        System.exit(1);
    }

    // Exercise the set
    s.addAll(Arrays.asList(args).subList(1, args.length-1));
    System.out.println(s);
}
```

While this program is just a toy, the technique that it demonstrates is very powerful. The toy program could easily be turned into a generic set tester that validates the specified Set implementation by aggressively manipulating one or more instances and checking that they obey the Set contract. Similarly, it could be turned into a generic set performance analysis tool. In fact, the technique that it demonstrates is sufficient to implement a full-blown *service provider framework* (Item 1). Most of the time, this technique is all that you need in the way of reflection.

You can see two disadvantages of reflection in the example. First, the example is capable of generating three run-time errors, all of which would have been compile-time errors if reflective instantiation were not used. Second, it takes twenty lines of tedious code to generate an instance of the class from its name, whereas a constructor invocation would fit neatly on a single line. These disadvantages are, however, restricted to the part of the program that instantiates the object. Once instantiated, it is indistinguishable from any other Set instance. In a real program, the great bulk of the code is thus unaffected by this limited use of reflection.

A legitimate, if rare, use of reflection is to break a class's dependencies on other classes, methods, or fields that may be absent at run time. This can be useful if you are writing a package that must run against multiple versions of some other package. The technique is to compile your package against the minimal environment required to support it, typically the oldest version, and to access any newer classes or methods reflectively. To make this work, you have to take appropriate action if a newer class or method that you are attempting to access does not exist at run time. Appropriate action might consist of using some alternate means to accomplish the same goal or operating with reduced functionality.

In summary, reflection is a powerful facility that is required for certain sophisticated system programming tasks, but it has many disadvantages. If you are writing a program that has to work with classes unknown at compile time you should, if at all possible, use reflection only to instantiate objects and access the objects using some interface or superclass that is known at compile time.

Item 36: Use native methods judiciously

The Java Native Interface (JNI) allows Java applications to call *native methods*, which are special methods written in *native programming languages* such as C or C++. Native methods can perform arbitrary computation in native languages before returning to the Java programming language.

Historically, native methods have had three main uses. They provided access to platform-specific facilities such as registries and file locks. They provided access to libraries of legacy code, which could in turn provide access to legacy data. Finally, native methods were used to write performance-critical parts of applications in native languages for improved performance.

It is legitimate to use native methods to access platform-specific facilities, but as the Java platform matures, it provides more and more features previously found only in host platforms. For example, the `java.util.prefs` package, added in release 1.4, offers the functionality of a registry. It is also legitimate to use native methods to access legacy code, but there are better ways to access some legacy code. For example, the JDBC API provides access to legacy databases.

As of release 1.3, it is rarely advisable to use native methods for improved performance. In early releases, it was often necessary, but JVM implementations have gotten much faster. For most tasks, it is now possible to obtain comparable performance without resorting to native methods. By way of example, when `java.math` was added to the platform in release 1.1, `BigInteger` was implemented atop a fast multiprecision arithmetic library written in C. At the time, this was necessary for adequate performance. In release 1.3, `BigInteger` was rewritten entirely in Java and carefully tuned. The new version is faster than the original on all of Sun's 1.3 JVM implementations for most operations and operand sizes.

The use of native methods has serious disadvantages. Because native languages are not *safe* (Item 24), applications using native methods are no longer immune to memory corruption errors. Because native languages are platform dependent, applications using native methods are no longer freely portable. Native code must be recompiled for each target platform and may require modification as well. There is a high fixed cost associated with going into and out of native code, so native methods can *decrease* performance if they do only a small amount of work. Finally, native methods are tedious to write and difficult to read.

In summary, think twice before using native methods. Rarely, if ever, use them for improved performance. If you must use native methods to access low-level resources or legacy libraries, use as little native code as possible and test it thoroughly. A single bug in the native code can corrupt your entire application.

Item 37: Optimize judiciously

There are three aphorisms concerning optimization that everyone should know. They are perhaps beginning to suffer from overexposure, but in case you aren't yet familiar with them, here they are:

> More computing sins are committed in the name of efficiency (without necessarily achieving it) than for any other single reason—including blind stupidity.
>
> —William A. Wulf [Wulf72]

> We *should* forget about small efficiencies, say about 97% of the time: premature optimization is the root of all evil.
>
> —Donald E. Knuth [Knuth74]

> We follow two rules in the matter of optimization:
>
> Rule 1.   Don't do it.
>
> Rule 2 (for experts only).   Don't do it yet—that is, not until you have a perfectly clear and unoptimized solution.
>
> —M. A. Jackson [Jackson75]

All of these aphorisms predate the Java programming language by two decades. They tell a deep truth about optimization: It is easy to do more harm than good, especially if you optimize prematurely. In the process, you may produce software that is neither fast nor correct and cannot easily be fixed.

Don't sacrifice sound architectural principles for performance. **Strive to write good programs rather than fast ones**. If a good program is not fast enough, its architecture will allow it to be optimized. Good programs embody the principle of *information hiding*: Where possible, they localize design decisions within individual modules, so individual decisions can be changed without affecting the remainder of the system (Item 12).

This does not mean that you can ignore performance concerns until your program is complete. Implementation problems can be fixed by later optimization, but pervasive architectural flaws that limit performance can be nearly impossible to fix without rewriting the system. Changing a fundamental facet of your design after the fact can result in an ill-structured system that is difficult to maintain and evolve. Therefore you should think about performance during the design process.

Strive to avoid design decisions that limit performance. The components of a design that are most difficult to change after the fact are those specifying interactions between modules and with the outside world. Chief among these design components are APIs, wire-level protocols, and persistent data formats. Not only are these design components difficult or impossible to change after the fact, but all of them can place significant limitations on the performance that a system can ever achieve.

Consider the performance consequences of your API design decisions. Making a public type mutable may require a lot of needless defensive copying (Item 24). Similarly, using inheritance in a public class where composition would have been appropriate ties the class forever to its superclass, which can place artificial limits on the performance of the subclass (Item 14). As a final example, using an implementation type rather than an interface in an API ties you to a specific implementation, even though faster implementations may be written in the future (Item 34).

The effects of API design on performance are very real. Consider the getSize method in the java.awt.Component class. The decision that this performance-critical method was to return a Dimension instance, coupled with the decision that Dimension instances are mutable, forces any implementation of this method to allocate a new Dimension instance on every invocation. Even though, as of release 1.3, allocating small objects is relatively inexpensive, allocating millions of objects needlessly can do real harm to performance.

In this case, several alternatives existed. Ideally, Dimension should have been immutable (Item 13); alternatively, the getSize method could have been replaced by two methods returning the individual primitive components of a Dimension object. In fact, two such methods were added to the Component API in the 1.2 release for performance reasons. Preexisting client code, however, still uses the getSize method and still suffers the performance consequences of the original API design decisions.

Luckily, it is generally the case that good API design is consistent with good performance. **It is a very bad idea to warp an API to achieve good performance**. The performance issue that caused you to warp the API may go away in a future release of the platform or other underlying software, but the warped API and the support headaches that it causes will be with you for life.

Once you've carefully designed your program and produced a clear, concise, and well-structured implementation, *then* it may be time to consider optimization, assuming you're not already satisfied with the performance of the program. Recall that Jackson's two rules of optimization were "Don't do it," and "(for experts only). Don't do it yet." He could have added one more: **Measure performance before and after each attempted optimization.**

You may be surprised by what you find. Often attempted optimizations have no measurable effect on performance; sometimes they make it worse. The main reason is that it's difficult to guess where your program is spending its time. The part of the program that you think is slow may not be at fault, in which case you'd be wasting your time trying to optimize it. Common wisdom reveals that programs spend 80 percent of their time in 20 percent of their code.

Profiling tools can help you decide where to focus your optimization efforts. Such tools give you run-time information such as roughly how much time each method is consuming and how many times it is invoked. In addition to focusing your tuning efforts, this can alert you to the need for algorithmic changes. If a quadratic (or worse) algorithm lurks inside your program, no amount of tuning will fix the problem. You must replace the algorithm with one that's more efficient. The more code in the system, the more important it is to use a profiler. It's like looking for a needle in a haystack: The bigger the haystack, the more useful it is to have a metal detector. The Java 2 SDK comes with a simple profiler, and several more sophisticated profiling tools are available commercially.

The need to measure the effects of optimization is even greater on the Java platform than on more traditional platforms, as the Java programming language does not have a strong *performance model*. The relative costs of the various primitive operations are not well defined. The "semantic gap" between what the programmer writes and what the CPU executes is far greater than in traditional compiled languages which makes it very difficult to reliably predict the performance consequences of any optimization. There are plenty of performance myths floating around that turn out to be half-truths or outright lies.

Not only is the performance model ill-defined, but it varies from JVM implementation to JVM implementation and from release to release. If you will be running your program on multiple JVM implementations, it is important that you measure the effects of your optimization on each. Occasionally you may be forced to make trade-offs between performance on different JVM implementations.

To summarize, do not strive to write fast programs—strive to write good ones; speed will follow. Do think about performance issues while you're designing systems and especially while you're designing APIs, wire-level protocols, and persistent data formats. When you've finished building the system, measure its performance. If it's fast enough, you're done. If not, locate the source of the problems with the aid of a profiler, and go to work optimizing the relevant parts of the system. The first step is to examine your choice of algorithms: No amount of low-level optimization can make up for a poor choice of algorithm. Repeat this process as necessary, measuring the performance after every change, until you're satisfied.

Item 38: Adhere to generally accepted naming conventions

The Java platform has a well-established set of *naming conventions*, many of which are contained in *The Java Language Specification* [JLS, 6.8]. Loosely speaking, naming conventions fall into two categories: typographical and grammatical.

There are only a handful of typographical naming conventions, covering packages, classes, interfaces, methods, and fields. You should rarely violate them and never without a very good reason. If an API violates these conventions, it may be difficult to use. If an implementation violates them, it may be difficult to maintain. In both cases, violations have the potential to confuse and irritate other programmers who work with the code and can cause faulty assumptions that lead to errors. The conventions are summarized in this item.

Package names should be hierarchical with the parts separated by periods. Parts should consist of lowercase alphabetic characters and, rarely, digits. The name of any package that will be used outside your organization should begin with your organization's Internet domain name with the top-level domain first, for example, `edu.cmu`, `com.sun`, `gov.nsa`. The standard libraries and optional packages, whose names begin with `java` and `javax`, are exceptions to this rule. Users must not create packages whose names begin with `java` or `javax`. Detailed rules for converting Internet domain names to package name prefixes can be found in *The Java Language Specification* [JLS, 7.7].

The remainder of a package name should consist of one or more parts describing the package. Parts should be short, generally eight or fewer characters. Meaningful abbreviations are encouraged, for example, `util` rather than `utilities`. Acronyms are acceptable, for example, `awt`. Parts should generally consist of a single word or abbreviation.

Many packages have names with just one part in addition to the internet domain name. Additional parts are appropriate for large facilities whose size demands that they be broken up into an informal hierarchy. For example, the `javax.swing` package has a rich hierarchy of packages with names such as `javax.swing.plaf.metal`. Such packages are often referred to as subpackages, although they are subpackages by convention only; there is no linguistic support for package hierarchies.

Class and interface names should consist of one or more words, with the first letter of each word capitalized, for example, `Timer` or `TimerTask`. Abbreviations are to be avoided, except for acronyms and certain common abbreviations like `max` and `min`. There is little consensus as to whether acronyms should be uppercase or have only their first letter capitalized. While uppercase is more common, a strong argument can be made in favor of capitalizing only the first letter. Even if multiple acronyms occur back-to-back, you can still tell where one word starts and the next word ends. Which class name would you rather see, `HTTPURL` or `HttpUrl`?

Method and field names follow the same typographical conventions as class and interface names, except that the first letter of a method or field name should be lowercase, for example, `remove`, `ensureCapacity`. If an acronym occurs as the first word of a method or field name, it should be lowercase.

The sole exception to the previous rule concerns "constant fields," whose names should consist of one or more uppercase words separated by the underscore character, for example, `VALUES` or `NEGATIVE_INFINITY`. A constant field is a static final field whose value is immutable. If a static final field has a primitive type or an immutable reference type (Item 13), then it is a constant field. If the type is potentially mutable, it can still be a constant field if the referenced object is immutable. For example, a typesafe enum can export its universe of enumeration constants in an immutable `List` constant (page 107). Note that constant fields constitute the *only* recommended use of underscores.

Local variable names have similar typographical naming conventions to member names, except that abbreviations are permitted, as are individual characters and short sequences of characters whose meaning depends on the context in which the local variable occurs, for example, `i`, `xref`, `houseNumber`.

For quick reference, Table 7.1 shows examples of typographical conventions.

Table 7.1: Examples of Typographical Conventions

Identifier Type	Examples
Package	`com.sun.medialib`, `com.sun.jdi.event`
Class or Interface	`Timer`, `TimerTask`, `KeyFactorySpi`, `HttpServlet`
Method or Field	`remove`, `ensureCapacity`, `getCrc`
Constant Field	`VALUES`, `NEGATIVE_INFINITY`
Local Variable	`i`, `xref`, `houseNumber`

The grammatical naming conventions are more flexible and more controversial than the typographical conventions. There are no grammatical naming conventions to speak of for packages. Classes are generally named with a noun or noun phrase, for example, `Timer` or `BufferedWriter`. Interfaces are named like classes, for example, Collection or Comparator, or with an adjective ending in "-able" or "-ible," for example, Runnable or Accessible.

Methods that perform some action are generally named with a verb or verb phrase, for example, append or drawImage. Methods that return a boolean value usually have names that begin with the word "is," followed by a noun, a noun phrase, or any word or phrase that functions as an adjective, for example, isDigit, isProbablePrime, isEmpty, isEnabled, isRunning.

Methods that return a nonboolean function or attribute of the object on which they're invoked are usually named with a noun, a noun phrase, or a verb phrase beginning with the verb "get," for example, size, hashCode, or getTime. There is a vocal contingent that claims only the third form (beginning with "get") is acceptable, but there is no basis for this claim. The first two forms usually lead to more readable code, for example,

```
if (car.speed() > 2 * SPEED_LIMIT)
    generateAudibleAlert("Watch out for cops!");
```

The form beginning with "get" is mandatory if the class containing the method is a *Bean* [JavaBeans], and it's advisable if you're considering turning the class into a Bean at a later time. Also, there is strong precedent for this form if the class contains a method to set the same attribute. In this case, the two methods should be named get*Attribute* and set*Attribute*.

A few method names deserve special mention. Methods that convert the type of an object, returning an independent object of a different type, are often called to*Type*, for example, toString, toArray. Methods that return a *view* (Item 4) whose type differs from that of the receiving object, are often called as*Type*, for example, asList. Methods that return a primitive with the same value as the object on which they're invoked are often called *type*Value, for example, intValue. Common names for static factories are valueOf and getInstance (Item 1, page 9).

Grammatical conventions for field names are less well established and less important than those for class, interface, and method names, as well-designed APIs contain few if any exposed fields. Fields of type boolean are typically named like boolean accessor methods with the initial "is" omitted, for example, initialized, composite. Fields of other types are usually named with nouns or noun phrases, such as height, digits, or bodyStyle. Grammatical conventions for local variables are similar to those for fields but are even weaker.

To summarize, internalize the standard naming conventions and learn to use them as second nature. The typographical conventions are straightforward and largely unambiguous; the grammatical conventions are more complex and looser. To quote from *The Java Language Specification* [JLS, 6.8], "These conventions should not be followed slavishly if long-held conventional usage dictates otherwise." Use common sense.

CHAPTER 8

Exceptions

WHEN used to best advantage, exceptions can improve a program's readability, reliability, and maintainability. When used improperly, they can have the opposite effect. This chapter provides guidelines for using exceptions effectively.

Item 39: Use exceptions only for exceptional conditions

Someday, if you are unlucky, you may stumble across a piece of code that looks something like this:

```
// Horrible abuse of exceptions. Don't ever do this!
try {
    int i = 0;
    while(true)
        a[i++].f();
} catch(ArrayIndexOutOfBoundsException e) {
}
```

What does this code do? It's not at all obvious from inspection, and that's reason enough not to use it. It turns out to be a horribly ill-conceived idiom for looping through the elements of an array. The infinite loop terminates by throwing, catching, and ignoring an `ArrayIndexOutOfBoundsException` when it attempts to access the first array element outside the bounds of the array. It's supposed to be equivalent to the standard idiom for looping through an array, instantly recognizable to any Java programmer:

```
for (int i = 0; i < a.length; i++)
    a[i].f();
```

So why would anyone use the exception-based idiom in preference to the tried and true? It's a misguided attempt to improve performance based on the faulty reasoning that, since the VM checks the bounds of all array accesses, the normal loop termination test (i < a.length) is redundant and should be avoided. There are three things wrong with this reasoning:

- Because exceptions are designed for use under exceptional circumstances, few, if any, JVM implementations attempt to optimize their performance. It is generally expensive to create, throw, and catch an exception.

- Placing code inside a try-catch block precludes certain optimizations that modern JVM implementations might otherwise perform.

- The standard idiom for looping through an array does not necessarily result in redundant checks; some modern JVM implementations optimize them away.

In fact, the exception-based idiom is far slower than the standard one on virtually all current JVM implementations. On my machine, the exception-based idiom runs seventy times slower than the standard one when looping from 0 to 99.

Not only does the exception-based looping idiom obfuscate the purpose of the code and reduce its performance, but it's not guaranteed to work. In the presence of an unrelated bug, the idiom can fail silently and mask the bug, greatly complicating the debugging process. Suppose the computation in the body of the loop contains a bug that results in an out-of-bounds access to some unrelated array. If a reasonable loop idiom were used, the bug would generate an uncaught exception, resulting in immediate thread termination with an appropriate error message. If the evil exception-based looping idiom were used, the bug-related exception would be caught and misinterpreted as a normal loop termination.

The moral of this story is simple: **Exceptions are, as their name implies, to be used only for exceptional conditions; they should never be used for ordinary control flow.** More generally, you should use standard, easily recognizable idioms in preference to overly clever ones that are purported to offer better performance. Even if the performance advantage is real, it may not remain in the face of steadily improving JVM implementations. The subtle bugs and maintenance headaches that come from overly clever idioms, however, are sure to remain.

This principle also has implications for API design. **A well-designed API must not force its client to use exceptions for ordinary control flow.** A class with a "state-dependent" method that can be invoked only under certain unpredictable conditions should generally have a separate "state-testing" method indicating whether it is appropriate to invoke the first method. For example, the `Iterator` class has the state-dependent `next` method, which returns the next element in the iteration, and the corresponding state-testing method `hasNext`. This enables the standard idiom for iterating over a collection:

```
for (Iterator i = collection.iterator(); i.hasNext(); ) {
    Foo foo = (Foo) i.next();
    ...
}
```

If `Iterator` lacked the `hasNext` method, the client would be forced to do the following instead:

```
// Do not use this hideous idiom for iteration over a collection!
try {
    Iterator i = collection.iterator();
    while(true) {
        Foo foo = (Foo) i.next();
        ...
    }
} catch (NoSuchElementException e) {
}
```

This should look very familiar after the array iteration example that began this item. Besides being wordy and misleading, the exception-based idiom is likely to perform significantly worse than the standard one and can mask bugs in unrelated parts of the system.

An alternative to providing a separate state-testing method is to have the state-dependent method return a distinguished value, such as `null`, if it is invoked with the object in an inappropriate state. This technique would not be appropriate for `Iterator`, as `null` is a legitimate return value for the `next` method.

Here are some guidelines to help you choose between a state-testing method and a distinguished return value. If an object is to be accessed concurrently without external synchronization or is subject to externally induced state transitions, it may be essential to use a distinguished return value, as the object's state could change in the interval between the invocation of a state-testing method and its corresponding state-dependent method. Performance concerns may dictate that a distinguished return value be used if a separate state-testing method would, of necessity, duplicate the work of the state-dependent method. All other things being equal, however, a state-testing method is mildly preferable to a distinguished return value. It offers slightly better readability, and inappropriate use is likely to be easier to detect and correct.

Item 40:   Use checked exceptions for recoverable conditions and run-time exceptions for programming errors

The Java programming language provides three kinds of throwables: *checked exceptions*, *run-time exceptions*, and *errors*. There is some confusion among programmers as to when each kind of throwable is appropriate. While the decision is not always clear-cut, there are some general rules that go a long way toward easing the choice.

The cardinal rule in deciding whether to use a checked or unchecked exception is: **Use checked exceptions for conditions from which the caller can reasonably be expected to recover.** By throwing a checked exception, you force the caller to handle the exception in a catch clause or to propagate it outward. Each checked exception that a method is declared to throw is thus a potent indication to the API user that the associated condition is a possible outcome of invoking the method.

By confronting the API user with a checked exception, the API designer presents a mandate to recover from the condition. The user can disregard this mandate by catching the exception and ignoring it, but this is usually a bad idea (Item 47).

There are two kinds of unchecked throwables: run-time exceptions and errors. They are identical in their behavior: Both are throwables that needn't, and generally shouldn't, be caught. If a program throws an unchecked exception or an error, it is generally the case that recovery is impossible and continued execution would do more harm than good. If a program does not catch such a throwable, it will cause the current thread to halt with an appropriate error message.

Use run-time exceptions to indicate programming errors. The great majority of run-time exceptions indicate *precondition violations*. A precondition violation is simply a failure by the client of an API to adhere to the contract established by the API specification. For example, the contract for array access specifies that the array index must be between zero and the array length minus one. ArrayIndexOutOfBoundsException indicates that this precondition was violated.

While the JLS does not require it, there is a strong convention that errors are reserved for use by the JVM to indicate resource deficiencies, invariant failures, or other conditions that make it impossible to continue execution [Chan98, Horstman00]. Given the almost universal acceptance of this convention, it's best not to implement any new Error subclasses. **All of the unchecked throwables you implement should subclass RuntimeException** (directly or indirectly).

It is possible to define a throwable that is not a subclass of `Exception`, `RuntimeException`, or `Error`. The JLS does not address such throwables directly, but specifies implicitly that they are behaviorally identical to ordinary checked exceptions (which are subclasses of `Exception` but not `RuntimeException`). So when should you use such a beast? In a word, never. It has no benefits over an ordinary checked exceptionality would serve merely to confuse the user of your API.

To summarize, use checked exceptions for recoverable conditions and runtime exceptions for programming errors. Of course, the situation is not always black and white. For example, consider the case of resource exhaustion, which can be caused by a programming error such as allocating an unreasonably large array or by a genuine shortage of resources. If resource exhaustion is caused by a temporary shortage or by temporarily heightened demand, the condition may well be recoverable. It is a matter of judgment on the part of the API designer whether a given instance of resource exhaustion is likely to allow for recovery. If you believe a condition is likely to allow for recovery, use a checked exception; if not, use a run-time exception. If it isn't clear whether recovery is possible, you're probably better off using an unchecked exception, for reasons discussed in Item 41.

API designers often forget that exceptions are full-fledged objects on which arbitrary methods can be defined. The primary use of such methods is to provide the code that catches the exception with additional information concerning the condition that caused the exception to be thrown. In the absence of such methods, programmers have been known to parse the string representation of an exception to ferret out additional information. This is extremely bad practice. Classes seldom specify the details of their string representations; thus string representations may differ from implementation to implementation and release to release. Therefore code that parses the string representation of an exception is likely to be nonportable and fragile.

Because checked exceptions generally indicate recoverable conditions, it's especially important for such exceptions to provide methods that furnish information that could help the caller to recover. For example, suppose a checked exception is thrown when an attempt to make a call on a pay phone fails because the caller has not deposited a sufficient quantity of money. The exception should provide an accessor method to query the amount of the shortfall so the amount can be relayed to the user of the phone.

Item 41: Avoid unnecessary use of checked exceptions

Checked exceptions are a wonderful feature of the Java programming language. Unlike return codes, they *force* the programmer to deal with exceptional conditions, greatly enhancing reliability. That said, overuse of checked exceptions can make an API far less pleasant to use. If a method throws one or more checked exceptions, the code that invokes the method must handle the exceptions in one or more `catch` blocks, or it must declare that it throws the exceptions and let them propagate outward. Either way, it places a nontrivial burden on the programmer.

The burden is justified if the exceptional condition cannot be prevented by proper use of the API *and* the programmer using the API can take some useful action once confronted with the exception. Unless both of these conditions hold, an unchecked exception is more appropriate. As a litmus test, ask yourself how the programmer will handle the exception. Is this the best that can be done?

```
} catch(TheCheckedException e) {
    throw new Error("Assertion error"); // Should never happen!
}
```

How about this?

```
} catch(TheCheckedException e) {
    e.printStackTrace();        // Oh well, we lose.
    System.exit(1);
}
```

If the programmer using the API can do no better, an unchecked exception would be more appropriate. One example of an exception that fails this test is `CloneNotSupportedException`. It is thrown by `Object.clone`, which should be invoked only on objects that implement `Cloneable` (Item 10). In practice, the `catch` block almost always has the character of an assertion failure. The checked nature of the exception provides no benefit to the programmer, but it requires effort and complicates programs.

The additional burden on the programmer caused by a checked exception is substantially higher if it is the *sole* checked exception thrown by a method. If there are others, the method must already appear in a `try` block, and this exception merely requires another `catch` block. If a method throws a single checked exception, this exception alone is responsible for the fact that the method must appear in a `try` block. Under these circumstances, it pays to ask yourself whether there isn't some way to avoid the checked exception.

One technique for turning a checked exception into an unchecked exception is to break the method that throws the exception into two methods, the first of which returns a `boolean` indicating whether the exception would be thrown. This API transformation transforms the calling sequence from this:

```
// Invocation with checked exception
try {
    obj.action(args);
} catch(TheCheckedException e) {
    // Handle exceptional condition
    ...
}
```

to this:

```
// Invocation with state-testing method and unchecked exception
if (obj.actionPermitted(args)) {
    obj.action(args);
} else {
    // Handle exceptional condition
    ...
}
```

This transformation is not always appropriate, but where it is appropriate it can make an API more pleasant to use. While the latter calling sequence is no prettier than the former, the resulting API is more flexible. In cases where the programmer knows the call will succeed or is content to let the thread terminate if the call fails, the transformation also allows this simple calling sequence:

```
obj.action(args);
```

If you suspect that the simple calling sequence will be the norm, then this API transformation may be appropriate. The API resulting from this transformation is essentially identical to the "state-testing method" API in Item 39 and the same caveats apply: If an object is to be accessed concurrently without external synchronization or it is subject to externally induced state transitions, this transformation is inappropriate, as the object's state may change between the invocations of `actionPermitted` and `action`. If a separate `actionPermitted` method would, of necessity, duplicate the work of the `action` method, the transformation may be ruled out by performance concerns.

Item 42: Favor the use of standard exceptions

One of the attributes that most strongly distinguishes expert programmers from less experienced ones is that experts strive for and usually achieve a high degree of code reuse. Exceptions are no exception to the general rule that code reuse is good. The Java platform libraries provide a basic set of unchecked exceptions that cover a large fraction of the exception-throwing needs of most APIs. In this item, we'll discuss these commonly reused exceptions.

Reusing preexisting exceptions has several benefits. Chief among these, it makes your API easier to learn and use because it matches established conventions with which programmers are already familiar. A close second is that programs using your API are easier to read because they aren't cluttered with unfamiliar exceptions. Finally, fewer exception classes mean a smaller memory footprint and less time spent loading classes.

The most commonly reused exception is `IllegalArgumentException`. This is generally the exception to throw when the caller passes in an argument whose value is inappropriate. For example, this would be the exception to throw if the caller passed a negative number in a parameter representing the number of times some action were to be repeated.

Another commonly reused exception is `IllegalStateException`. This is generally the exception to throw if the invocation is illegal, given the state of the receiving object. For example, this would be the exception to throw if the caller attempted to use some object before it had been properly initialized.

Arguably, all erroneous method invocations boil down to an illegal argument or illegal state, but other exceptions are standardly used for certain kinds of illegal arguments and states. If a caller passes `null` in some parameter for which null values are prohibited, convention dictates that `NullPointerException` be thrown rather than `IllegalArgumentException`. Similarly, if a caller passes an out-of-range value in a parameter representing an index into a sequence, `IndexOutOfBoundsException` should be thrown rather than `IllegalArgumentException`.

Another general-purpose exception worth knowing about is `ConcurrentModificationException`. This exception should be thrown if an object designed for use by a single thread or with external synchronization detects that it is being (or has been) concurrently modified.

A last general-purpose exception worthy of note is `UnsupportedOperationException`. This is the exception to throw if an object does not support an attempted operation. Its use is rare compared to that of other exceptions discussed in this item, as most objects support all the methods they implement. This exception is used by implementations of interfaces that fail to implement one or more optional operations defined by the interface. For example, an append-only `List` implementation would throw this exception if someone tried to delete an element.

Table 8.1 summarizes the most commonly reused exceptions.

Table 8.1:   Commonly Used Exceptions

Exception	Occasion for Use
`IllegalArgumentException`	Parameter value is inappropriate
`IllegalStateException`	Object state is inappropriate for method invocation
`NullPointerException`	Parameter value is null where prohibited
`IndexOutOfBoundsException`	Index parameter value is out of range
`ConcurrentModificationException`	Concurrent modification of object has been detected where prohibited
`UnsupportedOperationException`	Object does not support method

While these are by far are the most commonly reused exceptions in the Java platform libraries, other exceptions may be reused where circumstances warrant. For example, it would be appropriate to reuse `ArithmeticException` and `NumberFormatException` if you were implementing arithmetic objects like complex numbers or matrices. If an exception fits your needs, go ahead and use it, but only if the conditions under which you would throw it are consistent with the exception's documentation. Reuse must be based on semantics, not just on name. Also, feel free to subclass an existing exception if you want to add a bit more failure-capture information (Item 45).

Finally, be aware that choosing which exception to reuse is not always an exact science, as the "occasions for use" in the Table 8.1 are not mutually exclusive. Consider, for example, the case of an object representing a deck of cards. Suppose there were a method to deal a hand from the deck that took as an argument the size of the hand. Suppose the caller passed in this parameter a value that was larger than the number of cards remaining in the deck. This could be construed as an `IllegalArgumentException` (the `handSize` parameter value is too high) or an `IllegalStateException` (the deck object contains too few cards for the request). In this case the `IllegalArgumentException` feels right, but there are no hard-and-fast rules.

Item 43: Throw exceptions appropriate to the abstraction

It is disconcerting when a method throws an exception that has no apparent connection to the task that it performs. This often happens when a method propagates an exception thrown by a lower-level abstraction. Besides being disconcerting, this pollutes the API of the higher layer with implementation details. If the implementation of the higher layer is changed in a subsequent release, the exceptions that it throws may change as well, potentially breaking existing client programs.

To avoid this problem, **higher layers should catch lower-level exceptions and, in their place, throw exceptions that are explainable in terms of the higher-level abstraction.** This idiom, which we call *exception translation*, looks like this:

```
// Exception Translation
try {
    // Use lower-level abstraction to do our bidding
    ...
} catch(LowerLevelException e) {
    throw new HigherLevelException(...);
}
```

Here is an example of exception transaction taken from the AbstractSequentialList class, which is a *skeletal implementation* (Item 16) of the List interface. In this example, exception translation is mandated by the specification of the get method in the List interface:

```
/**
 * Returns the element at the specified position in this list.
 * @throws IndexOutOfBoundsException if the index is out of range
 *         (index < 0 || index >= size()).
 */
public Object get(int index) {
    ListIterator i = listIterator(index);
    try {
        return i.next();
    } catch(NoSuchElementException e) {
        throw new IndexOutOfBoundsException("Index: " + index);
    }
}
```

A special form of exception translation called *exception chaining* is appropriate in cases where the lower-level exception might be helpful to someone debugging the situation that caused the exception. In this approach, the lower-level exception is stored by the higher-level exception, which provides a public accessor method to retrieve the lower-level exception:

```
// Exception Chaining
try {
    // Use lower-level abstraction to do our bidding
    ...
} catch (LowerLevelException e) {
    throw new HigherLevelException(e);
}
```

As of release 1.4, exception chaining is supported by `Throwable`. If you're targeting release 1.4 (or a later one), you can take advantage of this support by having your higher-level exception's constructor chain to `Throwable(Throwable)`:

```
// Exception chaining in release 1.4
HigherLevelException(Throwable t) {
    super(t);
}
```

If you're targeting an earlier release, your exception must store the lower-level exception and provide an accessor:

```
// Exception chaining prior to release 1.4
private Throwable cause;

HigherLevelException(Throwable t) {
    cause = t;
}

public Throwable getCause() {
    return cause;
}
```

By naming the accessor `getCause` and using the shown declaration, you ensure that your exception will interoperate with the platform's chaining facility should you use the exception in a release like 1.4. This has the advantage of integrating the lower-level exception's stack trace into that of the higher-level exception in a standard fashion. Also, it allows standard debugging tools to access the lower-level exception.

While exception translation is superior to mindless propagation of exceptions from lower layers, it should not be overused. Where possible, the best way to deal with exceptions from lower layers is to avoid them entirely by ensuring that lower-level methods will succeed before invoking them. Sometimes you can do this by explicitly checking the validity of the higher-level method's arguments before passing them on to lower layers.

If it is impossible to prevent exceptions from lower layers, the next best thing is to have the higher layer silently work around these exceptions, insulating the caller of the higher-level method from the lower-level problem. Under these circumstances, it may be appropriate to log the exception using some appropriate logging facility such as `java.util.logging`, which was introduced in release 1.4. This allows an administrator to investigate the problem, while insulating the client code and the end user from it.

In situations where it is not feasible to prevent exceptions from lower layers or to insulate higher layers from them, exception translation should generally be used. Only if the lower-level method's specification happens to guarantee that all of the exceptions it throws are appropriate to the higher level should exceptions be allowed to propagate from the lower layer to the higher.

Item 44: Document all exceptions thrown by each method

A description of the exceptions thrown by a method comprises an important part of the documentation required to use the method properly. Therefore it is critically important that you take the time to carefully document all of the exceptions thrown by each method.

Always declare checked exceptions individually, and document precisely the conditions under which each one is thrown using the Javadoc @throws tag. Don't take the shortcut of declaring that a method throws some superclass of multiple exception classes that it may throw. As an extreme example, never declare that a method "throws Exception" or, worse yet, "throws Throwable." In addition to denying any guidance to the programmer concerning the exceptions that the method is capable of throwing, such a declaration greatly hinders the use of the method, as it effectively obscures any other exception that may be thrown in the same context.

While the language does not require programmers to declare the unchecked exceptions that a method is capable of throwing, it is wise to document them as carefully as the checked exceptions. Unchecked exceptions generally represent programming errors (Item 40), and familiarizing programmers with all of the errors they can make helps them avoid making these errors. A well-documented list of the unchecked exceptions that a method can throw effectively describes the *preconditions* for its successful execution. It is essential that each method's documentation describes its preconditions, and documenting its unchecked exceptions is the best way to satisfy this requirement.

It is particularly important that methods in interfaces document the unchecked exceptions they may throw. This documentation forms a part of the interface's *general contract* and enables common behavior among multiple implementations of the interface.

Use the Javadoc @throws tag to document each unchecked exception that a method can throw, but do not use the throws keyword to include unchecked exceptions in the method declaration. It is important that the programmer using your API be aware of which exceptions are checked and which are unchecked, as his responsibilities differ in these two cases. The documentation generated by the Javadoc @throws tag in the absence of the method header generated by the throws declaration provides a strong visual cue to help the programmer distinguish checked exceptions from unchecked.

It should be noted that documenting all of the unchecked exceptions that each method can throw is an ideal, not always achievable in the real world. When a class undergoes revision, it is not a violation of source or binary compatibility if an exported method is modified to throw additional unchecked exceptions. Suppose a class invokes a method from another, independently written class. The authors of the former class may carefully document all of the unchecked exceptions that each method throws, but if the latter class is revised to throw additional unchecked exceptions, it is quite likely that the former class (which has not undergone revision) will propagate the new unchecked exceptions even though it does not declare them.

If an exception is thrown by many methods in a class for the same reason, it is acceptable to document the exception in the class's documentation comment rather than documenting it individually for each method. A common example is `NullPointerException`. It is fine for a class's documentation comment to say "all methods in this class throw a `NullPointerException` if a null object reference is passed in any parameter," or words to that effect.

Item 45: Include failure-capture information in detail messages

When a program fails due to an uncaught exception, the system automatically prints out the exception's stack trace. The stack trace contains the exception's *string representation*, the result of its `toString` method. This typically consists of the exception's class name followed by its *detail message*. Frequently this is the only information that programmers or field service personnel investigating a software failure will have to go on. If the failure is not easily reproducible, it may be difficult or impossible to get any more information. Therefore it is critically important that the exception's `toString` method return as much information about the cause of the failure as possible. In other words, the string representation of an exception should capture the failure for subsequent analysis.

To capture the failure, the string representation of an exception should contain the values of all parameters and fields that "contributed to the exception." For example, an `IndexOutOfBounds` exception's detail message should contain the lower bound, the upper bound, and the actual index that failed to lie between the bounds. This information tells a lot about the failure. Any or all of the three values could be wrong. The actual index could be one less than the lower bound or equal to the upper bound (a "fencepost error"), or it could be a wild value, far too low or high. The lower bound could be greater than the upper bound (a serious internal invariant failure). Each of these situations points to a different problem, and it greatly aids in the diagnosis if the programmer knows what sort of error to look for.

While it is critical to include all of the pertinent "hard data" in the string representation of an exception, it is generally unimportant to include a lot of prose. The stack trace is intended to be analyzed in conjunction with the source files and generally contains the exact file and line number from which the exception was thrown, as well as the files and line numbers of all other method invocations on the stack. Lengthy prose descriptions of the failure are generally superfluous; the information can be gleaned by reading the source code.

The string representation of an exception should not be confused with a user-level error message, which must be intelligible to end users. Unlike a user-level error message, it is primarily for the benefit of programmers or field service personnel for use when analyzing a failure. Therefore information content is far more important than intelligibility.

One way to ensure that exceptions contain adequate failure-capture information in their string representations is to require this information in their constructors in lieu of a string detail message. The detail message can then be generated automatically to include the information. For example, *instead* of a `String` constructor, `IndexOutOfBoundsException` could have had a constructor that looks like this:

```
/**
 * Construct an IndexOutOfBoundsException.
 *
 * @param lowerBound the lowest legal index value.
 * @param upperBound the highest legal index value plus one.
 * @param index      the actual index value.
 */
public IndexOutOfBoundsException(int lowerBound, int upperBound,
                                 int index) {
    // Generate a detail message that captures the failure
    super(  "Lower bound: " + lowerBound +
          ", Upper bound: " + upperBound +
          ", Index: "       + index);
}
```

Unfortunately, the Java platform libraries do not make heavy use of this idiom, but it is highly recommended. It makes it easy for the programmer throwing an exception to capture the failure. In fact, it makes it hard for the programmer not to capture the failure! In effect, the idiom centralizes the code to generate a high-quality string representation for an exception in the exception class itself, rather than requiring each user of the class to generate the string representation redundantly.

As suggested in Item 40, it may be appropriate for an exception to provide accessor methods for its failure-capture information (`lowerBound`, `upperBound`, and `index` in the above example). It is more important to provide such accessor methods on checked exceptions than on unchecked exceptions because the failure-capture information could be useful in recovering from the failure. It is rare (although not inconceivable) that a programmer might want programmatic access to the details of an unchecked exception. Even for unchecked exceptions, however, it seems advisable to provide these accessors on general principle (Item 9, page 44).

Item 46: Strive for failure atomicity

After an object throws an exception, it is generally desirable that the object still be in a well-defined, usable state, even if the failure occurred in the midst of performing an operation. This is especially true for checked exceptions, from which the caller is expected to recover. **Generally speaking, a failed method invocation should leave the object in the state that it was in prior to the invocation**. A method with this property is said to be *failure atomic.*

There are several ways to achieve this effect. The simplest is to design immutable objects (Item 13). If an object is immutable, failure atomicity is free. If an operation fails, it may prevent a new object from getting created, but it will never leave an existing object in an inconsistent state because the state of each object is consistent when it is created and can't be modified thereafter.

For methods that operate on mutable objects, the most common way to achieve failure atomicity is to check parameters for validity before performing the operation (Item 23). This causes any exception to get thrown before object modification commences. For example, consider the Stack.pop method in Item 5:

```
public Object pop() {
    if (size == 0)
        throw new EmptyStackException();
    Object result = elements[--size];
    elements[size] = null; // Eliminate obsolete reference
    return result;
}
```

If the initial size check were eliminated, the method would still throw an exception when it attempted to pop an element from an empty stack. However it would leave the size field in an inconsistent (negative) state, causing any future method invocations on the object to fail. Additionally, the exception thrown by the pop method would be inappropriate to the abstraction (Item 43).

A closely related approach to achieving failure atomicity is to order the computation so that any part that may fail takes place before any part that modifies the object. This approach is a natural extension of the previous one when arguments cannot be checked without performing a part of the computation. For example, consider the case of TreeMap, whose elements are sorted according to some ordering. In order to add an element to a TreeMap, the element must be of a type that can be compared using the TreeMap's ordering. Attempting to add an incorrectly typed element will naturally fail with a ClassCastException as a result of searching for the element in the tree, before the tree has been modified in any way.

A third and far less common approach to achieving failure atomicity is to write *recovery code* that intercepts a failure occurring in the midst of an operation and causes the object to roll back its state to the point before the operation began. This approach is used mainly for persistent data structures.

A final approach to achieving failure atomicity is to perform the operation on a temporary copy of the object and replace the contents of the object with the temporary copy once the operation is complete. This approach occurs naturally when the computation can be performed more quickly once the data have been stored in a temporary data structure. For example, Collections.sort dumps its input list into an array prior to sorting to reduce the cost of accessing elements in the inner loop of the sort. This is done for performance, but, as an added benefit, it ensures that the input list will be untouched if the sort fails.

While failure atomicity is generally desirable, it is not always achievable. For example, if two threads attempt to modify the same object concurrently without proper synchronization, the object may be left in an inconsistent state. It would therefore be wrong to assume that an object was still usable after catching a ConcurrentModificationException. Errors (as opposed to exceptions) are generally unrecoverable, and methods need not even attempt to preserve failure atomicity when throwing errors.

Even where failure atomicity is possible, it is not always desirable. For some operations, it would significantly increase cost or complexity. However, it is often both free and easy to achieve failure atomicity once you're aware of the issue. As a rule, any exception that is part of a method's specification should leave the object in the same state it was in prior to the method invocation. Where this rule is violated, the API documentation should clearly indicate what state the object will be left in. Unfortunately, plenty of existing API documentation fails to live up to this ideal.

Item 47: Don't ignore exceptions

While this advice may seem obvious, it is violated often enough that it bears repeating. When the designers of an API declare a method to throw an exception, they are trying to tell you something. Don't ignore it! It is easy to ignore exceptions by surrounding the method invocation with a `try` statement with an empty `catch` block:

```
// Empty catch block ignores exception - Highly suspect!
try {
    ...
} catch (SomeException e) {
}
```

An empty catch block defeats the purpose of exceptions, which is to force you to handle exceptional conditions. Ignoring an exception is analogous to ignoring a fire alarm—and turning it off so no one else gets a chance to see if there's a real fire. You may get away with it, or the results may be disastrous. Whenever you see an empty `catch` block, alarm bells should go off in your head. **At the very least, the `catch` block should contain a comment explaining why it is appropriate to ignore the exception.**

An example of the sort of situation where it might be appropriate to ignore an exception is image rendering for animation. If the screen is being updated at regular intervals, the best way to deal with a transient fault may be to ignore it and wait for the next update.

The advice in this item applies equally to checked and unchecked exceptions. Whether an exception represents a predictable exceptional condition or a programming error, ignoring it with an empty `catch` block will result in a program that continues silently in the face of error. The program may then fail at an arbitrary time in the future, at a point in the code that may not bear any relation to the source of the problem. Properly handling an exception can avert failure entirely. Merely letting an unchecked exception propagate outwardly at least causes the program to fail swiftly, preserving information to aid in debugging the failure.

CHAPTER 9

Threads

$\mathbf{T}$HREADS allow multiple activities to proceed concurrently in the same program. Multithreaded programming is more difficult than single-threaded programming, so the advice of Item 30 is particularly applicable here: If there is a library class that can save you from doing low-level multithreaded programming, by all means use it. The java.util.Timer class is one example, and Doug Lea's util.concurrent package[Lea01] is a whole collection of high-level threading utilities. Even if you use such libraries where applicable, you'll still have to write or maintain multithreaded code from time to time. This chapter contains advice to help you write clear, correct, well-documented multithreaded programs.

Item 48: Synchronize access to shared mutable data

The synchronized keyword ensures that only a single thread will execute a statement or block at a time. Many programmers think of synchronization *solely* as a means of mutual exclusion, to prevent an object from being observed in an inconsistent state while it is being modified by another thread. In this view, an object is created in a consistent state (Item 13) and locked by the methods that access it. These methods observe the state and optionally cause a *state transition*, transforming the object from one consistent state to another. Proper use of synchronization guarantees that no method will ever observe the object in an inconsistent state.

This view is correct, but it doesn't tell the whole story. Not only does synchronization prevent a thread from observing an object in an inconsistent state, but it also ensures that objects progress from consistent state to consistent state by an orderly sequence of state transitions that appear to execute sequentially. Every thread entering a synchronized method or block sees the effects of all previous state transitions controlled by the same lock. After a thread exits the synchronized region, any thread that enters a region synchronized by the same lock sees the state transition caused by that thread, if any.

The language guarantees that reading or writing a single variable is *atomic* unless the variable is of type long or double. In other words, reading a variable other than a long or double is guaranteed to return a value that was stored into that variable by some thread, even if multiple threads modify the variable concurrently without synchronization.

You may hear it said that to improve performance, you should avoid the use of synchronization when reading or writing atomic data. This advice is dangerously wrong. While the atomicity guarantee ensures that a thread will not see a random value when reading atomic data, it does not guarantee that a value written by one thread will be visible to another: **Synchronization is required for reliable communication between threads as well as for mutual exclusion.** This is a consequence of a fairly technical aspect of the Java programming language known as the *memory model* [JLS, 17]. While the memory model is likely to undergo substantial revision in an upcoming release [Pugh01a], it is a near certainty that this fact will not change.

The consequences of failing to synchronize access to a shared variable can be dire even if the variable is atomically readable and writable. Consider the following serial number generation facility:

```
// Broken - requires synchronization!
private static int nextSerialNumber = 0;

public static int generateSerialNumber() {
    return nextSerialNumber++;
}
```

The intent of this facility is to guarantee that every invocation of generate-SerialNumber returns a different serial number, as long as there are no more than 2^{32} invocations. Synchronization is not required to protect the invariants of the serial number generator because it has none; its state consists of a single atomically writable field (nextSerialNumber), and all possible values of this field are legal. However, the method does not work without synchronization. The increment operator (++) both reads and writes the nextSerialNumber field so it is not atomic. The read and write are independent operations, performed in sequence. Multiple concurrent threads can thus observe the nextSerialNumber field with the same value and return the same serial number.

More surprisingly, it is possible for one thread to call `generateSerialNumber` repeatedly, obtaining a sequence of serial numbers from zero to *n*, after which another thread calls `generateSerialNumber` and obtains a serial number of zero. Without synchronization, the second thread might see *none* of the updates made by the first. This is a result of the aforementioned memory model issue.

Fixing the `generateSerialNumber` method is as simple as adding the `synchronized` modifier to its declaration. This ensures that multiple invocations won't be interleaved and that each invocation will see the effects of all previous invocations. To bulletproof the method, it might also be wise to use `long` instead of `int` or to throw an exception if `nextSerialNumber` were about to wrap.

Next, consider the process of stopping a thread. While the platform provides methods for involuntarily stopping a thread, these methods are deprecated because they are inherently *unsafe*—their use can result in object corruption. The recommended method of stopping a thread is simply to have the thread poll some field whose value can be changed to indicate that the thread is to stop itself. The field is typically a `boolean` or an object reference. Because reading and writing such a field is atomic, some programmers are tempted to dispense with synchronization when accessing the field. Thus it is not uncommon to see code that looks like this:

```
// Broken - requires synchronization!
public class StoppableThread extends Thread {
    private boolean stopRequested = false;

    public void run() {
        boolean done = false;

        while (!stopRequested && !done) {
            ... // do what needs to be done.
        }
    }

    public void requestStop() {
        stopRequested = true;
    }
}
```

The problem with this code is that in the absence of synchronization, there is no guarantee as to when, if ever, the stoppable thread will "see" a change in the the value of `stopRequested` that was made by another thread. As a result, the `requestStop` method might be completely ineffective. Unless you are running on a multiprocessor, you are unlikely to observe the problematic behavior in practice, but there are no guarantees. The straightforward way to fix the problem is simply to synchronize all access to the stopRequested field:

```
// Properly synchronized cooperative thread termination
public class StoppableThread extends Thread {
    private boolean stopRequested = false;

    public void run() {
        boolean done = false;

        while (!stopRequested() && !done) {
            ... // do what needs to be done.
        }
    }

    public synchronized void requestStop() {
        stopRequested = true;
    }

    private synchronized boolean stopRequested() {
        return stopRequested;
    }
}
```

Note that the actions of each of the synchronized methods are atomic: The synchronization is being used solely for its communication effects, not for mutual exclusion. It is clear that the revised code works, and the cost of synchronizing on each iteration of the loop is unlikely to be noticeable. That said, there is a correct alternative that is slightly less verbose and whose performance may be slightly better. The synchronization may be omitted if stopRequested is declared volatile. The volatile modifier guarantees that any thread that reads a field will see the most recently written value.

The penalty for failing to synchronize access to `stopRequested` in the previous example is comparatively minor; the effect of the `requestStop` method may be delayed indefinitely. The penalty for failing to synchronize access to mutable shared data can be much more severe. Consider the *double-check idiom* for lazy initialization:

```
// The double-check idiom for lazy initialization - broken!
private static Foo foo = null;

public static Foo getFoo() {
    if (foo == null) {
        synchronized (Foo.class) {
            if (foo == null)
                foo = new Foo();
        }
    }
    return foo;
}
```

The idea behind this idiom is that you can avoid the cost of synchronization in the common case of accessing the field (`foo`) after it has been initialized. Synchronization is used only to prevent multiple threads from initializing the field. The idiom does guarantee that the field will be initialized at most once and that all threads invoking `getFoo` will get the correct value for the object reference. Unfortunately, the object reference is not guaranteed to work properly. If a thread reads the reference without synchronization and then invokes a method on the referenced object, the method may observe the object in a partially initialized state and fail catastrophically.

That a thread can observe the lazily constructed object in a partially initialized state is wildly counterintuitive. The object is fully constructed before the reference is "published" in the field from which it is read by other threads (`foo`). But in the absence of synchronization, reading a "published" object reference does not guarantee that a thread will see all of the data that were stored in memory prior to the publication of the object reference. In particular, reading a published object reference does not guarantee that the reading thread will see the most recent values of the data that constitute the internals of the referenced object. In general, **the double-check idiom does not work**, although it does work if the shared variable contains a primitive value rather than an object reference [Pugh01b].

There are several ways to fix the problem. The easiest way is to dispense with lazy initialization entirely:

```
// Normal static initialization (not lazy)
private static final Foo foo = new Foo();

public static Foo getFoo() {
    return foo;
}
```

This clearly works, and the getFoo method is as fast as it could possibly be. It does no synchronization and no computation either. As discussed in Item 37, you should write simple, clear, correct programs, leaving optimization till last, and you should optimize only if measurement shows that it is necessary. Therefore dispensing with lazy initialization is generally the best approach. If you dispense with lazy initialization, measure the cost, and find that it is prohibitive, the next best thing is to use a properly synchronized method to perform lazy initialization:

```
// Properly synchronized lazy initialization
private static Foo foo = null;

public static synchronized Foo getFoo() {
    if (foo == null)
        foo = new Foo();
    return foo;
}
```

This method is guaranteed to work, but it incurs the cost of synchronization on every invocation. On modern JVM implementations, this cost is relatively small. However, if you've determined by measuring the performance of your system that you can afford neither the cost of normal initialization nor the cost of synchronizing every access, there is another option. The *initialize-on-demand holder class* idiom is appropriate for use when a static field is expensive to initialize and may not be needed, but will be used intensively if it is needed. This idiom is shown below:

```
// The initialize-on-demand holder class idiom
private static class FooHolder {
    static final Foo foo = new Foo();
}

public static Foo getFoo() { return FooHolder.foo; }
```

The idiom takes advantage of the guarantee that a class will not be initialized until it is used [JLS, 12.4.1]. When the getFoo method is invoked for the first time, it reads the field FooHolder.foo, causing the FooHolder class to get initialized. The beauty of this idiom is that the getFoo method is not synchronized and performs only a field access, so lazy initialization adds practically nothing to the cost of access. The only shortcoming of the idiom is that it does not work for instance fields, only for static fields.

In summary, **whenever multiple threads share mutable data, each thread that reads or writes the data must obtain a lock**. Do not let the guarantee of atomic reads and writes deter you from performing proper synchronization. Without synchronization, there is no guarantee as to which, if any, of a thread's changes will be observed by another thread. Liveness and safety failures can result from unsynchronized data access. Such failures will be extremely difficult to reproduce. They may be timing dependent and will be highly dependent on the details of the JVM implementation and the hardware on which it is running.

The use of the volatile modifier constitutes a viable alternative to ordinary synchronization under certain circumstances, but this is an advanced technique. Furthermore, the extent of its applicability will not be known until the ongoing work on the memory model is complete.

Item 49: Avoid excessive synchronization

Item 48 warns of the dangers of insufficient synchronization. This item concerns the opposite problem. Depending on the situation, excessive synchronization can cause reduced performance, deadlock, or even nondeterministic behavior.

To avoid the risk of deadlock, never cede control to the client within a synchronized method or block. In other words, inside a synchronized region, do not invoke a public or protected method that is designed to be overridden. (Such methods are typically abstract, but occasionally they have a concrete default implementation.) From the perspective of the class containing the synchronized region, such a method is *alien*. The class has no knowledge of what the method does and no control over it. A client could provide an implementation of an alien method that creates another thread that calls back into the class. The newly created thread might then try to acquire the same lock held by the original thread, which would cause the newly created thread to block. If the method that created the thread waits for the thread to finish, deadlock results.

To make this concrete, consider the following class, which implements a *work queue*. This class allows clients to enqueue work items for asynchronous processing. The enqueue method may be invoked as often as necessary. The constructor starts a background thread that removes items from the queue in the order they were enqueued and processes them by invoking the processItem method. When the work queue is no longer needed, the client invokes the stop method to ask the thread to terminate gracefully after completing any work item in progress.

```java
public abstract class WorkQueue {
    private final List queue = new LinkedList();
    private boolean stopped = false;

    protected WorkQueue() { new WorkerThread().start(); }

    public final void enqueue(Object workItem) {
        synchronized (queue) {
            queue.add(workItem);
            queue.notify();
        }
    }

    public final void stop()  {
        synchronized (queue) {
            stopped = true;
            queue.notify();
        }
    }
```

```java
    protected abstract void processItem(Object workItem)
        throws InterruptedException;

    // Broken - invokes alien method from synchronized block!
    private class WorkerThread extends Thread {
        public void run() {
            while (true) {  // Main loop
                synchronized (queue) {
                    try {
                        while (queue.isEmpty() && !stopped)
                            queue.wait();
                    } catch (InterruptedException e) {
                        return;
                    }

                    if (stopped)
                        return;

                    Object workItem = queue.remove(0);
                    try {
                        processItem(workItem); // Lock held!
                    } catch (InterruptedException e) {
                        return;
                    }
                }
            }
        }
    }
}
```

To use this class, you must subclass it to provide an implementation of the abstract processItem method. For example, the following subclass prints out each work item, printing no more than one item per second, no matter how frequently items are enqueued:

```java
class DisplayQueue extends WorkQueue {
    protected void processItem(Object workItem)
            throws InterruptedException {
        System.out.println(workItem);
        Thread.sleep(1000);
    }
}
```

Because the WorkQueue class invokes the abstract processItem method from within a synchronized block, it is subject to deadlock. The following subclass will cause it to deadlock by the means described above:

```
class DeadlockQueue extends WorkQueue {
    protected void processItem(final Object workItem)
            throws InterruptedException {
        // Create a new thread that returns workItem to queue
        Thread child = new Thread() {
            public void run() { enqueue(workItem); }
        };
        child.start();
        child.join(); // Deadlock!
    }
}
```

This example is contrived because there is no reason for the processItem method to create a background thread, but the problem is real. Invoking externally provided methods from within synchronized blocks has caused many deadlocks in real systems such as GUI toolkits. Luckily it is easy to fix the problem. Simply move the method invocation outside of the synchronized block, as shown:

```
// Alien method outside synchronized block - "Open call"
private class WorkerThread extends Thread {
    public void run() {
        while (true) {  // Main loop
            Object workItem = null;
            synchronized (queue) {
                try {
                    while (queue.isEmpty() && !stopped)
                        queue.wait();
                } catch (InterruptedException e) {
                    return;
                }
                if (stopped)
                    return;
                workItem = queue.remove(0);
            }
            try {
                processItem(workItem); // No lock held
            } catch (InterruptedException e) {
                return;
            }
        }
    }
}
```

An alien method invoked outside of a synchronized region is known as an *open call* [Lea00, 2.4.1.3]. Besides preventing deadlocks, open calls can greatly increase concurrency. An alien method might run for an arbitrarily long period, during which time other threads would unnecessarily be denied access to the shared object if the alien method were invoked inside the synchronized region.

As a rule, you should do as little work as possible inside synchronized regions. Obtain the lock, examine the shared data, transform the data as necessary, and drop the lock. If you must perform some time-consuming activity, find a way to move the activity out of the synchronized region.

Invoking an alien method from within a synchronized region can cause failures more severe than deadlocks if the alien method is invoked while the invariants protected by the synchronized region are temporarily invalid. (This cannot happen in the broken work queue example because the queue is in a consistent state when processItem is invoked.) Such failures do not involve the creation of a new thread from within the alien method; they occur when the alien method itself calls back in to the faulty class. Because locks in the Java programming language are *recursive*, such calls won't deadlock as they would if they were made by another thread. The calling thread already holds the lock, so the thread will succeed when it tries to acquire the lock a second time, even though there is another conceptually unrelated operation in progress on the data protected by the lock. The consequences of such a failure can be catastrophic; in essence, the lock has failed to do its job. Recursive locks simplify the construction of multithreaded object-oriented programs, but they can turn liveness failures into safety failures.

The first part of this item was about concurrency problems. Now we turn our attention to performance. While the cost of synchronization has plummeted since the early days of the Java platform, it will never vanish entirely. If a frequently used operation is synchronized unnecessarily, it can have significant impact on performance. For example, consider the classes StringBuffer and BufferedInputStream. These classes are thread-safe (Item 52) but are almost always used by a single thread, so the locking they do is usually unnecessary. They support fine-grained methods, operating at the individual character or byte level, so not only do these classes tend to do unnecessary locking, but they tend to do a lot of it. This can result in significant performance loss. One paper reported a loss close to 20 percent in a real-world application [Heydon99]. You are unlikely to see performance losses this dramatic caused by unnecessary synchronization, but 5 to 10 percent is within the realm of possibility.

Arguably this belongs to the "small efficiencies" that Knuth says we should forget about (Item 37). If, however, you are writing a low-level abstraction that will generally be used by a single thread or as a component in a larger synchronized object, you should consider refraining from synchronizing the class internally. Whether or not you decide to synchronize a class, it is critical that you document its thread-safety properties (Item 52).

It is not always clear whether a given class should perform internal synchronization. In the nomenclature of Item 52, it is not always clear whether a class should be made *thread-safe* or *thread-compatible*. Here are a few guidelines to help you make this choice.

If you're writing a class that will be used heavily in circumstances requiring synchronization and also in circumstances where synchronization is not required, a reasonable approach is to provide both synchronized (thread-safe) and unsynchronized (thread-compatible) variants. One way to do this is to provide a *wrapper class* (Item 14) that implements an interface describing the class and performs appropriate synchronization before forwarding method invocations to the corresponding method of the wrapped object. This is the approach that was taken by the Collections Framework. Arguably, it should have been taken by java.util.Random as well. A second approach, suitable for classes that are not designed to be extended or reimplemented, is to provide an unsynchronized class and a subclass consisting solely of synchronized methods that invoke their counterparts in the superclass.

One good reason to synchronize a class internally is because it is intended for heavily concurrent use and you can achieve significantly higher concurrency by performing internal fine-grained synchronization. For example, it is possible to implement a nonresizable hash table that independently synchronizes access to each bucket. This affords much greater concurrency than locking the entire table to access a single entry.

If a class or a static method relies on a mutable *static* field, it must be synchronized internally, even if it is typically used by a single thread. Unlike a shared instance, it is not possible for the client to perform external synchronization because there can be no guarantee that other clients will do likewise. The static method Math.random exemplifies this situation.

In summary, to avoid deadlock and data corruption, never call an alien method from within a synchronized region. More generally, try to limit the amount of work that you do from within synchronized regions. When you are designing a mutable class, think about whether it should do its own synchronization. The cost savings that you can hope to achieve by dispensing with synchronization is no longer huge, but it is measurable. Base your decision on whether the primary use of the abstraction will be multithreaded, and document your decision clearly.

Item 50: Never invoke `wait` outside a loop

The `Object.wait` method is used to make a thread wait for some condition. It must be invoked inside a synchronized region that locks the object on which it is invoked. **This is the standard idiom for using the `wait` method:**

```
synchronized (obj) {
    while (<condition does not hold>)
        obj.wait();

    ... // Perform action appropriate to condition
}
```

Always use the `wait` loop idiom to invoke the `wait` method. Never invoke it outside of a loop. The loop serves to test the condition before and after waiting.

Testing the condition before waiting and skipping the wait if the condition already holds are necessary to ensure *liveness*. If the condition already holds and `notify` (or `notifyAll`) method has already been invoked before a thread waits, there is no guarantee that the thread will *ever* waken from the wait.

Testing the condition after waiting and waiting again if the condition does not hold are necessary to ensure *safety*. If the thread proceeds with the action when the condition does not hold, it can destroy the invariants protected by the lock. There are several reasons a thread might wake up when the condition does not hold:

- Another thread could have obtained the lock and changed the protected state between the time a thread invoked `notify` and the time the waiting thread woke up.

- Another thread could have invoked `notify` accidentally or maliciously when the condition did not hold. Classes expose themselves to this sort of mischief by waiting on publicly accessible objects. Any `wait` contained in a synchronized method of a publicly accessible object is susceptible to this problem.

- The notifying thread could be overly "generous" in waking waiting threads. For example, the notifying thread must invoke `notifyAll` even if only some of the waiting threads have their condition satisfied.

- The waiting thread could wake up in the absence of a notify. This is known as a *spurious wakeup*. Although *The Java Language Specification*[JLS] does not mention this possibility, many JVM implementations use threading facilities in which spurious wakeups are known to occur, albeit rarely [Posix, 11.4.3.6.1].

A related issue is whether you should use `notify` or `notifyAll` to wake waiting threads. (Recall that `notify` wakes a single waiting thread, assuming such a thread exists, and `notifyAll` wakes all waiting threads.) It is often said that you should *always* use `notifyAll`. This is reasonable, conservative advice, assuming that all `wait` invocations are inside `while` loops. It will always yield correct results because it guarantees that you'll wake the threads that need to be awakened. You may wake some other threads too, but this won't affect the correctness of your program. These threads will check the condition for which they're waiting and, finding it false, will continue waiting.

As an optimization, you may choose to invoke `notify` instead of `notifyAll` if all threads that could be in the wait-set are waiting for the same condition and only one thread at a time can benefit from the condition becoming true. Both of these conditions are trivially satisfied if only a single thread waits on a particular object (as in the `WorkQueue` example, Item 50).

Even if these conditions appear true, there may be cause to use `notifyAll` in place of `notify`. Just as placing the `wait` invocation in a loop protects against accidental or malicious notifications on a publicly accessible object, using `notifyAll` in place of `notify` protects against accidental or malicious waits by an unrelated thread. Such waits could otherwise "swallow" a critical notification, leaving its intended recipient waiting indefinitely. The reason that `notifyAll` was *not* used in the `WorkQueue` example is that the worker thread waits on a *private* object (`queue`) so there is no danger of accidental or malicious waits.

There is one caveat concerning the advice to use `notifyAll` in preference to `notify`. While the use of `notifyAll` cannot harm correctness, it can harm performance. In fact, it systematically degrades the performance of certain data structures from linear in the number of waiting threads to quadratic. The class of data structures so affected are those for which only a certain number of threads are granted some special status at any given time and other threads must wait. Examples include *semaphores*, *bounded buffers*, and *read-write locks*.

If you are implementing this sort of data structure and you wake up each thread as it becomes eligible for "special status," you wake each thread once for a total of n wakeups. If you wake all n threads when only one can obtain special status and the remaining n-1 threads go back to waiting, you will end up with $n + (n - 1) + (n - 2) \ldots + 1$ wakeups by the time all waiting threads have been granted special status. The sum of this series is $O(n^2)$. If you know that the number of threads will always be small, this may not be a problem in practice, but if you have no such assurances, it is important to use a more selective wakeup strategy.

If all of the threads vying for special status are logically equivalent, then all you have to do is carefully use `notify` instead of `notifyAll`. If, however, only some of the waiting threads are eligible for special status at any given time, then you must use a pattern known as *Specific Notification* [Cargill96, Lea99]. This pattern is beyond the scope of this book.

In summary, always invoke `wait` from within a `while` loop, using the standard idiom. There is simply no reason to do otherwise. Usually, you should use `notifyAll` in preference to `notify`. There are, however, situations where doing so will impose a substantial performance penalty. If `notify` is used, great care must be taken to ensure liveness.

Item 51: Don't depend on the thread scheduler

When multiple threads are runnable, the thread scheduler determines which threads get to run and for how long. Any reasonable JVM implementation will attempt some sort of fairness when making this determination, but the exact policy varies greatly among implementations. Therefore well-written multithreaded programs should not depend on the details of this policy. **Any program that relies on the thread scheduler for its correctness or performance is likely to be nonportable**.

The best way to write a robust, responsive, portable multithreaded application is to ensure that there are few runnable threads at any given time. This leaves the thread scheduler with very little choice: It simply runs the runnable threads till they're no longer runnable. As a consequence, the program's behavior doesn't vary much even under radically different thread scheduling algorithms.

The main technique for keeping the number of runnable threads down is to have each thread do a small amount of work and then wait for some condition using `Object.wait` or for some time to elapse using `Thread.sleep`. Threads should not *busy-wait*, repeatedly checking a data structure waiting for something to happen. Besides making the program vulnerable to the vagaries of the scheduler, busy-waiting can greatly increase the load on the processor, reducing the amount of useful work that other processes can accomplish on the same machine.

The work queue example in Item 49 follows these recommendations: Assuming the client-provided `processItem` method is well behaved, the worker thread spends most of its time waiting on a monitor for the queue to become nonempty. As an extreme example of what not to do, consider this perverse reimplementation of `WorkQueue`, which busy-waits instead of using a monitor:

```
// HORRIBLE PROGRAM - uses busy-wait instead of Object.wait!
public abstract class WorkQueue {
    private final List queue = new LinkedList();
    private boolean stopped = false;

    protected WorkQueue() { new WorkerThread().start(); }

    public final void enqueue(Object workItem) {
        synchronized (queue) { queue.add(workItem); }
    }
    public final void stop()  {
        synchronized (queue) { stopped = true; }
    }
    protected abstract void processItem(Object workItem)
        throws InterruptedException;
```

```
private class WorkerThread extends Thread {
    public void run() {
        final Object QUEUE_IS_EMPTY = new Object();
        while (true) {  // Main loop
            Object workItem = QUEUE_IS_EMPTY;
            synchronized (queue) {
                if (stopped)
                    return;
                if (!queue.isEmpty())
                    workItem = queue.remove(0);
            }

            if (workItem != QUEUE_IS_EMPTY) {
                try {
                    processItem(workItem);
                } catch (InterruptedException e) {
                    return;
                }
            }
        }
    }
}
```

To give you some idea of the price you'd pay for this sort of implementation, consider the following microbenchmark, which creates two work queues and passes a work item back and forth between them. (The work item passed from one queue to the other is a reference to the former queue, which serves as a sort of return address.) The program runs for ten seconds before starting measurement to allow the system to "warm up" and then counts the number of round trips from queue to queue in the next ten seconds. On my machine, the final version of Work-Queue in Item 49 exhibits 23,000 round trips per second, while the perverse implementation above exhibits 17 round trips per second:

```
class PingPongQueue extends WorkQueue {
    volatile int count = 0;

    protected void processItem(final Object sender) {
        count++;
        WorkQueue recipient = (WorkQueue) sender;
        recipient.enqueue(this);
    }
}
```

```
public class WaitQueuePerf {
    public static void main(String[] args) {
        PingPongQueue q1 = new PingPongQueue();
        PingPongQueue q2 = new PingPongQueue();
        q1.enqueue(q2); // Kick-start the system

        // Give the system 10 seconds to warm up
        try {
            Thread.sleep(10000);
        } catch (InterruptedException e) {
        }

        // Measure the number of round trips in 10 seconds
        int count = q1.count;
        try {
            Thread.sleep(10000);
        } catch (InterruptedException e) {
        }
        System.out.println(q1.count - count);

        q1.stop();
        q2.stop();
    }
}
```

While the WorkQueue implementation above may seem a bit farfetched, it's not uncommon to see multithreaded systems with one or more threads that are unnecessarily runnable. The results may not be as extreme as those demonstrated here, but performance and portability are likely to suffer.

When faced with a program that barely works because some threads aren't getting enough CPU time relative to others, **resist the temptation to "fix" the program by putting in calls to Thread.yield**. You may succeed in getting the program to work, but the resulting program will be nonportable from a performance standpoint. The same yield invocations that improve performance on one JVM implementation might make it worse on another and have no effect on a third. Thread.yield has no testable semantics. A better course of action is to restructure the application to reduce the number of concurrently runnable threads.

A related technique, to which similar caveats apply, is adjusting *thread priorities*. **Thread priorities are among the least portable features of the Java platform.** It is not unreasonable to tune the responsiveness of an application by tweaking a few thread priorities, but it is rarely necessary, and the results will vary from JVM implementation to JVM implementation. It is unreasonable to solve a serious liveness problem by adjusting thread priorities; the problem is likely to return until you find and fix the underlying cause.

The only use that most programmers will ever have for `Thread.yield` is to artificially increase the concurrency of a program during testing. This shakes out bugs by exploring a larger fraction of the program's state-space, thus increasing confidence in the correctness of the system. This technique has proven highly effective in ferreting out subtle concurrency bugs.

In summary, do not depend on the thread scheduler for the correctness of your application. The resulting application will be neither robust nor portable. As a corollary, do not rely on `Thread.yield` or thread priorities. These facilities are merely hints to the scheduler. They may be used sparingly to improve the quality of service of an already working implementation, but they should never be used to "fix" a program that barely works.

Item 52: Document thread safety

How a class behaves when its instances or static methods are subjected to concurrent use is an important part of the contract that the class establishes with its clients. If you do not document this component of a class's behavior, the programmers who use the class will be forced to make assumptions. If those assumptions are wrong, the resulting program may perform insufficient synchronization (Item 48) or excessive synchronization (Item 49). In either case, serious errors may result.

It is sometimes said that users can determine the thread safety of a method by looking for the presence of the `synchronized` modifier in the documentation generated by Javadoc. This is wrong on several counts. While the Javadoc utility did include the `synchronized` modifier in its output in releases prior to 1.2, this was a bug and has been fixed. **The presence of the `synchronized` modifier in a method declaration is an implementation detail, not a part of the exported API.** Its presence does not reliably indicate that a method is thread safe; it is subject to change from release to release.

Moreover, the claim that the presence of the `synchronized` keyword is sufficient to document thread safety embodies the common misconception that thread safety is an all-or-nothing property. In fact, there are many levels of thread safety that a class can support. **To enable safe multithreaded use, a class must clearly document in prose the level of thread safety that it supports.**

The following list summarizes the levels of thread safety that a class can support. This list is not meant to be exhaustive, but it covers the common cases. The names used in this list are not standard because there are no widely accepted conventions in this area:

- **immutable**—Instances of this class appear constant to their clients. No external synchronization is necessary. Examples include `String`, `Integer`, and `BigInteger` (Item 13).

- **thread-safe**—Instances of this class are mutable, but all methods contain sufficient internal synchronization that instances may be used concurrently without the need for external synchronization. Concurrent invocations will appear to execute serially in some globally consistent order. Examples include `Random` and `java.util.Timer`.

- **conditionally thread-safe**—Like thread-safe, except that the class (or an associated class) contains methods that must be invoked in sequence without interference from other threads. To eliminate the possibility of interference, the client must obtain an appropriate lock for the duration of the sequence. Examples include `Hashtable` and `Vector`, whose iterators require external synchronization.

- **thread-compatible**—Instances of this class can safely be used concurrently by surrounding each method invocation (and in some cases, each sequence of method invocations) by external synchronization. Examples include the general purpose collection implementations, such as `ArrayList` and `HashMap`.

- **thread-hostile**—This class is not safe for concurrent use by multiple threads, even if all method invocations are surrounded by external synchronization. Typically, thread hostility stems from the fact that methods modify static data that affect other threads. Luckily, there are very few thread-hostile classes or methods in the platform libraries. The `System.runFinalizersOnExit` method is thread-hostile, and has been deprecated.

Documenting a conditionally thread-safe class requires care. You must indicate which invocation sequences require external synchronization and which lock (or in rare cases, which locks) must be acquired to exclude concurrent access. Typically it is the lock on the instance itself, but there are exceptions. If an object represents an alternative *view* on some other object, the client must obtain a lock on the backing object so as to prevent direct modifications to the backing object. For example, the documentation for `Hashtable.keys` should say something like this:

If there is any danger of another thread modifying this hash table, safely enumerating over its keys requires that you lock the `Hashtable` instance prior to calling this method, and retain the lock until you are finished using the returned `Enumeration`, as demonstrated in the following code fragment:

```
Hashtable h = ...;

synchronized (h) {
    for (Enumeration e = h.keys(); e.hasMoreElements(); )
        f(e.nextElement());
}
```

As of release 1.3, `Hashtable`'s documentation does not include this prose, but hopefully this situation will soon be remedied. More generally, the Java platform libraries could do a better job of documenting their thread safety.

While committing to the use of a publicly accessible lock object allows clients to perform a sequence of method invocations atomically, this flexibility comes at a price. A malicious client can mount a denial-of-service attack simply by holding the lock on the object:

```
// Denial-of-service attack
synchronized (importantObject) {
    Thread.sleep(Integer.MAX_VALUE); // Disable importantObject
}
```

If you are concerned about this denial-of-service attack, you should use a *private lock object* to synchronize operations:

```
// Private lock object idiom - thwarts denial-of-service attack
private Object lock = new Object();

public void  foo() {
    synchronized(lock) {
        ...
    }
}
```

Because the lock is obtained on an object that is inaccessible to clients, the containing object is immune from the denial-of-service attack shown above. Note that conditionally thread-safe classes are always prone to this attack because they must document the lock to be held when performing operation sequences atomically. Thread-safe classes, however, may be protected from this attack by the use of the private lock object idiom.

Using internal objects for locking is particularly suited to classes designed for inheritance (Item 15) such as the WorkQueue class in Item 49. If the superclass were to use its instances for locking, a subclass could unintentionally interfere with its operation. By using the same lock for different purposes, the superclass and the subclass could end up "stepping on each others' toes."

To summarize, every class should clearly document its thread-safety properties. The only way to do this is to provide carefully worded prose descriptions. The synchronized modifier plays no part in documenting the thread safety of a class. It is, however, important for conditionally thread-safe classes to document which object must be locked to allow sequences of method invocations to execute atomically. The description of a class's thread safety generally belongs in the class's documentation comment, but methods with special thread-safety properties should describe these properties in their own documentation comments.

Item 53: Avoid thread groups

Along with threads, locks, and monitors, a basic abstraction offered by the threading system is *thread groups*. Thread groups were originally envisioned as a mechanism for isolating applets for security purposes. They never really fulfilled this promise, and their security importance has waned to the extent that they aren't even mentioned in the seminal work on the Java 2 platform security model [Gong99].

Given that thread groups don't provide any security functionality to speak of, what functionality do they provide? To a first approximation, they allow you to apply Thread primitives to a bunch of threads at once. Several of these primitives have been deprecated, and the remainder are infrequently used. On balance, thread groups don't provide much in the way of useful functionality.

In an ironic twist, the ThreadGroup API is weak from a thread safety standpoint. To get a list of the active threads in a thread group, you must invoke the enumerate method, which takes as a parameter an array large enough to hold all the active threads. The activeCount method returns the number of active threads in a thread group, but there is no guarantee that this count will still be accurate once an array has been allocated and passed to the enumerate method. If the array is too small, the enumerate method silently ignores any extra threads.

The API to get a list of the subgroups of a thread group is similarly flawed. While these problems could have been fixed with the addition of new methods, they haven't been fixed because there is no real need; **thread groups are largely obsolete.**

To summarize, thread groups don't provide much in the way of useful functionality, and much of the functionality they do provide is flawed. Thread groups are best viewed as an unsuccessful experiment, and you may simply ignore their existence. If you are designing a class that deals with logical groups of threads, just store the Thread references comprising each logical group in an array or collection. The alert reader may notice that this advice appears to contradict that of Item 30, "Know and use the libraries." In this instance, Item 30 is wrong.

There is a minor exception to the advice that you should simply ignore thread groups. One small piece of functionality is available *only* in the ThreadGroup API. The ThreadGroup.uncaughtException method is automatically invoked when a thread in the group throws an uncaught exception. This method is used by the "execution environment" to respond appropriately to uncaught exceptions. The default implementation prints a stack trace to the standard error stream. You may occasionally wish to override this implementation, for example, to direct the stack trace to an application-specific log.

CHAPTER 10

Serialization

THIS chapter concerns the *object serialization* API, which provides a framework for encoding objects as byte streams and reconstructing objects from their byte-stream encodings. Encoding an object as a byte stream is known as *serializing* the object; the reverse process is known as *deserializing* it. Once an object has been serialized, its encoding can be transmitted from one running virtual machine to another or stored on disk for later deserialization. Serialization provides the standard wire-level object representation for remote communication, and the standard persistent data format for the JavaBeans™ component architecture.

Item 54: Implement `Serializable` judiciously

Allowing a class's instances to be serialized can be as simple as adding the words "`implements Serializable`" to its declaration. Because this is so easy to do, there is a common misconception that serialization requires little effort on the part of the programmer. The truth is far more complex. While the immediate cost to make a class serializable can be negligible, the long-term costs are often substantial.

A major cost of implementing `Serializable` is that it decreases the flexibility to change a class's implementation once it has been released. When a class implements `Serializable`, its byte-stream encoding (or *serialized form*) becomes part of its exported API. Once you distribute a class widely, you are generally required to support the serialized form forever, just as you are required to support all other parts of the exported API. If you do not go to the effort to design a *custom serialized form*, but merely accept the default, the serialized form will forever be tied to the class's original internal representation. In other words, if you accept the default serialized form, the class's private and package-private instance fields become part of its exported API, and the practice of minimizing access to fields (Item 12) loses its effectiveness as a tool for information hiding.

If you accept the default serialized form and later change the class's internal representation, an incompatible change in the serialized form may result. Clients attempting to serialize an instance using an old version of the class and deserialize it using the new version will experience program failures. It is possible to change the internal representation while maintaining the original serialized form (using `ObjectOutputStream.putFields` and `ObjectInputStream.readFields`), but it can be difficult and leaves visible warts in the source code. Therefore you should carefully design a high-quality serialized form that you are willing to live with for the long haul (Item 55). Doing so will add to the cost of development, but it is worth the effort. Even a well-designed serialized form places constraints on the evolution of a class; an ill-designed serialized form can be crippling.

A simple example of the constraints on evolution that accompany serializability concerns *stream unique identifiers*, more commonly known as *serial version UIDs*. Every serializable class has a unique identification number associated with it. If you do not specify the identification number explicitly by declaring a private static final `long` field named `serialVersionUID`, the system automatically generates it by applying a complex deterministic procedure to the class. The automatically generated value is affected by the class's name, the names of the interfaces it implements, and all of its public and protected members. If you change any of these things in any way, for example, by adding a trivial convenience method, the automatically generated serial version UID changes. If you fail to declare an explicit serial version UID, compatibility will be broken.

A second cost of implementing `Serializable` is that it increases the likelihood of bugs and security holes. Normally, objects are created using constructors; serialization is an *extralinguistic mechanism* for creating objects. Whether you accept the default behavior or override it, deserialization is a "hidden constructor" with all of the same issues as other constructors. Because there is no explicit constructor, it is easy to forget that you must ensure that deserialization guarantees all of the invariants established by real constructors and that it does not allow an attacker to gain access to the internals of the object under construction. Relying on the default deserialization mechanism can easily leave objects open to invariant corruption and illegal access (Item 56).

A third cost of implementing `Serializable` is that it increases the testing burden associated with releasing a new version of a class. When a serializable class is revised, it is important to check that it is possible to serialize an instance in the new release, and deserialize it in old releases, and vice versa. The amount of testing required is thus proportional to the product of the number of serializable classes and the number of releases, which can be large. These tests cannot be constructed automatically because, in addition to *binary compatibility*, you must test for *semantic compatibility*. In other words, you must ensure both that the serialization-deserialization process succeeds and that it results in a faithful replica of the original object. The greater the change to a serializable class, the greater the need for testing. The need is reduced if a custom serialized form is carefully designed when the class is first written (Item 55), but it does not vanish entirely.

Implementing the `Serializable` interface is not a decision to be undertaken lightly. It offers real benefits: It is essential if a class is to participate in some framework that relies on serialization for object transmission or persistence. Furthermore, it greatly eases the use of a class as a component in another class that must implement `Serializable`. There are, however, many real costs associated with implementing `Serializable`. Each time you implement a class, weigh the costs against the benefits. As a rule of thumb, value classes such as `Date` and `BigInteger` should implement `Serializable`, as should most collection classes. Classes representing active entities, such as thread pools, should rarely implement `Serializable`. As of release 1.4, there is an XML-based JavaBeans persistence mechanism, so it is no longer necessary for Beans to implement `Serializable`.

Classes designed for inheritance (Item 15) should rarely implement `Serializable`, and interfaces should rarely extend it. Violating this rule places a significant burden on anyone who extends the class or implements the interface. There are times when it is appropriate to violate the rule. For example, if a class or interface exists primarily to participate in some framework that requires all participants to implement `Serializable`, then it makes perfect sense for the class or interface to implement or extend `Serializable`.

There is one caveat regarding the decision *not* to implement `Serializable`. If a class that is designed for inheritance is not serializable, it may be impossible to write a serializable subclass. Specifically, it will be impossible if the superclass does not provide an accessible parameterless constructor. Therefore **you should consider providing a parameterless constructor on nonserializable classes designed for inheritance**. Often this requires no effort because many classes designed for inheritance have no state, but this is not always the case.

It is best to create objects with all of their invariants already established (Item 13). If client-provided information is required to establish these invariants, this precludes the use of a parameterless constructor. Naively adding a parameterless constructor and an initialization method to a class whose remaining constructors establish its invariants would complicate the class's state-space, increasing the likelihood of error.

Here is a way to add a parameterless constructor to a nonserializable extendable class that avoids these deficiencies. Suppose the class has one constructor:

```
public AbstractFoo(int x, int y) { ... }
```

The following transformation adds a protected parameterless constructor and an initialization method. The initialization method has the same parameters as the normal constructor and establishes the same invariants:

```
// Nonserializable stateful class allowing serializable subclass
public abstract class AbstractFoo {
    private int x, y; // The state
    private boolean initialized = false;

    public AbstractFoo(int x, int y) { initialize(x, y); }

    /**
     * This constructor and the following method allow subclass's
     * readObject method to initialize our internal state.
     */
    protected AbstractFoo() { }

    protected final void initialize(int x, int y) {
        if (initialized)
            throw new IllegalStateException(
                "Already initialized");
        this.x = x;
        this.y = y;
        ... // Do anything else the original constructor did
        initialized = true;
    }

    /**
     * These methods provide access to internal state so it can
     * be manually serialized by subclass's writeObject method.
     */
    protected final int getX() { return x; }
    protected final int getY() { return y; }

    // Must be called by all public instance methods
    private void checkInit() throws IllegalStateException {
        if (!initialized)
            throw new IllegalStateException("Uninitialized");
    }
    ... // Remainder omitted
}
```

All instance methods in `AbstractFoo` must invoke `checkInit` before going about their business. This ensures that method invocations fail quickly and cleanly if a poorly written subclass fails to initialize an instance. With this mechanism in place, it is reasonably straightforward to implement a serializable subclass:

```
// Serializable subclass of nonserializable stateful class
public class Foo extends AbstractFoo implements Serializable {
    private void readObject(ObjectInputStream s)
            throws IOException, ClassNotFoundException {
        s.defaultReadObject();

        // Manually deserialize and initialize superclass state
        int x = s.readInt();
        int y = s.readInt();
        initialize(x, y);
    }

    private void writeObject(ObjectOutputStream s)
            throws IOException {
        s.defaultWriteObject();

        // Manually serialize superclass state
        s.writeInt(getX());
        s.writeInt(getY());
    }

    // Constructor does not use any of the fancy mechanism
    public Foo(int x, int y) { super(x, y); }
}
```

Inner classes **(Item 18) should rarely, if ever, implement `Serializable`.** They use compiler-generated *synthetic fields* to store references to *enclosing instances* and to store values of local variables from enclosing scopes. How these fields correspond to the class definition is unspecified, as are the names of anonymous and local classes. Therefore, **the default serialized form of an inner class is ill-defined**. A *static member class* can, however, implement `Serializable`.

To summarize, the ease of implementing `Serializable` is specious. Unless a class is to be thrown away after a short period of use, implementing `Serializable` is a serious commitment that should be made with care. Extra caution is warranted if a class is designed for inheritance. For such classes, an intermediate design point between implementing `Serializable` and prohibiting it in subclasses is to provide an accessible parameterless constructor. This design point permits, but does not require, subclasses to implement `Serializable`.

Item 55: Consider using a custom serialized form

When you are producing a class under time pressure, it is generally appropriate to concentrate your efforts on designing the best API. Sometimes this means releasing a "throwaway" implementation, which you know you'll replace in a future release. Normally this is not a problem, but if the class implements `Serializable` and uses the default serialized form, you'll never be able to escape completely from the throwaway implementation. It will dictate the serialized form forever. This is not a theoretical problem. It happened to several classes in the Java platform libraries, such as `BigInteger`.

Do not accept the default serialized form without first considering whether it is appropriate. Accepting the default serialized form should be a conscious decision on your part that this encoding is reasonable from the standpoint of flexibility, performance, and correctness. Generally speaking, you should accept the default serialized form only if it is largely identical to the encoding that you would choose if you were designing a custom serialized form.

The default serialized form of an object is a reasonably efficient encoding of the *physical* representation of the object graph rooted at the object. In other words, it describes the data contained in the object and in every object that is reachable from this object. It also describes the topology by which all of these objects are interlinked. The ideal serialized form of an object contains only the *logical* data represented by the object. It is independent of the physical representation.

The default serialized form is likely to be appropriate if an object's physical representation is identical to its logical content. For example, the default serialized form would be reasonable for the following class, which represents a person's name:

```
// Good candidate for default serialized form
public class Name implements Serializable {
    /**
     * Last name.  Must be non-null.
     * @serial
     */
    private String lastName;

    /**
     * First name.  Must be non-null.
     * @serial
     */
    private String firstName;
```

```
/**
 * Middle initial, or '\u0000' if name lacks middle initial.
 * @serial
 */
private char   middleInitial;

    ... // Remainder omitted
}
```

Logically speaking, a name consists of two strings that represent a last name and first name and a character that represents a middle initial. The instance fields in Name precisely mirror this logical content.

Even if you decide that the default serialized form is appropriate, you often must provide a readObject method to ensure invariants and security. In the case of Name, the readObject method could ensure that lastName and first-Name were non-null. This issue is discussed at length in Item 56.

Note that there are documentation comments on the lastName, firstName, and middleInitial fields, even though they are private. That is because these private fields define a public API, the serialized form of the class, and this public API must be documented. The presence of the @serial tag tells the Javadoc utility to place this documentation on a special page that documents serialized forms.

Near the opposite end of the spectrum from Name, consider the following class, which represents a list of strings (ignoring for the moment that you'd be better off using one of the standard List implementations in the library):

```
// Awful candidate for default serialized form
public class StringList implements Serializable {
    private int size = 0;
    private Entry head = null;

    private static class Entry implements Serializable {
        String data;
        Entry  next;
        Entry  previous;
    }

    ... // Remainder omitted
}
```

Logically speaking, this class represents a sequence of strings. Physically, it represents the sequence as a doubly linked list. If you accept the default serialized form, the serialized form will painstakingly mirror every entry in the linked list and all the links between the entries, in both directions.

Using the default serialized form when an object's physical representation differs substantially from its logical data content has four disadvantages:

- **It permanently ties the exported API to the internal representation.** In the above example, the private `StringList.Entry` class becomes part of the public API. If the representation is changed in a future release, the `StringList` class will still need to accept the linked-list representation on input and generate it on output. The class will never be rid of the code to manipulate linked lists, even if it doesn't use them any more.

- **It can consume excessive space.** In the above example, the serialized form unnecessarily represents each entry in the linked list and all the links. These entries and links are mere implementation details not worthy of inclusion in the serialized form. Because the serialized form is excessively large, writing it to disk or sending it across the network will be excessively slow.

- **It can consume excessive time.** The serialization logic has no knowledge of the topology of the object graph, so it must go through an expensive graph traversal. In the example above, it would be sufficient simply to follow the `next` references.

- **It can cause stack overflows**. The default serialization procedure performs a recursive traversal of the object graph, which can cause stack overflows even for moderately sized object graphs. Serializing a `StringList` instance with 1200 elements causes the stack to overflow on my machine. The number of elements required to cause this problem may vary depending on the JVM implementation; some implementations may not have this problem at all.

A reasonable serialized form for `StringList` is simply the number of strings in the list, followed by the strings themselves. This constitutes the logical data represented by a `StringList`, stripped of the details of its physical representation. Here is a revised version of `StringList` containing `writeObject` and `readObject` methods implementing this serialized form. As a reminder, the `transient` modifier indicates that an instance field is to be omitted from a class's default serialized form:

```
// StringList with a reasonable custom serialized form
public class StringList implements Serializable {
    private transient int size   = 0;
    private transient Entry head = null;
```

```java
    // No longer Serializable!
    private static class Entry {
        String data;
        Entry  next;
        Entry  previous;
    }

    // Appends the specified string to the list
    public void add(String s) { ... }

    /**
     * Serialize this <tt>StringList</tt> instance.
     *
     * @serialData The size of the list (the number of strings
     * it contains) is emitted (<tt>int</tt>), followed by all of
     * its elements (each a <tt>String</tt>), in the proper
     * sequence.
     */
    private void writeObject(ObjectOutputStream s)
            throws IOException {
        s.defaultWriteObject();
        s.writeInt(size);

        // Write out all elements in the proper order.
        for (Entry e = head; e != null; e = e.next)
            s.writeObject(e.data);
    }

    private void readObject(ObjectInputStream s)
            throws IOException, ClassNotFoundException {
        s.defaultReadObject();
        int size = s.readInt();

        // Read in all elements and insert them in list
        for (int i = 0; i < size; i++)
            add((String)s.readObject());
    }

    ... // Remainder omitted
}
```

Note that the writeObject method invokes defaultWriteObject and the readObject method invokes defaultReadObject, even though all of StringList's fields are transient. **If all instance fields are transient, it is technically permissible to dispense with invoking defaultWriteObject and defaultReadObject, but it is not recommended.** Even if all instance fields are transient, invoking defaultWriteObject affects the serialized form, resulting in greatly enhanced flexibility. The resulting serialized form makes it possible to add nontransient instance fields in a later release while preserving backward and forward compatibility. If an instance is serialized in a later version and deserialized in an earlier version, the added fields will be ignored. Had the earlier version's readObject method failed to invoke defaultReadObject, the deserialization would fail with a StreamCorruptedException.

Note that there is a documentation comment on the writeObject method, even though it is private. This is analogous to the documentation comment on the private fields in the Name class. This private method defines a public API, the serialized form, and that public API should be documented. Like the @serial tag for fields, the @serialData tag for methods tells the Javadoc utility to place this documentation on the serialized forms page.

To lend some sense of scale to the earlier performance discussion, if the average string length is ten characters, the serialized form of the revised version of StringList occupies about half as much space as the serialized form of the original. On my machine, serializing the revised version of StringList is about two and one half times as fast as serializing the original version, again with a string length of ten. Finally, there is no stack overflow problem in the revised form, hence no practical upper limit to the size of a StringList that can be serialized.

While the default serialized form would be bad for StringList, there are classes for which it would be far worse. For StringList, the default serialized form is inflexible and performs badly, but it is *correct* in the sense that serializing and deserializing a StringList instance yields a faithful copy of the original object with all of its invariants intact. This is not the case for any object whose invariants are tied to implementation-specific details.

For example, consider the case of a hash table. The physical representation is a sequence of hash buckets containing key-value entries. Which bucket an entry is placed in is a function of the hash code of the key, which is not, in general, guaranteed to be the same from JVM implementation to JVM implementation. In fact, it isn't even guaranteed to be the same from run to run on the same JVM implementation. Therefore accepting the default serialized form for a hash table would constitute a serious bug. Serializing and deserializing the hash table could yield an object whose invariants were seriously corrupt.

Whether or not you use the default serialized form, every instance field that is not labeled transient will be serialized when the defaultWriteObject method is invoked. Therefore every instance field that can be made transient should be made so. This includes redundant fields, whose values can be computed from "primary data fields," such as a cached hash value. It also includes fields whose values are tied to one particular run of the JVM, such as a `long` field representing a pointer to a native data structure. **Before deciding to make a field nontransient, convince yourself that its value is part of the logical state of the object.** If you use a custom serialized form, most or all of the instance fields should be labeled `transient`, as in the `StringList` example shown above.

If you are using the default serialized form and you have labeled one or more fields `transient`, remember that these fields will be initialized to their *default values* when an instance is deserialized: `null` for object reference fields, zero for numeric primitive fields, and `false` for `boolean` fields [JLS, 4.5.5]. If these values are unacceptable for any transient fields, you must provide a `readObject` method that invokes the `defaultReadObject` method and then restores transient fields to acceptable values (Item 56). Alternatively, these fields can be lazily initialized the first time they are used.

Regardless of what serialized form you choose, declare an explicit serial version UID in every serializable class you write. This eliminates the serial version UID as a potential source of incompatibility (Item 54). There is also a small performance benefit. If no serial version UID is provided, an expensive computation is required to generate one at run time.

Declaring a serial version UID is simple. Just add this line to your class:

```
private static final long serialVersionUID = randomLongValue ;
```

It doesn't much matter which value you choose for *randomLongValue*. Common practice dictates that you generate the value by running the `serialver` utility on the class, but it's also fine to pick a number out of thin air. If you ever want to make a new version of the class that is *incompatible* with existing versions, merely change the value in the declaration. This will cause attempts to deserialize serialized instances of previous versions to fail with an `InvalidClassException`.

To summarize, when you have decided that a class should be serializable (Item 54), think hard about what the serialized form should be. Only use the default serialized form if it is a reasonable description of the logical state of the object; otherwise design a custom serialized form that aptly describes the object. You should allocate as much time to designing the serialized form of a class as you allocate to designing its exported methods. Just as you cannot eliminate exported methods from future versions, you cannot eliminate fields from the serialized form; they must be preserved forever to ensure serialization compatibility. Choosing the wrong serialized form can have permanent, negative impact on the complexity and performance of a class.

Item 56: Write `readObject` methods defensively

Item 24 contains an immutable date-range class containing mutable private date fields. The class goes to great lengths to preserve its invariants and its immutability by defensively copying `Date` objects in its constructor and accessors. Here is the class:

```
// Immutable class that uses defensive copying
public final class Period {
    private final Date start;
    private final Date end;

    /**
     * @param  start the beginning of the period.
     * @param  end the end of the period; must not precede start.
     * @throws IllegalArgument if start is after end.
     * @throws NullPointerException if start or end is null.
     */
    public Period(Date start, Date end) {
        this.start = new Date(start.getTime());
        this.end   = new Date(end.getTime());

        if (this.start.compareTo(this.end) > 0)
          throw new IllegalArgumentException(start +" > "+ end);
    }

    public Date start () { return (Date) start.clone(); }

    public Date end ()   { return (Date) end.clone(); }

    public String toString() { return start + " - " + end; }

    ... // Remainder omitted
}
```

Suppose you decide that you want this class to be serializable. Because the physical representation of a `Period` object exactly mirrors its logical data content, it is not unreasonable to use the default serialized form (Item 55). Therefore, it might seem that all you have to do to make the class serializable is to add the words "implements `Serializable`" to the class declaration. If you did so, however, the class would no longer guarantee its critical invariants.

The problem is that the `readObject` method is effectively another public constructor, and it demands all of the same care as any other constructor. Just as a constructor must check its arguments for validity (Item 23) and make defensive copies of parameters where appropriate (Item 24), so must a readObject method. If a readObject method fails to do either of these things, it is a relatively simple matter for an attacker to violate the class's invariants.

Loosely speaking, readObject is a constructor that takes a byte stream as its sole parameter. In normal use, the byte stream is generated by serializing a normally constructed instance. The problem arises when readObject is presented with a byte stream that is artificially constructed to generate an object that violates the invariants of its class. Assume that we simply added "implements Serializable" to the class declaration for Period. This ugly program generates a Period instance whose end precedes its start:

```
public class BogusPeriod {
    // Byte stream could not have come from real Period instance
    private static final byte[] serializedForm = new byte[] {
    (byte)0xac, (byte)0xed, 0x00, 0x05, 0x73, 0x72, 0x00, 0x06,
    0x50, 0x65, 0x72, 0x69, 0x6f, 0x64, 0x40, 0x7e, (byte)0xf8,
    0x2b, 0x4f, 0x46, (byte)0xc0, (byte)0xf4, 0x02, 0x00, 0x02,
    0x4c, 0x00, 0x03, 0x65, 0x6e, 0x64, 0x74, 0x00, 0x10, 0x4c,
    0x6a, 0x61, 0x76, 0x61, 0x2f, 0x75, 0x74, 0x69, 0x6c, 0x2f,
    0x44, 0x61, 0x74, 0x65, 0x3b, 0x4c, 0x00, 0x05, 0x73, 0x74,
    0x61, 0x72, 0x74, 0x71, 0x00, 0x7e, 0x00, 0x01, 0x78, 0x70,
    0x73, 0x72, 0x00, 0x0e, 0x6a, 0x61, 0x76, 0x61, 0x2e, 0x75,
    0x74, 0x69, 0x6c, 0x2e, 0x44, 0x61, 0x74, 0x65, 0x68, 0x6a,
    (byte)0x81, 0x01, 0x4b, 0x59, 0x74, 0x19, 0x03, 0x00, 0x00,
    0x78, 0x70, 0x77, 0x08, 0x00, 0x00, 0x00, 0x66, (byte)0xdf,
    0x6e, 0x1e, 0x00, 0x78, 0x73, 0x71, 0x00, 0x7e, 0x00, 0x03,
    0x77, 0x08, 0x00, 0x00, 0x00, (byte)0xd5, 0x17, 0x69, 0x22,
    0x00, 0x78 };

    public static void main(String[] args) {
        Period p = (Period) deserialize(serializedForm);
        System.out.println(p);
    }

    // Returns the object with the specified serialized form
    public static Object deserialize(byte[] sf) {
        try {
            InputStream is = new ByteArrayInputStream(sf);
            ObjectInputStream ois = new ObjectInputStream(is);
            return ois.readObject();
        } catch (Exception e) {
            throw new IllegalArgumentException(e.toString());
        }
    }
}
```

The byte array literal used to initialize serializedForm was generated by serializing a normal Period instance and hand-editing the resulting byte stream. The details of the stream are unimportant to the example, but if you're curious, the serialization byte stream format is described in the *Java™ Object Serialization Specification* [Serialization, 6]. If you run this program, it prints "Fri Jan 01 12:00:00 PST 1999 - Sun Jan 01 12:00:00 PST 1984." Making Period serializable enabled us to create an object that violates its class invariants. To fix this problem, provide a readObject method for Period that calls defaultReadObject and then checks the validity of the deserialized object. If the validity check fails, the readObject method throws an InvalidObjectException, preventing the deserialization from completing:

```
private void readObject(ObjectInputStream s)
        throws IOException, ClassNotFoundException {
    s.defaultReadObject();

    // Check that our invariants are satisfied
    if (start.compareTo(end) > 0)
        throw new InvalidObjectException(start +" after "+ end);
}
```

While this fix prevents an attacker from creating an invalid Period instance, there is a more subtle problem still lurking. It is possible to create a mutable Period instance by fabricating a byte stream that begins with a byte stream representing a valid Period instance and then appends extra references to the private Date fields internal to the Period instance. The attacker reads the Period instance from the ObjectInputStream and then reads the "rogue object references" that were appended to the stream. These references give the attacker access to the objects referenced by the private Date fields within the Period object. By mutating these Date instances, the attacker can mutate the Period instance. The following class demonstrates this attack:

```
public class MutablePeriod {
    // A period instance
    public final Period period;

    // period's start field, to which we shouldn't have access
    public final Date start;

    // period's end field, to which we shouldn't have access
    public final Date end;
```

```
    public MutablePeriod() {
        try {
            ByteArrayOutputStream bos =
                new ByteArrayOutputStream();
            ObjectOutputStream out =
                new ObjectOutputStream(bos);

            // Serialize a valid Period instance
            out.writeObject(new Period(new Date(), new Date()));

            /*
             * Append rogue "previous object refs" for internal
             * Date fields in Period. For details, see "Java
             * Object Serialization Specification," Section 6.4.
             */
            byte[] ref = { 0x71, 0, 0x7e, 0, 5 }; // Ref #5
            bos.write(ref); // The start field
            ref[4] = 4;     // Ref # 4
            bos.write(ref); // The end field

            // Deserialize Period and "stolen" Date references
            ObjectInputStream in = new ObjectInputStream(
            new ByteArrayInputStream(bos.toByteArray()));
            period = (Period) in.readObject();
            start  = (Date)   in.readObject();
            end    = (Date)   in.readObject();
        } catch (Exception e) {
            throw new RuntimeException(e.toString());
        }
    }
}
```

To see the attack in action, run the following program:

```
public static void main(String[] args) {
    MutablePeriod mp = new MutablePeriod();
    Period p = mp.period;
    Date pEnd = mp.end;

    // Let's turn back the clock
    pEnd.setYear(78);
    System.out.println(p);

    // Bring back the 60's!
    pEnd.setYear(69);
    System.out.println(p);
}
```

Running this program produces the following output:

```
Wed Mar 07 23:30:01 PST 2001 - Tue Mar 07 23:30:01 PST 1978
Wed Mar 07 23:30:01 PST 2001 - Fri Mar 07 23:30:01 PST 1969
```

While the Period instance is created with its invariants intact, it is possible to modify its internal components at will. Once in possession of a mutable Period instance, an attacker might cause great harm by passing the instance on to a class that depends on Period's immutability for its security. This is not so farfetched: There are classes that depend on String's immutability for their security.

The source of the problem is that Period's readObject method is not doing enough defensive copying. **When an object is deserialized, it is critical to defensively copy any field containing an object reference that a client must not possess.** Therefore every serializable immutable class containing private mutable components must defensively copy these components in its readObject method. The following readObject method suffices to ensure Period's invariants and to maintain its immutability:

```
private void readObject(ObjectInputStream s)
    throws IOException, ClassNotFoundException {
    s.defaultReadObject();

    // Defensively copy our mutable components
    start = new Date(start.getTime());
    end   = new Date(end.getTime());

    // Check that our invariants are satisfied
    if (start.compareTo(end) > 0)
        throw new InvalidObjectException(start +" after "+ end);
}
```

Note that the defensive copy is performed prior to the validity check and that we did not use Date's clone method to perform the defensive copy. Both of these details are required to protect Period against attack (Item 24). Note also that defensive copying is not possible for final fields. To use the readObject method, we must make the start and end fields nonfinal. This is unfortunate, but it is clearly the lesser of two evils. With the new readObject method in place and the final modifier removed from the start and end fields, the MutablePeriod class is rendered ineffective. The above attack program now generates this output:

```
Thu Mar 08 00:03:45 PST 2001 - Thu Mar 08 00:03:45 PST 2001
Thu Mar 08 00:03:45 PST 2001 - Thu Mar 08 00:03:45 PST 2001
```

There is a simple litmus test for deciding whether the default `readObject` method is acceptable. Would you feel comfortable adding a public constructor that took as parameters the values for each nontransient field in your object and stored the values in the fields with no validation whatsoever? If you can't answer yes to this question, then you must provide an explicit `readObject` method, and it must perform all of the validity checking and defensive copying that would be required of a constructor.

There is one other similarity between `readObject` methods and constructors, concerning nonfinal serializable classes. A `readObject` method must not invoke an overridable method, directly or indirectly (Item 15). If this rule is violated and the method is overridden, the overriding method will run before the subclass's state has been deserialized. A program failure is likely to result.

To summarize, any time you write a `readObject` method, adopt the mind-set that you are writing a public constructor that must produce a valid instance regardless of what byte stream it is given. Do not assume that the byte stream represents an actual serialized instance. While the examples in this item concern a class that uses the default serialized form, all of the issues that were raised apply equally to classes with custom serialized forms. Here, in summary form, are the guidelines for writing a bulletproof `readObject` method:

- For classes with object reference fields that must remain private, defensively copy each object that is to be stored in such a field. Mutable components of immutable classes fall into this category.

- For classes with invariants, check invariants and throw an `InvalidObjectException` if a check fails. The checks should follow any defensive copying.

- If an entire object graph must be validated after it is deserialized, the `ObjectInputValidation` interface should be used. The use of this interface is beyond the scope of this book. A sample use may be found in *The Java Class Libraries, Second Edition, Volume 1* [Chan98, p. 1256].

- Do not invoke any overridable methods in the class, directly or indirectly.

The `readResolve` method may be used as an alternative to a defensive `readObject` method. This alternative is discussed in Item 57.

Item 57: Provide a `readResolve` method when necessary

Item 2 describes the *Singleton* pattern and gives the following example of a single-ton class. This class restricts access to its constructor to ensure that only a single instance is ever created:

```
public class Elvis {
    public static final Elvis INSTANCE = new Elvis();

    private Elvis() {
        ...
    }

    ...  // Remainder omitted
}
```

As noted in Item 2, this class would no longer be a singleton if the words "`implements Serializable`" were added to its declaration. It doesn't matter whether the class uses the default serialized form or a custom serialized form (Item 55), nor does it matter whether the class provides an explicit `readObject` method (Item 56). Any `readObject` method, whether explicit or default, returns a newly created instance, which will not be the same instance that was created at class initialization time. Prior to the 1.2 release, it was impossible to write a serial-izable singleton class.

In the 1.2 release, the `readResolve` feature was added to the serialization facility [Serialization, 3.6]. If the class of an object being deserialized defines a `readResolve` method with the proper declaration, this method is invoked on the newly created object after it is deserialized. The object reference returned by this method is then returned in lieu of the newly created object. In most uses of this feature, no reference to the newly created object is retained; the object is effec-tively stillborn, immediately becoming eligible for garbage collection.

If the `Elvis` class is made to implement `Serializable`, the following `readResolve` method suffices to guarantee the singleton property:

```
private Object readResolve() throws ObjectStreamException {
    // Return the one true Elvis and let the garbage collector
    // take care of the Elvis impersonator.
    return INSTANCE;
}
```

This method ignores the deserialized object, simply returning the distinguished Elvis instance created when the class was initialized. Therefore the serialized form of an Elvis instance need not contain any real data; all instance fields should be marked transient. This applies not only to Elvis, but to all singletons.

A readResolve method is necessary not only for singletons, but for all other *instance-controlled* classes, in other words, for all classes that strictly control instance creation to maintain some invariant. Another example of an instance-controlled class is a *typesafe enum* (Item 21), whose readResolve method must return the canonical instance representing the specified enumeration constant. As a rule of thumb, if you are writing a serializable class that contains no public or protected constructors, consider whether it requires a readResolve method.

A second use for the readResolve method is as a conservative alternative to the defensive readObject method recommended in Item 56. In this approach, all validity checks and defensive copying are eliminated from the readObject method in favor of the validity checks and defensive copying provided by a normal constructor. If the default serialized form is used, the readObject method may be eliminated entirely. As explained in Item 56, this allows a malicious client to create an instance with compromised invariants. However, the potentially compromised deserialized instance is never placed into active service; it is simply mined for inputs to a public constructor or static factory and discarded.

The beauty of this approach is that it virtually eliminates the extralinguistic component of serialization, making it impossible to violate any class invariants that were present before the class was made serializable. To make this technique concrete, the following readResolve method can be used in lieu of the defensive readObject method in the Period example in Item 56:

```
// The defensive readResolve idiom
private Object readResolve() throws ObjectStreamException {
    return new Period(start, end);
}
```

This readResolve method stops both of the attacks described Item 56 dead in their tracks. The defensive readResolve idiom has several advantages over a defensive readObject. It is a *mechanical* technique for making a class serializable without putting its invariants at risk. It requires little code and little thought, and it is guaranteed to work. Finally, it eliminates the artificial restrictions that serialization places on the use of final fields.

While the defensive `readResolve` idiom is not widely used, it merits serious consideration. Its major disadvantage is that it is not suitable for classes that permit inheritance outside of their own package. This is not an issue for immutable classes, as they are generally final (Item 13). A minor disadvantage of the idiom is that it slightly reduces deserialization performance because it entails creating an extra object. On my machine, it slows the deserialization of `Period` instances by about one percent when compared to a defensive `readObject` method.

The accessibility of the `readResolve` method is significant. If you place a `readResolve` method on a final class, such as a singleton, it should be private. If you place a `readResolve` method on a nonfinal class, you must carefully consider its accessibility. If it is private, it will not apply to any subclasses. If it is package-private, it will apply only to subclasses in the same package. If it is protected or public, it will apply to all subclasses that do not override it. If a `readResolve` method is protected or public and a subclass does not override it, deserializing a serialized subclass instance will produce a superclass instance, which is probably not what you want.

The previous paragraph hints at the reason the `readResolve` method may not be substituted for a defensive `readObject` method in classes that permit inheritance. If the superclass's `readResolve` method were final, it would prevent subclass instances from being properly deserialized. If it were overridable, a malicious subclass could override it with a method returning a compromised instance.

To summarize, you must use a `readResolve` method to protect the "instance-control invariants" of singletons and other instance-controlled classes. In essence, the `readResolve` method turns the `readObject` method from a de facto public constructor into a de facto public static factory. The `readResolve` method is also useful as a simple alternative to a defensive `readObject` method for classes that prohibit inheritance outside their package.

References

[Arnold00]   Arnold, Ken, James Gosling, David Holmes. *The Java*™ *Programming Language, Third Edition.* Addison-Wesley, Boston, 2000. ISBN: 0201704331.

[Beck99]   Beck, Kent. *Extreme Programming Explained: Embrace Change.* Addison-Wesley, Reading, MA, 1999. ISBN: 0201616416.

[Bloch99]   Bloch, Joshua. Collections. In *The Java*™ *Tutorial Continued: The Rest of the JDK*™. Mary Campione, Kathy Walrath, Alison Huml, and the Tutorial Team. Addison-Wesley, Reading, MA, 1999. ISBN: 0201485583. Pages 17–93. Also available as <http://java.sun.com/docs/books/tutorial/collections/index.html>.

[Campione00]   Campione, Mary, Kathy Walrath, Alison Huml. *The Java*™ *Tutorial Continued: A Short Course on the Basics.* Addison-Wesley, Boston, MA, 2000. ISBN: 0201703939. Also available as <http://java.sun.com/docs/books/tutorial/index.html>.

[Cargill96]   Cargill, Thomas. Specific Notification for Java Thread Synchronization. *Proceedings of the Pattern Languages of Programming Conference*, 1996.

[Chan00]   Chan, Patrick. *The Java*™ *Developers Almanac 2000*, Addison-Wesley, Boston, MA, 2000. ISBN: 0201432994.

[Chan98]   Chan, Patrick, Rosanna Lee, and Douglas Kramer. *The Java*™ *Class Libraries Second Edition, Volume 1*, Addison-Wesley, Reading, MA, 1998. ISBN: 0201310023.

[Collections]   *The Collections Framework*. Sun Microsystems. March 2001.
<http://java.sun.com/j2se/1.3/docs/guide/collections/index.html>.

[Doclint]   *Doclint*. Ernst de Haan. March, 2001.
<http://www.znerd.demon.nl/doclint/>.

[Flanagan99]   Flanagan, David. *Java™ in a Nutshell, Third Edition*, O'Reilly and
Associates, Sebastopol, CA, 1999. ISBN: 1565924878.

[Gamma95]   Gamma, Erich, Richard Helm, Ralph Johnson, and John Vlissides.
Design Patterns: Elements of Reusable Object-Oriented Software,
Addison-Wesley, Reading, MA, 1995. ISBN: 0201633612.

[Gong99]   Gong, Li. *Inside Java™ 2 Platform Security*, Addison-Wesley,
Reading, MA, 1999. ISBN: 0201310007.

[Heydon99]   Allan Heydon and Marc A. Najork. Performance Limitations of the
Java Core Libraries. In *ACM 1999 Java Grande Conference,* pages
35–41. ACM Press, June 1999. Also available as
<http://research.compaq.com/SRC/mercator/papers/Java99/
final.pdf>

[Horstman00]   Horstmann, Cay, and Gary Cornell. *Core Java™ 2: Volume II—
Advanced Features*, Prentice Hall, Palo Alto, CA, 2000. ISBN:
0130819344.

[HTML401]   *HTML 4.01 Specification*. World Wide Web Consortium.
December 1999.
<http://www.w3.org/TR/1999/REC-html401-19991224/>.

[J2SE-APIs]   *Java™ 2 Platform, Standard Edition, v 1.3 API Specification*. Sun
Microsystems. March 2001.
<http://java.sun.com/j2se/1.3/docs/api/overview-summary.html>.

[Jackson75]   Jackson, M.A. *Principles of Program Design*, Academic Press,
London, 1975. ISBN: 0123790506.

[JavaBeans] *JavaBeans™ Spec*. Sun Microsystems. March 2001.
            <http://java.sun.com/products/javabeans/docs/spec.html>.

[Javadoc-a] *How to Write Doc Comments for Javadoc*. Sun Microsystems.
            January 2001.
            <http://java.sun.com/j2se/javadoc/writingdoccomments/>.

[Javadoc-b] *Javadoc Tool Home Page*. Sun Microsystems. January, 2001.
            <http://java.sun.com/j2se/javadoc/index.html>.

[JLS]   Gosling, James, Bill Joy, Guy Steele, Gilad Bracha. *The Java™
            Language Specification, Second Edition*, Addison-Wesley, Boston,
            2000. ISBN: 0201310082.

[Kahan91]   Kahan, William, and J. W. Thomas. *Augmenting a Programming
            Language with Complex Arithmetic*, UCB/CSD-91-667, University
            of California, Berkeley, 1991.

[Knuth74]   Knuth, Donald. Structured Programming with go to Statements.
            Computing Surveys 6 (1974): 261–301.

[Lea01]   *Overview of Package util.concurrent Release 1.3.0*. State
            University of New York, Oswego. January 12, 2001.
            <http://g.oswego.edu/dl/classes/EDU/oswego/cs/dl/util/concurrent/
            intro.html>.

[Lea00]   Lea, Doug. *Concurrent Programming in Java™: Design Principles
            and Patterns, Second Edition*, Addison-Wesley, Boston, 2000.
            ISBN: 0201310090.

[Lieberman86] Lieberman, Henry. Using Prototypical Objects to Implement
            Shared Behavior in Object-Oriented Systems. *Proceedings of the
            First ACM Conference on Object-Oriented Programming Systems,
            Languages, and Applications*, pages 214–223, Portland, September
            1986. ACM Press.

[Meyers98]   Meyers, Scott. *Effective C++, Second Edition: 50 Specific Ways to Improve Your Programs and Designs.* Addison-Wesley, Reading, MA, 1998. ISBN: 0201924889.

[Parnas72]   Parnas, D.L. On the Criteria to Be Used in Decomposing Systems into Modules. *Communications of the ACM* 15 (1972): 1053–1058.

[Posix]   9945-1:1996 (ISO/IEC) [IEEE/ANSI Std. 1003.1 1995 Edition] Information Technology—Portable Operating System Interface (POSIX)—Part 1: System Application: Program Interface (API) [C Language] (ANSI), IEEE Standards Press, ISBN: 1559375736.

[Pugh01a]   *The Java Memory Model.* Ed. William Pugh. University of Maryland. March 2001.
                <http://www.cs.umd.edu/~pugh/java/memoryModel/>.

[Pugh01b]   *The "Double-Checked Locking is Broken" Declaration.* Ed. William Pugh. University of Maryland. March 2001.
                <http://www.cs.umd.edu/~pugh/java/memoryModel/ DoubleCheckedLocking.html>.

[Serialization] *Java™ Object Serialization Specification.* Sun Microsystems. March 2001.
                <http://java.sun.com/j2se/1.3/docs/guide/serialization/spec/ serialTOC.doc.html>.

[Smith62]   Smith, Robert. Algorithm 116 Complex Division.
                In *Communications of the ACM*, 5.8 (August 1962): 435.

[Snyder86]   Synder, Alan. Encapsulation and Inheritance in Object-Oriented Programming Languages. In *Object-Oriented Programming Systems, Languages, and Applications Conference Proceedings*, 38–45, 1986. ACM Press.

[Thomas94]   Thomas, Jim, and Jerome T. Coonen. Issues Regarding Imaginary Types for C and C++. In *The Journal of C Language Translation*, 5.3 (March 1994): 134–138.

[Vermeulen00] Vermeulen, Allan, Scott W. Ambler, Greg Bumgardener, Eldon Metz, Trevor Mesfeldt, Jim Shur, Patrick Thompson. *The Elements of Java™ Style*, Cambridge University Press, Cambridge, United Kingdom, 2001. ISBN: 0521777682.

[Weblint] *The Weblint Home Page*. Weblint.org. March 2001. <http://www.weblint.org/>.

[Wulf72] Wulf, W. A Case Against the GOTO. *Proceedings of the 25th ACM National Conference* 2 (1972): 791–797.

Index of Patterns and Idioms

Index

The Java™ Series

ISBN 0-201-70433-1   ISBN 0-201-31005-8   ISBN 0-201-70323-8   ISBN 0-201-70393-9   ISBN 0-201-74622-0   ISBN 0-201-48558-3

ISBN 0-201-43299-4   ISBN 0-201-75282-4   ISBN 0-201-75484-3   ISBN 0-201-71623-2   ISBN 0-201-31002-3   ISBN 0-201-31003-1

ISBN 0-201-48552-4   ISBN 0-201-71102-8   ISBN 0-201-70329-7   ISBN 0-201-30955-6   ISBN 0-201-31000-7   ISBN 0-201-31008-2

ISBN 0-201-63456-2   ISBN 0-201-70277-0   ISBN 0-201-31009-0   ISBN 0-201-70502-8   ISBN 0-201-32577-2   ISBN 0-201-43294-3

ISBN 0-201-70267-3   ISBN 0-201-74627-1   ISBN 0-201-70456-0   ISBN 0-201-71041-2   ISBN 0-201-43321-4

ISBN 0-201-43328-1   ISBN 0-201-70969-4   ISBN 0-201-72617-3

Please see our web site (http://www.awl.com/cseng/javaseries)
for more information on these titles.

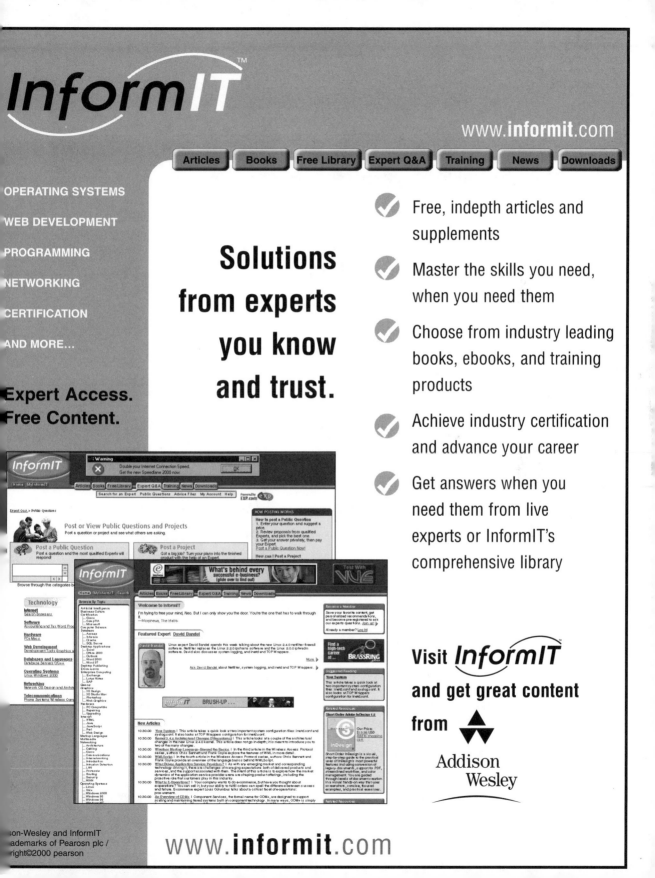